International African Library 18
General Editors: J. D. Y. Peel and David Parkin

AN AFRICAN NICHE ECONOMY

International African Library

General Editors

J. D. Y. Peel *and* David Parkin

The International African Library is a major monograph series from the International African Institute and complements its quarterly periodical *Africa*, the premier journal in the field of African studies. Theoretically informed ethnographies, studies of social relations 'on the ground' which are sensitive to local cultural forms, have long been central to the Institute's publications programme. The *IAL* maintains this strength but extends it into new areas of contemporary concern, both practical and intellectual. It includes works focused on problems of development, especially on the linkages between the local and national levels of society; studies along the interface between the social and environmental sciences; and historical studies, especially those of a social, cultural or interdisciplinary character.

AN AFRICAN NICHE ECONOMY

FARMING TO FEED IBADAN, 1968-88

JANE I. GUYER

EDINBURGH UNIVERSITY PRESS
for the International African Institute, London

© Jane I. Guyer, 1997

Edinburgh University Press Ltd
22 George Square, Edinburgh

Typeset in Linotronic Plantin
by Koinonia, Bury, and
printed and bound in Great Britain
at the University Press, Cambridge

A CIP record for this book is available
from the British Library

ISBN 0 7486 0931 8 (hardback)
ISBN 0 7486 1033 2 (paperback)

CONTENTS

LIST OF MAPS, TABLES AND FIGURES

Figures

PREFACE

A study such as this, based on two visits decades apart, catches the life of the community at two arbitrary moments. Life may be quite contradictory at those moments, offering no clear sense of direction. My first visit coincided with the later years of the Civil War and the Agbekoya farmers' revolt against increased taxes. Action on both scores was minor in Western Ibarapa. A few windows were broken at government offices in Igbo-Ọra, and I left an almost deserted town in August 1969, as people judiciously withdrew to the farm villages until the tax troubles were over. But that era had also brought the first piped water, from the new dam at Eruwa: a boon of great value for an area where river beds dessicated in the dry season and all water had to be head-loaded.

Political issues heated up again during the creation of new states in 1976, when the membership of Ibarapa in Oyo or Ogun States was in dispute, along with the status of the ọbas on the list of beaded crowns of Yorubaland. At the same moment, however, the new fleet of cheap vehicles, running on subsidised petrol, was poised to open up new commercial possibilities as never before.

My second visit in 1988 coincided with the economic turbulence and political ambiguity of the early years of Babangida's presidency of Nigeria. The phased transition to democracy (1988–93) was gearing up. By 1991 the President had mandated the creation of two – and only two – political parties, and two spacious party headquarters duly went up in Igbo-Ọra, one on each side of town. From my first time back in 1987, a certain mood of optimism about the renewed opportunity for engagement with government was unmistakable, in spite of the sudden lurch of inflation and the return of adult children from the cities as jobs dried up following structural adjustment. There was a rural roads policy, and 1988 promised to bring rural electrification as the long rows of pylons stretched out beside the main roads from one town to the next.

By the time I write this preface, the sense that political conflicts can coexist with social and economic gains has faded. Running water has long ago been given up in favour of compound wells. Petrol is often in short supply. Electricity depends on personally-owned generators now that great lengths of cable have been stolen from the relay lines near to Ibadan. There is no recourse and no positive intervention.

It is tempting, as hindsight offers clearer contours to the multiple directions of the research moment, to allow that pattern to shape the entire interpretation. Instead I have tried to retain the sense of both challenge and possibility that I knew in 1988, and that I could hear in all the narratives of change over the intervening twenty years. No one knew what would work, but a repertoire of local templates was applied to new circumstances, and it is this engagement that I want to capture rather than prioritising an apparent overall direction of change. From the kind of account I give one can understand the capacity for growth and also anticipate some alternative scenarios for retrenchment under adversity, rather than being forced – when 'trends' start going off-track or reversing – into the crisis terminology of things falling apart into an 'anarchy' that has never been very far from Western images of African social life. In fact, social and productive life goes on.

It may be the inevitable middle age of the long-term researcher that makes such persistence seem striking and even miraculous. Personal longevity also accounts for the conviction that only the synthesis, the composition, is one's own work. All the components of the research have their several authors, from the farmers who made mental records of work done and money earned, to the readers who pruned and shaped the manuscript, by way of dozens of others whose voices I still recognise in the text. Its first and foremost authors are the people whose community is depicted. I am indebted to the ọbas of Ibarapa who made me welcome, encouraged the research and allowed me to study their farms: Onidere Akintaro in 1968, Onidere Amos Ẹniọla Ọlawọorẹ, Olunloye II, in 1988, and Eleruwa Ọlaniyan in 1988. Akintaro chose a mentor for me from the community. Over the entire twenty years and for both periods of field research, Silas Okunlọla Lasunsi, now Mogaji of Idere, offered hospitality, guided the pragmatics of life and discussed untold numbers of issues. The expertise of Joel Oduọla made it possible to synthesise a history from all the compound narratives. For farming history, as well as hospitality during both studies, I benefited from the particular insights of Ezekiel Ojẹrinde, James Oni, Joel Adediran, and the Balẹ Agbẹ of Idere, Adeṣọpẹ. In recognition of the contributions that different farmers made to my understanding, I have shortened but not changed their names in the text. In fact, it is space alone that prohibits mentioning everyone.

My research assistants took considerable initiative on their own parts of the project. In 1968, James Ọlabiyi, and in 1988, Adegboyega Ojẹtọla, maintained records in my absence as well as acting as general assistants. Ọdunyẹmi Ọladokun and Nasiru Iṣọla carried out specific studies. In 1988 Olukẹmi Idowu interviewed the large and corporate farmers and their workers in eastern Ibarapa.

For both projects I benefited from affiliation and collegiality in Nigeria. In 1968, I was an occasional student in the Department of Sociology, University of Ibadan, under the supervision of Francis Okediji. In 1988, I was a visiting researcher at the International Institute of Tropical Agricul-

ture in Ibadan, under the directorship of Larry Steifel, in the department
headed by Dunstan Spencer, and at the Institute of African Studies, University of Ibadan, under the directorship of Bolanle Awẹ. Akin Mabogunjẹ
made me feel as if I were affiliated with all his many endeavours, even
though I was not a formal student or collaborator. He regularly challenged
me to think harder, do more and relate my findings more acutely to
prospects for the future of the Nigerian rural areas. Peter Ay was a fund of
information on the technical history of rural production in Africa. LaRay
Denzer maintained not only friendship but an insistent demand for detailed
realism to which she contributed with newspaper cuttings and regular commentary. Adigun Agbaje sent materials on the political and administrative
changes of the later 1980s. William Brieger, as long-time resident of Igbo-
Ọra, has been a constant part of the second project, offering hospitality,
collaboration, commentary and willingness to check up on neglected details.

In the United States, I owe much to my dissertation adviser Robert
Merrill (since deceased) and Alfred Harris of the University of Rochester.
The various works that have already been published from my second
research have benefitted from the critique of so many colleagues that a full
review is impractical. Sara Berry, Pauline Peters, Paul Richards, Achille
Mbembe, Karin Barber, Murray Last and John Peel have all inspired the
rethinking of more than one, if not most. Nearly all of that work was carried
out while I was faculty at Boston University, and my colleagues there have
listened and answered back to great effect. I was fortunate to have Eric
Lambin as a BU colleague in the early 1990s, to carry out the remote sensing
analysis. Mimi Wan not only helped with my data analysis, but subsequently
carried out her own research in Ibadan; her findings have helped me to
clarify my own. This final manuscript has been honed and pruned by John
Peel, Paul Richards, and two other reviewers. They do not necessarily endorse the approach or the interpretation, but their critique has made clearer
what it is that I take final responsibility for.

The research was financed in 1968 by a grant and fellowship from the
National Institute of Mental Health for Field Research Training in Anthropology (TO1 MH11744-01). In 1987 I had a summer fellowship to plan the
new study from the Joint Committee on African Studies of the Social
Science Research Council/American Council of Learned Societies. The
main research was financed by a grant from the National Science Foundation, Anthropology Programs (BNS-8704188).

My family has put in the same almost-thirty years of work on this project
as I have, which for my children encompasses their entire lives. Bernie has
participated from first to last; Sam originates in Nigeria, and Kate in
Cameroon; Nathan took field photographs in 1988. To say that this book is
partly theirs is also to say that we all owe more than can be explicitly
described and acknowledged, to our engagements with Africa.

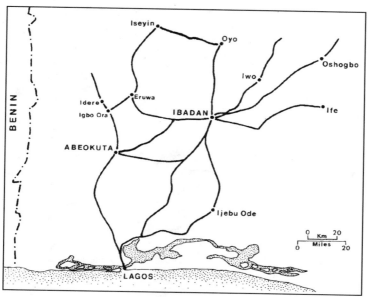

Map 1 Western Nigeria

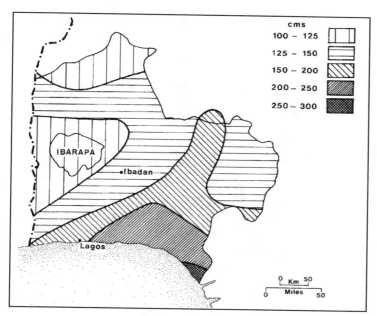

Map 2 Western Nigeria, mean annual rainfall pattern

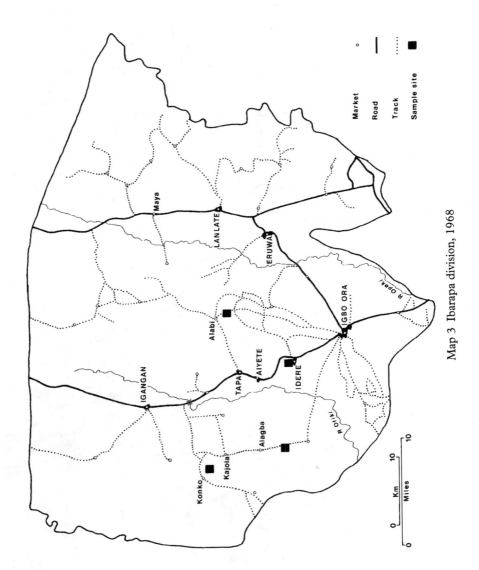

Map 3 Ibarapa division, 1968

PART I
LOCATIONS

1

URBAN HINTERLANDS AND COMPETITIVE ECONOMIES

The supply of food to a great city is among the most remarkable of social phenomena – full of instruction on all sides ... . (Dodd 1856:1, writing of London)

(T)he riches of the country depend on agriculture, pursued with assi-duity, to nourish and enrich the city population, which is counted in hundreds of thousands and millions of heads, and, surely, to do this is no little thing. (Frobenius 1913 (1966 edition): 149–50, writing of Yorubaland)

The period of urban growth in Europe during the nineteenth century raised both the proportion of non-agricultural workers in the population and the sensibility of commentators to the intricacies of production and organisation in the food sector that made this possible. George Dodd's mid-century London, according to his title page, was 'a community of two millions and a half', for which 'a Hundred and Fifty Millions ... scarcely send ships enough to supply the ever-increasing consumption.' There is still a great deal to be learned about comparable processes during Africa's period of rapid urban growth. The present study of one small producing community in the supply hinterland of Ibadan, over a period of twenty years of convulsive economic change, argues that innovations are specific, surprising and deeply depend-ent on competitive processes whose organisation long predates the present challenge and will be highly influential in the shaping of the future.

The classic studies of production and markets in Africa are grounded in the twin problematics of subsistence and exports, the two great concerns of the colonial period, rather than in the domestic market.[1] On the whole these studies demonstrated important achievements on the part of African farm-ers, that were given a particular boost during the 1950s when favourable climatic and price conditions combined with intensified political aspirations to hold out the promise of a continuing upward trajectory. The period of accelerated urban growth which followed coincided with an increased inci-dence of drought, fluctuating prices attendant on the currency and trade instabilities of the post-Bretton Woods era, and subjection to the crippling politics of autocracy. The idea of an agricultural crisis in Africa began to permeate the literature, where population dynamics of natural increase and rural–urban migration seemed dangerously out of synchronisation with an apparent worsening of climate instabilities, poor price incentives to producers, and regime entrenchment that ensured powerlessness to the rural voice. The urgency of development initiatives intensified, to prevent or at least buffer the effects of worsening situations in Africa as much of the rest of the world moved into green or communications revolutions, and the 'Asian miracle'.

As the global economy now reconfigures around new currency markets and new regulatory structures codified in the General Agreement on Tariffs and Trade and the various measures of the European Union, it becomes clear that there is no agreed vision any more of a plausible trajectory of development for the economies of West Africa, which show less and less likelihood of transformation along known industrial lines. And yet urbanisation proceeds apace. Ibadan and Lagos have probably at least tripled in population over the past twenty years, each now being very considerably larger than London in the nineteenth century, and growing at a far faster rate. The population of London did not even double over the entire eighteenth century (Wrigley 1985: 693), whereas West African urbanisation from 1960 and 1980 'occurred at three times the highest rate achieved by Europe during the industrial revolution' (Arnaud, quoted in Snrech 1995: 62). Under these conditions the rural–urban relationship is not only a 'glorious opportunity of dynamic interchange' (Hart 1982a: 153) but possibly the single most generative locus for the creation of the new commercial and social orders beyond the state within which ordinary populations must create their future (Hart 1992).

The current urbanisation in West Africa is not obviously a stage in a process of transformation that is recognisable from the world historical record. The patterns of change in food supply systems do not necessarily break down neatly along the lines of classic models of the development of a home market: differentiated, specialised, intensified, increasingly capitalised and subjected directly or indirectly to management plans from government. And yet production and distribution systems have grown over the past several decades, and possibly at a rate that compares favourably with other historical cases, even if not with the great spurt achieved in Asia through green revolution technologies. The food system has responded to demand despite difficulties of transport, no refrigeration, a narrow range of storage techniques and no commodity futures market. So even if up to 20 per cent (see Morrison 1984:16) of food has been imported at certain moments, even if some of the urban poor fail to meet adequate nutritional standards, and even if many urban inhabitants also farm, in comparative and historical terms the feeding of Nigerian towns across the great waves of macro-economic and political fluctuation has been an impressive achievement of productive technique and social organisation.

This leaves scholars with the descriptive and theoretical challenge of returning to the old terrain of 'markets in Africa' (Bohannan and Dalton 1962) with new questions and with the heightened sensibility to novelty that Dodd, Frobenius and other contemporary writers and scholars brought to the study of urban food supply in the nineteenth century. A phase of important empirical description in market studies in the 1950s and 1960s (Bauer 1954; Güsten 1968; Hodder and Ukwu 1969), and a bold assimilation of moments of commercial growth to the terms of analysis applied to capitalism (Hill 1970; Tiffen 1976), coincided with a phase of intense theoretical debate within anthropology. In response to the taxonomy of Bohannan and Dalton, Dupré and Rey (1968), the 'market principle' could never be understood shorn of its longer social and political history. By the mid-to-late 1980s enough economic history had been explored, and enough theoreticians from different disciplines had entered the arena of debate, that a series of reviews written over a period of several years in the mid-1980s could chart the emerging originality of African configurations at the overlap between competing perspectives: agro-ecologies and a social management of productive knowledge based on a persistent diversity (Richards 1985; Dommen 1988); technical and socio-political resistance to recognisable forms of capitalist development in agriculture (Williams 1988; Bernstein 1990); an ongoing negotiability and therefore indeterminate value of the social relations of production that severely limited the predictive power of micro-economic analysis (Berry 1984); and a much wider variety of engagements with markets than any single summary could encompass, based on differences of environment (Tosh 1980), popular processes internal to ethno-political groups (Dupré 1985) and colonial socio-political history (Guyer 1987). Underlying narratives began to address crisis and stagnation (Watts 1989), or to reflect such an immense and complex patchwork of variety that new efforts would be required if it were ever to be integrated into new interpretations. For Nigeria during the oil boom of the 1970s and early 1980s, Watts concluded that 'the Nigerian agricultural sector expanded and varied new forms of accumulation took place in the countryside', and yet there are 'black spaces ... which severely impoverish our understanding of agrarian change' (Watts 1987: 7,33).

Slowly, cautiously and surprisingly some long-term local studies are now returning patterns of growth to the descriptive and interpretive agenda (Haugerud 1989; Netting et al. 1989; Stone et al. 1990; Linares 1992; Moore and Vaughan 1994; Tiffen et al. 1994). 'Black spaces' begin to take their place in what Swindell refers to cautiously but optimistically as 'a mosaic of production and exchange relations' (1988: 98) in urban subregions, characterised by 'the essentially anarchic vigour of African rural life'

(Siddle and Swindell 1990: 201). The latest interpretation of West African urbanisation suggests that overal supply is almost keeping up with demand: 'food production is lagging only three years behind population growth' (Snrech 1995: xii). But if patterns of change are neither simply ecologically adaptive nor economically capitalist, and they do not feed a capitalist market for raw materials or wage goods, in what terms are they to be described and understood?

This question begs for a response that spans the methodological spectrum – including cultural as well as quantitative analysis – but that is also informed by an ambition to address the sociological issues that loom beyond. These home markets are not just the 'informal sector' in some generic sense, but the social and economic horizon for the foreseeable future. It is the growing importance of an emergent commercial order/disorder in West Africa's social future that forces us out of descriptive and interpretive modes that direct a divining rod only towards signs of the familiar: pragmatic 'adaptation to conditions', imminent transformation along one or other of the known pathways, or embattled reduction of longer-term strategies to the short-term tactics of what de Certeau (1984) refers to as 'making do' in the interstices of an otherwise dominant order. Trying to bridge the theoretical chasms inherited from the 1970s and 1980s, Mamdani suggests that 'the free peasant economy lay at the *interstices* of markets and compulsions' (1996: 147, emphasis added). The connection he insists on between political and economic interventions is basic, but the comprehensiveness of the influence of administrative and economic policy over regional markets is still at issue. As Berry (1993) has explored for the internal politics of agrarian states, Hibou (1996) shows in detail for economic protectionism *vis-à-vis* the world, and Guyer (1993) suggested for the application of regulatory models from the metropolitan to the African context, the domination of national and world orders in Africa is an extraordinarily complex and aleatory process that has created institutional gaps and logical hiatuses – of the 'you can't get there from here' variety – that describe a social mosaic more internally complex than any imagery of interstices or margins can adequately express.

Two careful syntheses from the mid-1990s (Chauveau 1995; Wiggins 1995) suggest some characteristics of the African peasantry living under these conditions: producers are deeply engaged with markets, and most successfully with the domestic rather than the export market; both production patterns and local institutions have proved diverse and flexible; growth has involved combinations of multiple different strategies, rather than a single major innovation; and the social mediation of the configurations of change within and between groups has involved a persistent 'ordinary politics' of ongoing engagement with one another and the institutional nexus (Chauveau 1995: 47). Both scholars also conclude that understanding these processes of mediation between society and markets will demand more work: 'the processes are less clear and simple' (Wiggins 1995: 834), and certainly 'it is illusory to pull from (macro-economic) results and non-empirical extrapolations the "how" of the process' (Chauveau 1995: 47). These two studies orient us particularly towards a focus on understanding diversity as a process, in a way than can link the local agro-economy of crop studies (Moock and Rhoades 1992) to the macro-sociology of 'uni- or multi-modal' development (Gladwin and Truman 1989), and that can suggest relationships amongst the diversity of plants in a field, the diversity of farmer strategies in a community, the diversity of regional specialisations, and the differentiation of the larger economy according to resource endowment and control of wealth.

As research and analysis edges closer to clarity on the issues that could well guide a new phase of both thinking and action, an inductive approach to a single case has much to offer again: that is, an approach in which field data are accorded primacy, and specific propositions from the literature are faced as they arise, as distinct from an approach that relies on guiding propositions and thereby over-frames the research. Long-term field data from the producing communities are arguably our scarcest resource by comparison with theoretical commentaries, which are now relatively profuse and varied. The models certainly explain something, but they do not explain enough, and – insofar as they have surprised us – it must often be the unexplained residual that has given rise to innovation. As Tom Forrest has put it simply with respect to concepts for analysis at the national level: 'Although these perspectives capture aspects of Nigeria's political economy, they do not give the whole picture' (1995: 6). 'The market' is a particularly frustrating topic to address from a single analytical vantage point, since it is such an enormously complex phenomenon. The differing approaches are numerous and, each in its own way, explanatory but also limited. Working assumptions of rationality and embeddedness are both necessary (see Granovetter 1993), but neither is sufficient for understanding how circuits of commerce and society are reshaping one another in the conditions of West Africa today.

With the purpose of addressing both the rationalities of short-run market response and the capacity of market engagement to reshape collective life in permanent and pervasive ways, I take the risk here of returning to a much-criticised method: the village study, with its attendant 'problem of the "bounded" village' (Roseberry 1989: 108). Even very recently Amanor has cautioned about the propensity of village studies to bracket 'the location of these settlements in the political and economic life of the region' (1994: 31). My own is deliberately a focused study, but within a surrounding field that is constantly refered to: I take the location of the village as one of its central characteristics; I attempt to identify generative processes that connect to others in rural and urban Nigeria that lie outside both my focus and my methodological expertise; and I end by suggesting connections with other kinds of study, of other phenomena, that were not envisaged at the outset but which turn out to be essential to a broader and richer understanding. I start by asking simply: what have been the cutting edges of market expansion in a producer community over a period of commercial growth, and then try to extrapolate a descriptive model of the competitive dynamics that have mediated the processes identified.

The method draws on the old social anthropological heuristic of patterns of behaviour as the explanandum, and is experimental – that is, as comprehensive as possible within the confines of current thinking – about the explanans. The impressive power of what people do, persistently and resiliently and imaginatively, over long periods of time, is the discipline's most basic subject matter. But in the turbulence of the present world, the 'reproduction of the status quo' that was once seen as 'custom' may be better analysed as 'a brilliantly innovative achievement' in the face of swirling uncertainties (Richards 1993). The contours of 'reason' – rational adaptation to environment; passive resistance to a predatory state; faithfulness to cultural principle or ancestral dictates – are buried behind the repetition of actions and their shifting patterns. For these phenomena, the methods of a qualified empiricism and positivism (see Peel 1978; Cohen 1980) still have something to offer because the image of 'what is to be understood' has clarity and can be subjected to critique and debate on a variety of grounds, from factual to philosophical. Avoidance of the old twin pitfalls of, on the one hand radical particularism ('this is its own system'), and on the other, artificially mechanistic generality ('this is a case of ...'), can only depend on the power of the case itself to add to the conceptual and comparative repertoire and to suggest new lines of enquiry. And the empiricist problem of naive creation of categories for description can only bring itself up against the resistance of the material. African originality has afforded these possibilities often enough in the past (see Bates et al. 1993) that the researcher trusts that it can instruct again: the writer, up to her limits, and beyond that, the reader and critic.

BACKGROUND TO THE STUDY

In a previous volume (Guyer 1987), a group of scholars addressed patterns in the growth of urban provisioning in Africa, taking the urban-centre vantage point and focusing particularly on the creation and management of the large differentiated categories of producer and consumer, peasant and planter, government and trader. The present study examines a microcosm: a single producer community as it has changed and developed over the twenty years between 1968 and 1988 when the urban area to which it sells tripled its size and extended its social and economic reach. It covers one set of actors, within a much larger differentiated social field, who are encouraged by the proximity of the urban market and forced by the weakness of the state institutions of local governance, to create and manage their own social and economic diversity.

The idea of studying the small Yoruba town of Idere was contingent on my own research career. I had studied its economy in 1968–69 to explore the economic implications of the domestic group cycle, counterposing the differing models of Fortes and Chayanov (Guyer 1972). In the 1970s I worked at reconstructing a local history of change in the food supply hinterland of Yaoundé, capital of Cameroon, using secondary sources to augment oral recollections of the past (Guyer 1984; 1987). With the limitations of that experience in mind, it seemed imperative – as time passed – to return to the Nigerian data I had collected as they themselves were rapidly becoming historical evidence. There was clearly a need for evidence from the past that was more varied and quantified than could be provided by memory and previous studies, done under different conditions by different scholars. At the same time as working on the Nigeria project, I experimented with the ancillary data that would be needed to make strong circumstantial arguments about change in the staple food economy by returning to the Southern Cameroon case material (Guyer 1991), and pursued another project, on pre-colonial currencies, to help expand my horizons with respect to how money and markets might have worked in different social historical contexts (Guyer 1993; 1995a).

To return to Nigeria, and to carry out a restudy, offered a unique opportunity: to use my own data as a basis for study, of a different urban dynamic in a different society and culture. The rural population of Western Nigeria has been highly responsive to urban demand, and without the intervention of the major policies and projects that marked the history of Yaoundé. Studies suggest the early development of some specialisation in the Ibadan food hinterland, primarily according to forest or savanna ecology, and secondarily by location within broad zones. The establishment of cocoa throughout the forest to the south and east of the city limited the potential for substantial growth in forest food crops for the market. Indeed, Galletti et al.'s (1956) study of Nigerian cocoa farmers in the 1950s shows that these rural areas were food importers themselves before the end of the colonial period. Cattle and cowpeas were already produced primarily in the north; wheatflour was already imported (Jones 1972; Andrae and Beckman 1985). The closer hinterland had also developed particular axes of supply: yam sales were important in the slightly drier savannas and well-drained soils to the north of Ibadan, from Iseyin to Ilorin; Ife and Ilesha, within the forest belt, provided plantain, fruit and vegetables; Ibadan Rural District, of which Ibarapa is a part, emphasised cassava (Gusten 1968: 218,264).

By 1972 it was already clear that the area north and west of Ibadan, and a corridor southward according with lower population density and savanna agro-ecologies, was disproportionately responsible for feeding the great cities of the south (Güsten 1968: 265; Jones 1972: 90). '(T)he west and Ibarapa account for the larger part of total sales' (Güsten 1968: 219, 223) to Ibadan city from the Ibadan Rural local government area. Already in the 1960s, 20 per cent of Ibarapa's total food production was estimated to be destined for the urban market (Güsten 1968: 222).

The meteoric growth of the Southern Nigerian cities after about 1974 was a function of the oil boom and post-Civil War efforts at democratisation. Over the next decade the Nigerian minority groups poured back in, augmented by immigrants from all over West Africa, searching for escape from the Sahelian drought, the Ghanaian penury and growing disorder in Liberia, or simply taking advantage of opportunities created by the borders between a stable franc CFA and an increasingly over-valued Nigerian naira. The interaction between a community that had belonged to the periphery of the Ibadan system described by Güsten and Jones for the 1960s and the vast and frenetic metropoles of the 1980s describes one of those spaces in the social geography (or 'black holes' in the 'mosaic') which, by virtue of government disinterest, can become a kind of internal frontier for local initiative. In his provocative work on the 'African frontier' Kopytoff (1987) suggested the pervasive importance of mobility, novelty and rebuilding in African pre-colonial history, and Barnes (1987) applied the idea to the uncharted and uninhabited institutional spaces that opened up in early urban communities in Nigeria. In the 1970s and 1980s comparable spaces opened up between demand and supply in the urban food supply sector.

Idere, in the administrative district of Ibarapa,[2] is one of hundreds of Yoruba settlements that have been in the Ibadan supply hinterland ever since the fall of Oyo in about 1837, when both Ibadan and its surrounding settlements were founded and Ibadan gained its disproportionate population and commanding military reputation (Awe 1967). Its interest lies not in an argument one could make about its representativeness, but to the contrary, in the relative precision with which its specificity can be defined: its location within a political-economic region, the ecological basis of production, and the cultural history of its people. Idere is sixty miles from Ibadan, in the savanna about twenty miles beyond the forest border. At least by the mid-nineteenth century the Yoruba towns on either side of the ecological border, and oriented towards established trade routes, were known for their own particular products. Ibarapa itself is probably named for the vine of the egusi-melon, bàrà, whose high-value and low-transportation-cost seeds were amongst the first commercialised contributions to the urban food market and remain an important component of the crop repertoire. By virtue of its open country and comparatively low population densities it has always been a favoured source of bush-meat. When Johnson listed the Yoruba subgroups by their 'special characteristics' in 1897, whereas all the other groups were accorded characteristics such as 'shrewd', 'docile' or loving 'ease', he wrote only of the Ibarapas that they were 'laborious farmers' (1921: xxii). In the twentieth century Ibarapa has been marginal to the great centres of power and cocoa wealth in the forest. It was the transport revolution of the 1970s oil boom that brought this area into more intense relationship to the urban areas.

For ultimately comparative purposes then, Idere is as ordinary a place as hundreds of others in the Yoruba rural areas. It has not been the originator of any sudden leap forward, the locus of any large and bold coordinated experiment or the recipient of any major development project. By its own standards it is not yet as successful as people hope. Its historical–mythical links to Aye, the 'world', the goddess-mother of the founder of the royal family, was first committed to writing in 1877 by S. W. Doherty, an African pastor based in Abeokuta, who quoted the ọba as claiming 'in this place God created the world'.[3] The links to Aye and the ritual primacy of the Onidere (the ọba, or king) within the chieftaincy hierarchy of Ibarapa have been reiterated repeatedly over the past century and more, and protected from bureaucratic revision in the recent past,[4] but they have not been accompanied either by particular demographic growth or unusual economic or political prominence. If one were searching for unusual or rapid innovations one would choose a different sector and probably another place. However, for an experiment in thinking about the frontiers of small, general and indigenously-created change, in relatively poor communities, in relation to historical shifts in the regional system, the absence of heroic scenarios or major tragedies can be an advantage. The modest nature of change enforces concentration on the solid parameters of the mundane.

AN INDUCTIVE APPROACH

Deciding on the basic form of description for an inductive approach to change poses no great problem: it has to follow some kind of narrative. The narrative form that offered the most possibilities for assessing alternative interpretations, and also lent itself to an anthropology based on people's self-conscious agency or 'performance' (Richards 1993) rather than abstract forces, was one based on the categories of actors in the local economy, and particularly on their moments of maximum innovation. Each set of participants was studied, particularly with respect to moments of either novelty or retrenchment.

The more challenging problems were interpretive and theoretical: first, to define the alternative or complementary interpretive frameworks that should guide data collection and analysis, and second, to decide on the criteria – other than exhaustion of author, reader or material – by which, in what would inevitably be a circumstantial argument, a case could finally rest. The first part of this section is devoted to a strategy of drawing on alternative frameworks through triangulation, and the second makes explicit the criteria for drawing the inferences back together into a single interpretation.

Triangulation

A full treatment of market dynamics requires 'tack(ing) backwards and for-
wards between descriptions ... without privileging either' the theoretical or
the indigenous models, as Alexander (1992: 84) advocates with respect to
addressing 'the market' in the post-1989 world. Tacking back and forth,
however, demands coordinates, otherwise the indeterminacies that may well
be 'out there' become deeply confused with the indeterminacies of one's
own vantage point. In Ibarapa I did not find any of the established narratives
in the literature on African agricultural change to be clearly the leading
explanatory contender for change: the development of marked regional
specialisation in response to calculations of comparative advantage, progressive social differentiation, deepening intensification of production,
growing occupational straddling or the feminisation of farming. At the same
time there are instances of almost every conceivable dynamic ever posited
with respect to peasant change: mechanisation and the development of large
plantations in a small-farmer economy, with a few instances of small-scale
sabotage and theft as one response and local organisational innovation with
respect to labour recruitment as another; the vicissitudes of unpredictable
changes in transport conditions and prices; volatilities of climate; growing
population; sudden changes in the gender division of labour; shifts in the
overal occupational structure, with increasing recourse to wage labour, by
farmers as employers and by their children as workers, along with attendant
bargaining; and competition with other rural producers altogether, in this
case, pastoralists trying to use the same environment as holding pastures for
the urban meat market.

Due to theoretical controversies and complex real situations, the expectations for market development represented in the literature are quite varied
and even contradictory. In an elegant overview of path-dependent theories
of economic growth through market development, Hirschman (1986) has
pointed out how diametrically opposed to one another theories of market
development can be: that markets create civil association and that they
destroy it, that they are shackled by 'feudal remnants' and that they are
catalysed by them. His conclusion is particularistic, that one 'needs to be
aware of both lines of influence, and [that] the balance is likely to be different in each concrete historical situation' (1986: 139). What constitutes,
however, a 'historical situation', and by what criteria should they be compared? Competitive dynamics in the informal sector of both production and
trade are likely to demonstrate patterns across cases rather than a multitude
of variety, but we have few suggestions of what these might be, other than
the confirmation of Hirschman's view – which is important, given the tendency to revert to evolutionism with respect to Africa – that specific long-
term histories of regional social structure and local traditions of production,
trade and political dynamics are clearly relevant to ongoing developments

(Skinner 1964–65; Trager 1985: 278; Mortimore 1993). We have no counter-part yet of the new work in the economic sociology of competition in indus-trial economies, that points out that even in the home of 'the theory of the firm', firms have followed distinctly different successive models for control over a century of change, that determine 'the nature of markets, competition and what courses of action would ensure ... survival' (Fligstein 1990: 123).

My working solution is to keep referring back to three strong arguments from the literature. First is the agro-ecological adaptive argument that in-creased population and market pressure on resources lead to innovations that intensify production. This is based on Boserup's (1965) theory and has been extended by Netting (1993), Turner et al. (1993) and Tiffen et al. (1994). Second there is the socio-economic argument, comprising both re-gional economic analysis based ultimately on the classic work of von Thünen (1966) and the politically-focused literature on peasants, that spe-cialisation of production follows predictable patterns based on modes of incorporation. Third, the social/cultural constructivist argument is based on the expectation that all negotiated trajectories forward in material and eco-nomic life will be mediated in ways that are culturally specific, a position that was developed in cultural ecological studies and finds careful development in the work of, for example, Stone (1993). All are relevant, so I am not attempting to play them off against one another in any global sense. People themselves can rarely afford to entertain an opposition between culture and rationality (in the conventional economic sense of cost–benefit calculation). They try to keep an eye on prices at the same time as an ear to the voice of the gods, and they struggle to make short-run responsiveness a meaningful phase in a long-run career. Rather I draw on the terms and predictions of these arguments to guide description and analysis and provoke different plausible interpretations. To be usable in that way each needs to be given a more precise content.

The Savanna Ecology: The Primacy of Crops

As evidence builds, it seems that analysis of change in West African farming is poorly served by theories that grant primacy to the measurement of inten-sification, judged according the shortening of fallow and concomitant rise in labour and capital inputs per unit area. In the 1960s, geographers such as Morgan and Moss (1965) were pointing out the complexity of adaptations on the forest–savanna border. Burnham's (1980) review article endorses that view for a broader landscape, arguing that humid savanna societies characteristically work with multiple cropping regimes at once. Dommen took the argument further to suggest that under the low resource conditions of Africa it is shift in crop mixes within crop regimes that characteristically constitutes the leading edge of intensification and 'paves the way' (1988: 103) for increased inputs and major innovations, if these eventually occur. A

recent analysis of Sierra Leone data concludes that fallow practices are not
related to population density, that they vary within communities, and that
shortening of fallow is not necessarily a sign of either improvement or deterioration in agro-ecological conditions (Gleave 1996).[5]

All these works support a similar conclusion: that techniques for managing the soil through investments of labour and capital are surpassed in Africa
by techniques based on investment in knowledge of crops, varieties and the
management of mixes and sequences. 'Extensive agriculture' with long
fallows is not only a function of low population densities but also a strategy
suited to an ecology that has particularly difficult soils and uniquely unpredictable rainfall. The soils are said to be 'chemically and physically very
fragile', 'poor to average' in agricultural value, making problematic any
pathways of change that are 'based more on the use of soil management
under low fertility levels than on fully exploiting the climatic and plant
genetic resources' (Kowal and Kassam 1978: 185,23,34). The most sensitive resource of all in savanna West Africa is rain. In temperate climates 'the
coefficient of variation of rainfall is about 15 per cent while 30 per cent is
typical for the tropics ... [and in addition] the moisture-holding capacity of
the soil is often low' (MacArthur 1980: 22).

Crop innovation for adaptation to rainfall is identifiable very early in
African agricultural history, in varietal improvement in cereal production
that maximises the use of limited moisture (Harlan 1980: 339). Recent
studies of crop varieties confirm that current farmers match varietal use to
resource stress (Adesina 1992; Voss 1992). Adoption of root crops buffers
the need for intensification of land use, under conditions where land is fragile (Turner et al. 1977: 391,393). Goldman explicitly mentions this tactic
with respect to Igbo farming at high population densities: 'technological
changes may be adopted as a means to help forestall a reduction in fallow
periods' (1993: 290). Overall, Ruthenberg (1980: 67) warned that in the
humid savannas there are very limited known ways of intensifying land use
further from a system of four years cultivation and eight years fallow without
crop failure and land degradation setting in.

Thus the crop change that characterises West African agricultural histories
is not just a convenient narrative device for economies without cadastral
surveys and Domesday books that describe the land. It should be thought of
as the leading edge of real strategies for controlling the pace of intensification where soils are fragile and rainfall variable. Zeleza hardly pauses to
justify such a stance, so self-evident does it seem: 'It can be argued that
many African societies witnessed a kind of agricultural revolution in the
nineteenth century: new foods and cash crops were widely adopted and old
indigenous cultigens spread within and across regions' (1993: 116). In one
of the earliest detailed analyses of 'shifting cultivation', de Schlippe noted
how the recent introduction of cassava and groundnuts 'led to the amalga-

mation of two pseudorotations into one', and cotton 'lengthened the duration of cultivation from two to three or four years' (1956: 225,231). Scholars exploring population pressure find that, over the second half of the twentieth century, '(t)he use of new cultigens has led not only to increased yields of production but to substantial dietary changes as well. In almost all of the sites major dietary shifts have taken place ...', as well as major shifts in marketed crops (Turner et al. 1993: 403). Other scholars exploring growth that they argue results from market response rather than resource pressure, also stress a particular crop: in this case maize (Goldman and Smith 1995).

The importance of crop dynamics in changing resource use has been announced by Richards (1996) and Chauveau (1995). In fact, Richards prefigured the position much earlier: 'the production, application and ownership of ecological knowledge rivals access to land, labor and equipment as a focus for analytical attention ... [where] intercropping ... is one of the great glories of African science' (1983: 24,27). In the West African savannas, crops lead, the characteristically flexible and varied social organisation of labour follows, and the two combined have permitted land use and capital investment to be conservative (or perhaps conservationist) in a pattern that contrasts markedly with land use inventiveness in Asian and European systems, combined with extreme social conservatism such that 'the peasant household' survived for almost a millenium.[6]

Indigenous knowlege and experience with crop innovations should therefore be very much at the centre of concern in the research on patterns of change in the expanding food supply hinterlands of the humid savannas. Cassava is an obvious example from Southern Nigeria. It is rapidly becoming the major commercial crop, whereas it is not even mentioned in Samuel Johnson's list of cultigens in his *History of the Yorubas*, written at the end of last century (1921: 177–8). In 1934 Forde noted that 'cassava ... has only recently been adopted by the Yoruba' (1934: 154). In Ibarapa, the introduction of cassava processing from the Egba to the south took place within living memory of old people, whereas now cassava varietal experimentation is on the frontier of current agricultural change. In this whole region, crop change has been remarkable over the past century (Mabogunje and Gleave 1964).

One would hardly expect, then, the precipitation of rings of specialised production to develop around the city, according to land use intensity of either the economic kind (driven by land/transport costs in relation to producer prices) or the ecological kind (driven by population pressures on land resources and self-provisioning needs). On the other hand, we should expect economic and ecological adjustments of some sort, and judging from history and inference, crops and combinations should stand at the centre of farmers' strategies. Have they, however, been free to follow an indigenous ecological–economic rationality?

The Ibadan Hinterland: Aleatory Policy

Even in the past, the Southern Nigerian towns have laid a much lighter, more indirect and intermittent political hand on their rural hinterlands than the cases included in our volume on *Feeding African Cities* (Guyer 1987), and than other urban centres now described in the literature (e.g. Woldemariam 1994, for Addis Ababa). Historically all manner of policy, either direct or indirect, has been relatively weak, diffuse or transient in effect because the economy was already large, varied and competitive before the rise of the great modern regional centres. 'Until the Second World War direct intervention by the colonial state in agricultural production and marketing was very limited' (Forrest 1981: 222).[7] In the 1960s scholars from abroad (Güsten 1968) and at home (Olatunbosun 1975) were pointing out 'Nigeria's neglected rural majority', rather than its dominated and exploited one. Only after the end of the civil war in 1970 did policy turn to the food sector with any comprehensive approach (Forrest 1981: 239). Even then, most of the efforts were wasteful rather than either positively or negatively effective. One cannot help imagining the scene, for example, in 1976 when Operation Feed the Nation suddenly assigned 30,000 students to spend the long vacation in the service of the state agriculture ministries, whose personnel 'struggled to find employment for them on state farms, schools and vegetable gardens' (Forrest 1981: 249). The discouraging effects on farmers' own investment in agriculture of the high agricultural taxation mediated by the export crop marketing boards are more serious and perhaps more pervasive. Berry (1985) argues persuasively that in the 1970s the export-crop peasantry was in danger of disappearing. Production of food crops may not have been as hard hit, although people's confidence in the returns to their investments is probably set by a broad knowledge of the region as well as particular experience of their own situation within it.[8]

New rural policies in the mid-1980s were perhaps the most influential that there have ever been in the food sector: the limits placed on grain imports, the investment in accessibility through the Directorate for Food, Roads and Rural Infrastructure, and the impetus to food processing through a series of interventions including most notably the Better Life for Rural Women policy. Most of these efforts provided stimuli to farmers rather than increasing opportunities for direct administrative control on a permanent basis. Only the Agricultural Development Projects financed by the World Bank, and the River Basin Development Authorities, took direct administrative blueprints to the farmers, but these have been locally circumscribed efforts. During the period of study, the Oyo North Development Project and the Ogun River Basin Development Authority were the main regional representatives of these national-level policies in the western savanna. Over the modern history of the Ibadan hinterland even quite large government schemes – such as cassava starch and gari production in World War II, the farm settlement production of the 1960s, subsidised rice distribution under the Essential Commodities Board in the early 1980s and the ADPs – have probably constituted at most tributaries to the vast stream of goods flowing into the urban markets through the indigenous system of production and distribution. Williams reaches the same conclusion with respect to private large-scale farmers in the 1980s: 'their contribution to agricultural production, especially of export crops and staple foods, is marginal' (1988: 386).

Until the 1970s, Ibadan was the largest city in sub-Saharan Africa (Lloyd et al. 1967), and it still ranks amongst the top few. A million in the mid-1960s, its population was estimated as three-and-a-half million in the mid-1980s. The largely self-employed urban population is criss-crossed by every possible social delineation. At independence it was already a multi-occupational, multi-ethnic, sprawlingly entrepreneurial city whose population was in constant, intense and reciprocal relationship with the rest of the country and beyond. The Nigerian borders have been completely porous, and cattle, people, commodities of all kinds including petrol all move into and out of Nigeria in response to the price of money as well as the price of goods.

In this situation government and the wider world economic order are by no means irrelevant to the trajectories of change, but the effects of policy are caused by a diverse configuration of measures that do not necessarily, or even frequently, create a coherent set of parameters at the national level (Forrest 1995) or economically effective government at the local level (Olowu 1990). On the producers' side, there have been no large-scale political or lobbying organisations in the food market as there have been in cacao, no boycotts or withdrawals in response to direct government management strategies of the kind that comes up in the history of food supply to Yaoundé and Dar es Salaam. Farmers believe that prices are influenced by the weather and by unidentifiable market forces, not by parastatals or an official price *mercuriale*. Incorporation into the food market involves a daily elaboration of competitive processes already in place and familiar to the participants, rather than a battle of the peasant versus the state or domination by a careless and/or predatory élite in a tragically lopsided class struggle (Woldemariam 1994). In this situation one can realistically draw on the predictions of central place theory that characteristic rings of some sort will develop according to a price calculus. How, then, do prices work in the local society and economy?

Yoruba Society and Economy

When Hill, Tiffen, Bauer and others who addressed African rural entrepreneurship in the 1950s and 1960s launched the then-polemic idea that this was 'rural capitalism', their case ran aground on the social historical critique that capacities for growth were highly socially contingent rather than emanating from a built-in systemic capitalist dynamic (e.g. Berry 1975). But subsequently, apart from neo-Marxist forays into a general/universal theory of petty commodity production, there was little attempt to develop an elaborated theory of the competitive market economies of the historically commercialised regions of West Africa that did not rest on capitalist categories of analysis.[9] Ethnographic work was illuminating, but stayed within the domain of social relationships in particular sectors (Trager 1981; 1985), and was suggestive of theoretical directions rather than developing them fully.

The lack of a model of market production and trade for the small producers of the African past is important, because most of the new market theories then have to resort to an evolutionary approach to modern market development: 'there is a desire to exchange'; 'some difference in personal tastes, endowments or both suggest the opportunity for traders to gain from exchange'; 'informal economies develop a strong knowledge base'; 'non-material resources, such as skills and knowledge, are available and relatively plentiful' (Cantor et al. 1992: 23,35,109). Ensminger (1992: 25) emphasises the mediation of transaction costs as trade networks widen from a narrow base. To the contrary, Yoruba scholars were emphatic, from the very first studies, that local markets did not grow out of local propensities to barter but rather out of the conditions of long-distance trade which both provided the monetary means, in cowries imported from the Atlantic trade, and demand, in passing caravans (Hodder and Ukwu 1969: 30). The cowry regime dates from well before the eighteenth century (Mabogunje 1968: 75). At Old Ọyọ at the beginning of the nineteenth century Clapperton described 'seven different markets, which are held every evening ... The chief articles for sale are yams, corn, calavances, plantains, bananas, vegetable butter, seeds of the colycynth, which forms a great article of food, sweetmeats, goats, fowls, sheep and lambs; and also cloth of the manufacture of the country, and their various instruments of agriculture' (1829: 59), all purchases being made in cowries. By at least the mid-century great quantities of goods were produced for widely-attended regional markets. In the 1850s Clarke describes the Ijẹṣa market of Okeibode with its 'hundreds of caravans', 'representatives of nearly all the Yoruba ... [from] the towns and cities for a diameter of more than one hundred miles' (1972: 125–7). In Ila, he saw huge mounds of cotton destined for the market (1972: 152), and found artisanal production so various as to be too 'tedious to mention' (1972: 275).[10] Pre-colonial oral texts and proverbs announced that 'nothing can be better known to you than money. It is what is closest to you; the starting point, in comparison with which other relationships and other knowledge can be assessed' (Barber 1995: 205).

Specialisation by occupation in Yoruba society long preceded even the cowry economy. I know of no comprehensive work on this topic, but the division of labour is so pervasively taken for granted in all sources on all topics that it must at least go back to the origins of Yoruba urbanism in the middle ages, or as early as the tenth century (Mabogunje 1968: 82–5). Fadipe writes: 'the division of labour has been carried to a very elaborate length – an elaboration which probably dates back, at least, to the eighteenth century' (Fadipe 1970: 151). Forde refers to a village where 'more than a hundred craftsmen devote themselves entirely to iron production' (1934: 165).

The historical sources are therefore at odds with the terms of evolutionary interpretation which assume a 'rational/responsive' emergence of a know-ledge/skill/identity profile for specialised production and exchange. By producing for the present urban market, Yoruba farmers are certainly responding to prices, but through their own conceptual and social organisa-tional capacities and histories: to mobilise resources, develop skills, redefine schedules of work, rethink standards and styles of consumption, evaluate prices, define and invest in 'assets', re-create community institutions and envisage a future. A whole panoply of local practice is at play.

One particular process that must demand attention is competition. In the abstract, competition stands at the centre of market theory, and substantive processes of negotiation have been a major topic in recent research in Africa. Surveying the contentious scenario that competition presents, Berry (1993) has emphasised the development and intensification of negotiability as a pervasive feature of social and economic processes, where rules and mean-ings as well as resource use are all at play. I concur, but with a proviso that comes out of the case study. Those who emphasise 'fluidity and ambiguity' have not yet defined the limits, either of the phenomenon or the concepts.[11] What, and how much of, the contention is a function, not only of recent local and national political frictions and contradictions, but of processes of competitive market expansion that are more or less familiar to people, and even generative? Market competition must have a thoroughly localised sociology and culture. For example, Belasco writes of a Yoruba economic culture in the nineteenth century, long before colonial incursions, in which negotiation and uncertainty are foundational assumptions about markets: 'the Yoruba anticipate its disorder because the indigenous view is that the market, in contrast to its Western antithesis, is characterized by a natural tendency towards disequilibrium. ... Uncertainty among the Yoruba is not fixed on the unpredictability of profit in a market enterprise, but rather it is concerned with the possibility of existential reversals' (1980: 26,32).

For the most part, attention to local cultures and styles of market growth have focused on craft specialisation and trade. It is taken for granted by an economic historian of the market in West Africa, Anthony Hopkins, that the development of trade demanded a 'moral code to sanction and control commercial relationships ... a blueprint' (1973: 64). The creation of 'tradi-tional' specialists involved guilds, patron–client relationships, networks mediated by religion and so on (Lloyd 1953). The 1950s saw a sudden profusion of new craft skills and organisations in the new metropolitan centres (Callaway 1967) that owed much to the social and cultural legacy from the past. Witness, for example, Waterman, who writes on the growth of popular urban music by invoking craft development: 'Juju groups ... [resemble] the organisations established by practitioners of modern crafts'; they have created a 'stylistic trajectory [that] has for over fifty years been grounded in processes of urban adaptation, including the creation of economic niches ...' (1990: 157,228). For export crop producers also, the literature of the 1960s was about innovation within a local style and social organisation.

For peasantries growing food crops, however, there has been no consistent attempt to define emergent, specifically commercial, moralities that might comprise indigenous attempts to give competition an expected value or to direct it along some pathways rather than others, over a period of growth and change. Although scholars have argued that farming innovations show a great deal of continuity with the past (e.g. Mortimore 1993), the social and cultural focus has been less on their specifically commercial leading edges or competitive dynamics than on their repertoires of adaptability and processes of agro-ecological innovation. For the West African populations to whom the commercial frontier was familiar, it is at least arguable that similar social and cultural processes might be applied to staple crop production as to other domains of the economy. As in moments of intense change in those other domains, themes and resolutions may well be emerging as well as arenas of enervating dispute, as people work from traditions that are *about* change, traditions *of* change, ways of investing innovation and competition with familiar modes of operation even if not with predictable outcomes.[12]

I did not arrive at the concept of a 'niche economy' through prior conviction, or from ideas put forward subsequently in economic sociology (Burt and Talmud 1993). Anthropologists have described the rational logic of product niches in market trade (Plattner 1982; Byrne 1985), but not their cultural logic over time. It was rather the actions and experiences of different participants in the economy, their narratives of novelty over the twenty years of change and expansion that suggested this interpretation. Beyond and encompassing adaptation to environment, response to prices and coping with instability, there is evidence for a local dynamic of market response that shows remarkable consonance with the modern craft dynamics and broader Yoruba cultural themes. An implicit evolutionism that constructs a trajectory from subsistence to crafts, from rural to urban, traditional to modern, is inapposite. Staple food production is part of a differentiated and diversified productive economy that comprises an expanding variety of practitioners in all its sectors, including farming. Working on the classic topic of 'the division of labour in society', one lifts some emphasis off 'labour' and vertical relations of resource control, in order to bring to the foreground the process of 'division' and both vertical and horizontal coordinates of mutual access.

Synthesis

The growth of farming is made up of a multiplicity of components: new transport, the entry of new categories of producer into the economy, the reduction in part-time farming, the expansion of men's farms, changes in crop varieties and cropping patterns, use of tractors, increase in farm labour, contention over land law and so on. I argue that the generative rubrics are more parsimonious than this seems, and that there are recurrent processes at work across a variety of arenas. There is a characteristic developmental process of market participation, whose ultimate form is occupational association. But it also permeates the competitive process at all the less formalised stages of skill/specialist development, from identification of a domain of activity, through naming of it to valuation, social organisational implementation and onwards through a sequence of well-known steps.

Because my argument emerges from inductive reasoning it is made up of a set of inferences whose consonance is argued circumstantially. That is, other possible interpretations of the farming data are found to be less persuasive or 'necessary but not sufficient', and the contours that we *can* see are shown to resonate powerfully with major Yoruba cultural themes as described in other studies. But there are other reasons besides intellectual aesthetics to wring a strong – and maybe even overdrawn – interpretation out of a limited study of one small place in a large regional economy over one short era of its history.

A major challenge of social science in modern Africa is to describe and explain the conditions of coexistence, interpenetration and mutual shaping of the forms of economic organisation that are rooted in the regulatory processes of state and capital, and those that derive their dynamics from emergent localised practice. Commercial process in the regional circuits of West Africa clearly operates in structurally different ways from the capitalism to which it is linked. In a helpful logical exploration of commoditisation, Hart (1982b) suggests that instead of thinking in binary fashion about 'types' of economic system that can be posited as mutually exclusive and counterposed to one another, one should think about a set of 'steps' towards greater abstractness of the commodity form, whose permutations and combinations are historically configured in varying ways.

The Western Nigerian staple food economy has its own configuration of market attributes that overlaps with Western monetisation and competition, but differs most notably in the virtual absence – except for certain key enclaves – of capitalist financial institutions such as the corporate form of productive organisation, banking, insurance, a complex tax code, local government assets and interventions, and land valuation as a basic element in both public and private asset formation.[13] By now these differences are best seen not as a 'traditional' condition but as an outcome of long-term engagement with the formal institutions. The 'marginalisation' of African economic processes is defined along that complex frontier between what can still be referred to roughly as the formal and informal sectors (or more precisely, the bankable and the non-bankable, the regulated-in and the non-regulated or regulated-out). The social terrain along that frontier is shifting and seems increasingly dangerous. Urban provisioning is one of its most successful and peacefully routine dynamics, by comparison, for example, with the ebb and flow of regulation and taxation, and the tumultuous history of the creation and management of wealth.

In the present context then, to push the argument as far as possible towards a *systemic* rather than an *adaptive* understanding of market processes is not primarily inspired by a populist wish to endorse the 'resilience' of local society in the face of the kind of incoherent policy described by Forrest (1995) and the yawning chasms of wealth, which in the case of Nigeria span dollar fortunes in private overseas accounts and tiny naira gains in local farmers' pockets. Rather I am convinced that the study of engagements across the interface to which I aspire in economic anthropology demands maximum space for the apprehension of local agency – individual, collective and systemic – in their fully constructive, rather than simply reactive, modes. The assumption of system facilitates an understanding of agency as having long-term and ramifying social consequences in addition to performative expressiveness and short term means–ends goals. For this reason it seems more fruitful to make bold claims for a social-systemic logic to production for regional markets than to remain so tentative that rational-adaptive, 'making do' interpretations can suffice. A century of social theory suggests the unlikelihood that social creativity – in however desperate or marginal a situation – will be without 'order', even if that order is difficult to conceptualise or to connect to the 'indiscipline' (Mbembe 1996) and fluidities that others have described for Africa's present and future.

The experience of these farmers is an extended illustration of the fact that people with a long engagement with markets are using them to recreate ways of life – careers and communities – as well as making a living through their work as food producers supplying one of the great cities of Africa.

NOTES

1. The key works that shaped scholarship on production over the late 1950s and early 1960s were De Schlippe (1956), Bohannan (1954), Jones (1959), Hill (1963), Allan (1965), Meillassoux (1960) and Miracle (1966). They are summarised in provocative ways by Boserup (1970) and Hopkins (1973), who, however, do not bring out the commercial food system for separate analysis.
2. Now Ifeloju; the district has been administratively redefined since the study.
3. CMS Yoruba Mission Papers, Birmingham University Library, CA 2,O 35, 12. I am indebted to J. D. Y. Peel for the passage from Doherty's journal.

4. During the local government reorganisations of 1976 the Onidere was not initially listed as amongst the beaded crown ǫbas of the newly-created Oyo State, presumably because of the size of the community. His claims were successfully defended, based in part on the mention of the town in Ifa verses.

5. Individuality and experimentation as one source of variety in 'traditional agriculture' was pointed out by Johnson over twenty years ago (1972). The fact that farmers elsewhere than in Africa maintain crop and field-type diversity even as they adopt new techniques (Brush 1992) offers opportunities for study of the comparative dynamics of what, and how, is saved.

6. Of course crops and varieties figure in agricultural histories elsewhere, but techniques of land and water management and the class basis of material resource control figure far more prominently as the cutting edge of historically-relevant innovation. See for example Slicher Van Bath (1963). Thirsk's (1978; 1985) emphasis on crop change in relation to small changes in consumption in England in the sixteenth and seventeenth centuries is not widely cited in relation to development issues.

7. For the wartime interventions see Falola (1989), and Guyer (1993).

8. The proper context in which to understand African farmers' investment strategies has been a source of much debate. Certain studies find low investment in agriculture (e.g. Flinn and Zuckerman 1981), but one of Berry's (1993) main contributions has been to set such findings in historical context. See also Forrest (1981: 232).

9. While illuminating in many ways, the applicability of Bernstein's (1990) review of simple commodity production to pre-colonial Africa depends on what one understands 'under capitalism' to mean. As Meillassoux (1991) has insisted, several centuries of slave history in Africa are in some sense part of expanding capitalism. The very cowries that made commercialisation possible in Yorubaland were imported through the slave trade networks (Hogendorn and Johnson 1986).

10. In fact, there has been a retreat from the general – the African mode of production (Coquery-Vidrovitch 1972), the lineage mode (Rey 1975) – to the particular and diverse with respect to pre-colonial economies. Zeleza (1993) concentrates on the *variety* of production and integration into world markets.

11. For example, Watts and Schroeder move from 'tensions and contradictions', to 'tensions and struggles', to 'struggles among competing local interests', to 'a battlefield of representations' (1991: 66–7).

12. The argument that Yoruba hermeneutics of power were oriented towards change as well as conservation, is advanced by Apter (1992). Studies of Africa wrestle continuously the concept of 'tradition' (Vansina 1990; Diagne 1993).

13. Bevan et al. contrast African economies in structural terms with 'salient features of the United States'; they are 'small, open economies with weak domestic financial markets, subject to a variety of government controls and liable to periodic temporary shocks in their terms of trade' (1990: 1,2).

14. Formal/informal are not just social science categories. A Nigerian business correspondent reported that in 1995 only about 7 per cent of the currency in circulation went through the banking system (Ndiulor 1995).

2

THE CHALLENGES AND METHODS
OF A RESTUDY

DESCRIPTIVE METHODS

The scientific potential in a restudy is maximised by a strict duplication of method that allows the closest possible comparability of data, whereas – for the anthropology of the last third of the twentieth century – the interpretive potential is maximised by a strict methodological critique that subjects those data to new theoretical contextualisation. My first study in 1968–69 was carried out under the premises of processual structural-functionalism and the second under a historicised political economy. The first was simply exploring how to link family and farm for an African market-oriented population; the second could take advantage of the great expansion of the library on African economic history and peasant production dynamics. The promise that a restudy held out therefore meant that only a combination of old and new methods would suffice, and by addition of new elements rather than by substitution of different approaches.

Creating coherence to that combination, as well as facing the fact that this angle of enquiry could illuminate only so much, involved a clear recognition of the theoretical basis on which the whole study rested. The methods from 1968 rested on the actor-based orientations of the processual social anthropology of the late 1960s, where structures were seen as reproduced and transformed through negotiation from within. The intervening years had seen the demise of actor-based analysis in favour of the study of constraints, especially from extra-local forces, and then its revival and reworking under the rubric of practice theory and agency in a world that was seen as far more unstable and capricious in its boundaries and dynamics than either the micro-structuralism of social anthropology or the macro-structuralism of political economy could adequately comprise. As a result, the individualism of method fom the 1960s did not seem as completely anachronistic in 1988 as it would have been in 1978, but it did demand serious new contextualisation.

The conclusions of the earlier study were reached at the cost of selectively detailed attention to what was ultimately a very small and under-contextualised microcosm. The farmers of Idere had been producing for the food market for several decades when I first studied the productive economy. Sales and cash income were essential components of my data, but it was the relationship between family and farm that guided the research questions in 1968–69. Although I was in Nigeria during the Civil War, the conditions of polity and market impinged on the pragmatics of my travel and on the content of my descriptions while figuring hardly at all in the interpretation of my data. Under the urban curfew, the few rather dilapidated market lorries that had escaped requisition by the army were prevented from leaving the cities or returning during darkness, so I, like the farmers and traders, had to adjust to tight schedules and very scarce space. Towards the end of my stay the army established a basic training camp on one of the market paths, which subjected all our travels to inspection and the farming villages to the presence of runaway recruits.

At that time, rather than dwelling on current conditions and their place in local history, I was posing an analytical problem, assessing two differing models of the life-cyclical relationship between family and farming: the developmental cycle of domestic groups developed by Goody, Fortes and others (1958), and the demographic cycle of labour and dependency developed by Chayanov (1966). The purpose was to explore whether, and how, productive life was planned in accordance with the domestic cycle, seen by Fortes as a function of the political-jural domain (in other words, kinship and politics) that was external to the household, and by Chayanov as a function of the worker-dependent ratio that was internal to family demography. Both the demographic and incorporative dynamics were at the centre of enquiry, but they were conceptualised as pertaining to small social units rather than to regional ecologies or market systems.

Almost immediately I started work 'the domestic group' had to be dropped as a major analytical tool because people were mobile from one house to another, and their income-earning, including farming, was individuated. Even if some aspect of domestic relations would eventually become important to the interpretation, at the pragmatic level of research method 'the household' was unmanageable. A survey of sixty farms (sixty-six farmers), in Idere and three of its satellite farming villages, focused on individuals and was planned to cover as much variation in the community as posssible in order to capture the importance of status (in accordance with Fortes), the importance of life cycle (in accordance with Chayanov), and the importance of possible variations in agro-ecology (in accordance with any materially-based theory). Starting from the Balè Agbè, the chief for the farmers, I worked outwards to include old men and teenagers, male farmers and a very few women, farmers in varying micro-ecologies, chiefs and ordinary people, artisans with part-time farms and full-time farmers. Work and budget diaries were kept for the six months of the first and most important growing season for twelve full-time savanna-crop farms (fifteen farmers altogether), all men, in three locations. One died in an accident during the period of study, which reduced the final sample of farms for all cumulative data to eleven. The rest of the data came from classic anthropological method: interviews, oral history, attendance at meetings, markets and court cases, and extensive observation.

What emerged from this study of individuals and their most immediate social context was a different and unsuspected way in which collective life was relevant, one that confirmed Fortes rather than Chayanov, albeit without the domestic group as the key unit. Variation in farm styles and personal budgets seemed in those days to have more to do with the possibilities and obligations of the farmer's seniority within the ceremonial and administrative system than with the nature or cyclical stage of either production or consumption 'groups'. In other words, they were career-specific. Basic needs were covered fairly easily in this humid savanna environment with its two growing seasons, multiple staple crops (yams, cassava, maize and guinea-corn) and a large variety of vegetables, oil seeds, cowpeas and fruit. Witness the fact that the artisans who farmed part-time for family subsistence had farms that were less than half the size of those who farmed to earn their entire living. Any effect of family size on food requirements was swamped by other factors: the kind of market orientation of the farmer and his ambitions with respect to a social career. My final interpretation was that men's aspirations and responsibilities within the kinship and political order beyond the domestic unit largely defined their work styles, income and expenditure patterns. Some farmers could envisage and were actively seeking future social prominence as heads of compound segments or even as chiefs. Others had already arrived at such positions, with all the attendant absences from farm and expenditure needs that were entailed. And for others ambition was much less evident in either social life or farming style.

At that time, though, I saw all their economic practice in synchronic style as entirely related to the social structure and its ongoing negotiations, and not – as I had to redesign the 1988 study to explore – as a particular moment in community history. In retrospect, I see these people in 1968 as turned inwards, devoted to shaping very localised careers not because they were members of a self-contained community but because the outward expansion of their horizons was suddenly contained by war-time conditions. The early 1960s was the nationalist period, marked by widening urban and regional involvement, road and bridge development, the foundation of migrant farm labour institutions, contract farming, elected local government and free primary education. All this history needed to be filled in around the decisions and negotiations in the microcosms of social and productive life.

There was one obvious way of doing this, simply by documenting regional change in greater detail. But, in keeping with the focus on agency and individuals from the earlier study, the other way was to broaden the sample of actors, so that the 'social context' for those I had concentrated on in 1968 was described not in terms of events and forces but in terms of other categories of actors. The society and economy I describe here are radically more populated than in my earlier work. In part this was a reflection of real change between 1968 and 1988, but in part it is a result of method. The core of the research design in 1988 involved restudy of the same sample as in 1968. The same people were interviewed, their farms were re-measured, their villages re-studied, work diaries kept and budgets re-collected on the same format as in 1968. Additional samples were then added: younger men who had come into the economy since 1968 (including returned migrants fom urban jobs), women, mid-scale farmers, farm labourers, owners of élite and corporate farms, tractor owners and transporters, landowners and produce traders. The result is like moving back from the detail of a small group of workers in a Brueghel painting of the peasant countryside, to take in the whole scene: the landscape all the way to the horizon, and all its other inhabitants.

There are three major limitations of such a research design, which I will discuss below, but first the following subsections summarise the samples and methods. The fieldwork in 1968–69 was done from September to the following August, and in the 1988 restudy, initial preparatory work was done in June–July 1987, the main restudies were done in January–March 1988, and monitored, reviewed and updated in June–July of 1988, and during short visits in 1989 and 1991.

Surveys and Interviews

Unless otherwise specified, all the studies were done by myself, assisted by James Ọlabiyi in 1968 and Adegboyega Ọjẹtọla in 1988.

1968
Sixty farms (sixty-six farmers, of whom two were women), in four locations (see map).

1988
1. Re-tracing of the same sample:
    – thirty-five were still living and farming (including the two women);
    – twelve had died;
    – eight had moved away and could not be found;
    – three had moved but were interviewed;
    – five were unable to farm from old age or disease, but were interviewed;
    – two were too sick to be interviewed;
    – one was still farming but elusive.
2. Seventeen men under the age of 45, from the same locations, to represent the younger generation.
3. Forty women's farms (forty-one women), from the same locations, many the wives, sisters and daughters of the men in the samples.

4. Nine local mid-scale farmers, representing all the most important men in this category.
5. Six very large farms in Ibarapa, four of them corporate enterprises and two the personal farms of local dignitaries (study carried out with Olukemi Idowu).
6. Groups of farm labourers from different ethnic backgrounds.
7. Three tractor-owners.
8. Three landowners and a lawyer who deals in land transactions.
9. Two-hundred-and-twenty-two women for two brief interviews about their entry into farming, being all the resident women in four town compounds, one from each town quarter, during their stay in town for an annual festival (study carried out with Odunyemi Ọladokun).
10. Market traders in the Igbo-Ọra Markets (with Nasiru Iṣọla).

Diary Study

1969

Twelve farms (fifteen full time, arable farmers), in three locations, kept daily work, income and expenditure diaries for the six months from 1 March to 31 August. None was literate, so all records were kept by weekly interview. Farms were measured three times, and intermittent longer interviews were done to clarify cumulative points. James Ọlabiyi kept the records during a period of my absence; otherwise I did the record-keeping myself, visiting each farmer weekly.

1988

Twenty-two full time farmers (including three women), in all four locations, kept the same records for the same six months. The fourth village, one in which cocoa was grown, was included because food cultivation had become a much more important part of the crop repertoire since 1968. The farmers included two older men and three now-adults, who had belonged to the initial diary sample in 1968. A few younger men kept their own written records, in Yoruba, but all were visited weekly. Ọjẹtọla kept the records over a period of my absence.

Remote Sensing Data

Data for this area had been collected in December 1987, just prior to the restudy. Analysis was carried out by Dr Eric Lambin. His summary of methods is included as Appendix A.

Regional and National Data

National trade statistics are used to inform an understanding of changes in the transport conditions. The Ibadan consumer price series is used as a rough measure of price changes. It is tabulated and discussed in Appendix B.

PROBLEMS AND LIMITATIONS

In the end there are three related problems which I find disconcerting, and whose resolution would require new work on a different design. The one consolation is that the present work shows exactly how important such work would be and where it needs to be focused.

The first is the familiar difficulty of all individualist methods: the problem of aggregation. Institutions are not identified a priori or studied separately, nor does one assume that one collectivity is necessarily more relevant to economic life than another. In my own view this leaves, for example, savings institutions and the customary courts under-described, for someone like myself who is not theoretically committed to individualism. One sees their influence mainly where they intervene in farmers' ongoing work. Otherwise, they are represented, although from a classic ethnographic perspective quite schematically, in Chapter 13, which is devoted to local public institutions and collective processes in general.

The second problem is more serious because the terms to engage with it do not emerge from the rest of the text, and that is my own reservations about whether the terms of description for farmers' activities in 1968 were 'right enough' on all points to warrant duplication. They were based on definitions of variables and more-or-less standard measures for a peasant economy: land and labour, income and expenditure. To illustrate the issue, let me briefly describe the problem of farm size. It seemed important in 1968 to collect these data. The literature treated them as fundamental to the calculation of what then concerned scholars: the capacity to expand production beyond self-provisioning and the labour thresholds on growth. I had difficulties from the outset because a man's farm reflected the rhythm of his capacity and ambition. Given the permissiveness of a bimodal rainfall pattern, the farm would be different sizes at different times of year. Methodological rigour with respect to farm size would then depend on doing all the measurements of any survey at the same time of year or in doing multiple measurements of the same farms, each at a different season. And for each farm a judgement also had to be made about whether very bushy fallow land, with a few stalks of cassava, qualified as part of the farm or not. For the farmer, it clearly was farmland, *oko*, in verbal concept and as a product of his past actions. But on a day-to-day schedule of planting, tending and weeding – that is, for determining the land/labour relationship – it hardly figured at all. Obviously, any defensible argument about the relationship between labour input and the size of enterprise (in the structural mode of the late 1960s), and any judgement about 'growth' over time (in the processual/historical mode of the late 1980s) would depend critically on how this very ordinary measurement issue was addressed.

The solution in 1968 was to cut out all land that had not been weeded at all over that year, to do the entire survey in the dry season to make all the measurements comparable in relation to the annual cycle, and to make three separate seasonal measurements of the fields of the diary sample in order to have some idea of change in farm size over the main growing season. At least this was clear. But I was still puzzled about how to deal adequately with the variable of 'farm size' and I did greatly appreciate Dovring's (1967) analogous reservations about measurement of labour in peasant studies (intensity of effort or amount of time?), and subsequent Scandinavian geographers' insistence on the documentation of timing, as distinct from either effort or amount of time spent. I never mustered a more profound revision of received definitions at that time, nor innovated conceptually on the boundaries of descriptive technique. But, even though farm measurement allowed some crucially important inferences to be made, I was clearly in some major sense doing the 'wrong thing' by measuring farm size in standard ways, and spent an inordinate amount of fieldwork time doing it, in both 1968 and 1988.

The conditions of restudy demanded that I do the same again, although farms were now composed differently, with different cultivation techniques and crop rotations on different plots. Even as small a shift as the change of the final crop from cassava (which needs little weeding after a certain point) to a crop that requires somewhat more care (such as pigeon peas), brings the near-fallow category of land within the criteria of 'the farm'. The fact that such small changes by farmers should have such large implications for measurement, in systems where small calibrations and reconfigurations are the object of the research, means that the methods are still too blunt for the phenomena.

Again, to give another graphic example that comes up several times in my exposition: my working assumption, for the purposes of exact repetition of method, that the six months from 1 March to 31 August could be treated the same in 1988 as in 1968 turned out to be quite wrong, although for reasons that were not obvious at the outset. I knew that the crop repertoire had changed, but this was still rainfed agriculture so the rainfall pattern still mandated the planting seasons, and the growth pattern of the crops mandated the time of harvest. What I had not accounted for was that the rainfall pattern had become much more unpredictable since the great West African drought of the mid-1970s, and that farmers planted very tentatively rather than confidently in March. The aggregate pattern showed that they had effectively shifted the entire economy three weeks later into the calendar. This affected the comparability of my results on every variable, including the timing of income from sales, which – for the old market crop of egusi – had shifted until even later into the year because of other factors altogether. Every result had to be recontextualised. Again 'standard' methods and the terms of rigorous comparisons were inflexible relative to the reality.

Thinking through the dilemmas and frustrations, one cannot help but note that the variables we address in the study of economic life tend to be those that would be reachable by policy, if the economic systems were vertically integrated. They are policy instruments under specific structural conditions: relative prices, wages, interest rates, tax levels and contract law, the mandated calendrics of national bureaucracy and also, though less directly, population growth and concentration, land access, and thereby farm size. In Nigeria, as I indicated in the introduction, the policy reach for shaping the magnitude and direction of producers' responsiveness has been limited, as well as inconsistently used. Should we abandon the effort of difficult and perhaps inapposite measurement, and thereby sacrifice comparative possibilities, or try to 'refine' the measures? As I draw out throughout the book, there are advantages to having tried to work with standard variables, but in the end one is aware of their limits and distortions.

This brings me finally to issues with which I remain most dissatisfied, phenomena that are ill-described because their importance was not seen until too late, or quite simply gaps in ethnographic coverage. One gap is no longer possible to fill adequately. As I pointed out, some of the patterns in the quantitative data surprised me and I found far too little commentary in my field notes to illuminate people's own understandings of them. Here I rely on other Yoruba sources and on Yoruba colleagues to flesh out the cultural logic. In the spirit of critical exploration, where I do see these problems I simply go as far as possible and then suggest directions for more comprehensive study in the future. Most importantly, my relatively short time in the field and my limited proficiency in the Yoruba language, especially beyond the vocabulary and conversation relative to farm and market, place constraints on culturally-based interpretation. Although I could follow certain conversations fairly accurately, all farm interviews were done with the help of an assistant/interpreter. As a result, when in doubt on the cultural front I defer to other sources as well as my own, and do not push the analysis further than my own confidence in it. Time in the field was one year in 1968–69, and a total of seven months for the restudy, spread over four visits, the main efforts being made over two continuous stays of three and two months between January and August 1988. I have had the good fortune of being able to remain in close correspondence and to visit for short periods since then, which has allowed me to firm up certain points.

THE FORMAT OF THE BOOK

The book is written to maximise what can be learned from an individualist method, where the main field data are first presented by actor and then aggregated at the end, in the context of issues about ecological and social systems that have arisen in the Yoruba and comparative literature. But since the meaning of 'individual' or 'career' is a necessarily social one, I round out the introductory section with a history of the town itself, as it is told, as one

of personal careers and social aggregations. The changing bases for occupation, identity and social organisation in the transformation from an older
division of labour to an agricultural, urban provisioning, economy, form the
beginning and end of the narrative, and indeed of the analysis.

In Part II, each chapter centres on the productive activities of one set of
people over the twenty years between 1968 and 1988. The sequence follows
the chronology of their entry into the hinterland economy: Fulani herders,
Idoma migrant labourers, formal sector organisations to promote incorporation through the 1960s, the farmers of 1968–69, and then all the varied
participants in the subsequent expansion, including new migrant farm labourers, tractor-owners and the other functionaries of the vehicle expansion
of the late 1970s, mid-scale farmers and large-scale corporate and agribusiness ventures, youth returning from the declining economies of the
cities after the crises of the mid-1980s, women, and the small-scale male
farmers who anchor the system. The male farmers, labourers, contract
farmers and a few women farmers were already established in 1968, as were
a few lorry transporters. The vehicle expansion of the 1970s is the fulcrum of
change. The chapter on transporters stands at the centre, followed by the
new participants in the food economy who moved in as accessibility improved and Idere moved structurally from the peripheral to the accessible
hinterland.

I do not attempt to balance the length of the descriptive chapters. Each is
as long as I have something to contribute, as far as possible in a detail that is
commensurate with the importance of the protagonists in the regional
economy. Each chapter is in the nature of a vignette, refering only in limited
ways to the others. The synergies and systemic inter-relations are picked up
in Part III, the final chapter of which summarises the organisational characteristics and cultural foundations of the niche economy.

An inductive approach involves laying out the evidence from which alternative arguments could be made, which perhaps burdens the exposition.
And, when the theme is the changing shape of diversity, it is bound to seem
over-detailed and diffuse to some readers at some points, and others at other
points. In the light of the inevitable challenge, I have concluded each chapter
not with a summary but with an interpretation that links the chapters to one
another, and to the final section, which draws the threads together.

3

IDERE: AN INVENTED COMMUNITY

Yoruba towns preserve and invoke the history of their foundation, often in a past that is fairly recent by comparative standards of agricultural communities in Europe or China. Many have been at their current sites for a hundred years or less at the time of the great colonial project of imposing immobility. The invention of community is a particularly apposite term for the hundreds of new Yoruba-speaking communities that were founded in the wake of the fall of Ọyọ in the 1837, and the Yoruba Wars of the nineteenth century. Many never managed to establish themselves as new communities. Some, of which Idere is one relatively small example, became the established rural communities of modern Western Nigerian social and economic life, their present stability a misleading guide to a preserved past of multiple personal pathways and aggregative moments, committed alliances and proudly remembered divergent ancestral origins (see Barber 1991). Ratification from the 1860s and into the colonial era by its overlord, Ibadan, confirmed its continuity in the regional political economy (Akintoye 1971: xviii, 212).

While introducing the town of Idere in this chapter, I am highlighting its deliberate creation because the operative principles of diversity and differentiation are critically relevant to later arguments about the economy. The constitution of the town, *ilú*, was the main subject of debate and consensus in the early nineteenth century. The operation of precedence and authority, *oyè* and *agbà* – succession to office, the powers of the ọba, relationship to other towns in the district and to the colonial authorities – was deeply contentious in the late nineteenth and early twentieth centuries. At the same time the social principles governing occupational association and differentiation, *ẹgbẹ́*, were applied to recruit and organise the population. Contention was intrinsic to the playing out of all social dynamics because decisions established precedent.

That goes for writing an official version of the collective history as well as interpreting the composite story to be gleaned from individual, compound and quarter historical sources. In a meeting with one of the notables of Idere in 1988, he described how their project of writing a town history had run aground on fundamental disagreement over who the first inhabitant of 'Idere' had been. Having studied town history in 1968 through collecting the histories of fifty-seven of the sixty-nine compounds and the four quarters,

I had a basic knowledge and interpretation from which to hazard my own suggestion as a contribution to the debate and as a possible way of breaking the deadlock. Idere, I argued, came closer than any other case I knew of to the theory of the Social Contract. The name comes from *dè*, meaning tied or bound, and was given when the three main groups of socially heterogeneous refugees from the Yoruba Wars came together in about 1840 in this new site in the savanna, far to the south of Old Oyo from whence came the largest single contingent. As I collected the varied histories of compounds, quarters, occupations and chieftaincy titles there had emerged a remarkable process of community creation; 'airy thinness', in the words of Shakespeare in *The Tempest*, had been given 'a local habitation and a name'. The idea of a constitutional conference came to mind, whereby an older model of political life was self-consciously replicated, to use Kopytoff's (1987) phrase, or probably negotiated, by the entire motley collection of first inhab- itants and later in-migrants, recruits and affines. My 'social contract' sug- gestion was greeted with little enthusiasm, however. Foundation definitively matters in a conception of the world permeated with seniority and precedence, above all where military ambition does not supercede civilian principles, under the defensive, civilian, more consensual conditions that Drewal and Drewal (1983) have recently argued to be characteristic of Western Yorubaland.

There was no major military leader of the Idere people. The first ọba, Olufiji, emerges rather as an extraordinarily skilled manager of the social principles and relationships of Yoruba civil society. His compromises still stand. Others' claims to high rank, that he negotiated downwards in the gradations of status in order to demarcate a single royal line, are still repre- sented in ritual and in the names of compounds but they are no longer actionable claims to the title. The leeway he gave for the *de facto* strength of certain individuals to be permanently recognised, irrespective of formal status, still exists in family control over certain titles. The basis for quarter (*àdúgbò*) organisation lies in recognition given to the pre-existing groupings of the refugees, and the freedom of compounds to recruit their own new branches through friendship rather than descent appears in several com- pound histories. The Orò cult through which the population used to control royal power was instituted very early, possibly during his reign. Thus, al- though the outcome was royal and hierarchical, the process shows clear evi- dence of populist negotiation.

THE FOUNDATION OF IDERE

The question of foundation is in part a question of the origins of the moral authority by which ties became perpetually binding. And indeed they have been so, in ways that no contract theory alone can explain. As early as 1890 the entire, barely fifty-year-old town was evacuated and destroyed by the invading Dahomean army. The citizens fled to Iseyin, and some stayed there when the rest returned to the old site to rebuild. Both groups preserved the tradition as it had been already established, rather than using the moment to re-create either new communities or new hierarchical relationships. The Iseyin contingent has retained for a hundred years its right to propose a candidate for the ọba's title when their own royal line's turn comes around. And the returnees rebuilt their compounds on the exact foundations, in the same town quarters, from which they had fled three years earlier.[1] An era of negotiation about formal hierarchy and identity had been superceded by one in which people accepted and identified with certain bounds and commitments that had been put in place at the moment that was culturally recognised as foundational.

There were three parties to foundation of the community at the site of the town: the royal line, the descendants of the hunter Adanatu who – all agree – used the region as a hunting ground before the establishment of any settlement, and the descendants of one Jọoda, who claimed a toll in cowries along the trade route that ran north–south. There were no other pre-existing settlements to deal with.[2] The royal claims to founder status rest not on their subsequent role as constitutional architects, but on their early presence in the area combined with possession of insignia from the politico-religious centre of Ile-Ife. The narrative of foundation has great symbolic importance for support of their authority, and is concretised in royal rights – that have recently been defended in court – to the site of their first settlement at Ibona, to which all deceased ọbas are returned to be buried.[3] According to the royal family's own history, three ọbas died and were buried at Ibona, during which time they designated other settlement sites for incoming refugees. It is said to be the fifth ọba that moved the settlement to the rocks above the present site of Idere and created a properly constituted town. At the outside limit it could not have been much more than thirty years between settlement at Ibona and movement down into the valley at the present site, and was probably much shorter, since CMS missionary S. W. Doherty noted Idere in 1877 as 'an ancient royal town of all the Barapa territory but now a small village at the foot of a rocky hill where they had lately descended from'.[4]

It was in their search for a new site, under threat from the Fulani, that the royal group ran across the fire of Adanatu, the hunter, founder of Ile Ajagba. Adanatu's hunting territory became one of the largest areas available to Idere's farmers, and indeed his son, Lala, was said to live largely from the ìṣákọ́lè tribute paid to him by the new farming population that Idere brought to his land. The third major contender for founding status is the family of Jọoda, said to be the bálè of the first constituted settlement near to the present site of the town. A refugee from Ọyọ, where his family had been rafter-makers at the palace, he gathered around himself a collection of other

refugees to exact cowry tolls on passing caravans. His first relationship with
the royal family was the classic alliance of marriage: his daughter married a
brother's son of Olufiji. Afterwards they were offered a title (Balẹ Onígbió),
but refused in favour of another with more prestigious connotations
(Ọdọfin).

These three, together, constitute Idere's founding moment: royalty, terri-
torial knowledge and control, and the strength of a solid location on regional
networks. The town they built was probably quite small. It was enumerated
at just under 3000 inhabitants in 1934 (Childs 1934: 23), and in the 1960s
at about 6000, living in sixty-nine compounds. If the nineteenth century
population had been around 2000, they constructed a remarkably complex
system for such small size. Indeed Kopytoff's 'replication' was taken to ex-
tremes. Four quarters were instituted, each with its own chieftaincy hierarchy, along with a set of military titles. Altogether there were at least nine
titles in the Ẹgbẹ Balogun (the military hierarchy) and seventeen for Ilu (the
town), including the Iyalode for women. Some of the rights to a title were
brought by the refugees from their original homes and incorporated into the
Idere system. Only three (Ṣobaloju, Ikolaba and Asalu) had been created
since the foundation by the time I collected the historical narratives in 1968.
In the beginning, then, there was probably at least one major Idere title per
ninety or so inhabitants – men, women and children – and on the average, at
least one for every three compounds. Possibly one in twenty adult men of all
ages was given a major title in either the civilian or military hierarchies.

One clue to the early proliferation of titles is their subsequent fate. Almost
immediately the lesser titles failed to find incumbents. While there had been
eleven Baloguns up to 1968, nine Jaguns, six Ọdọfins and nine Onideres
(the ọba), there had only been two Bansas. The first died in suspicious circumstances and no one else wanted the position. The title of Ekerin was
once left vacant because the in-fighting was so fierce that everyone became
afraid of evil medicine. Dilemmas were freqent and the political need less
insistent,[5] so that by the time the colonialists were setting up the Native
Court system the number of chiefs had fallen so low that the people had to
be ordered to fill the positions. By then, the foundational purposes had long
since been fulfilled and the meaning of chieftaincy was in an era of re-
creation.

Even for the titles that were continuously occupied, the first decades
seem to have been quite experimental in the order of succession. The two
alternating lines of the royal house – Ala and Ija – were not set up until the
third succession after Idere was founded, but it was a determined and
deliberate move by the Afọbajẹ, the kingmakers (Ọdọfin, Baasin, Jagun,
Aṣipa and Balogun) that was vigorously defended at several junctures.[5] Other
titles were experimental in other ways. Ọdọfin followed the same pattern as
Onidere, alternating from a patrilineal descent line to one traced through a

female link. Jagun, on the other hand, although it is now the head chieftaincy for two quarters, Koso and Apa, was originally given to a particular person as an honour, then passed on at his request to his friend, and only then instituted more formally as a title for the two original incumbents' quarters. In brief, there are many cases where the chieftaincy was clearly instituted long before the bases for succession were clarified and formulated.

The foundational moment was an inclusive one. Every family who brought a title or laid a claim that was consonant with the pre-eminence of the royal family was accommodated. It was simply more than anyone needed or wanted or could become deeply invested in during the troubled and defensive times of the mid- and late-nineteenth century. Then in the colonial period the pressures to provide functionaries combined with the desire to maintain a high regional profile, and a new punctiliousness was introduced: into the filling of positions and into the rigour of the rules. It was Onidere Oyerogba, Idere's first literate ọba, who created two new chieftaincy positions and developed wider regional networks before he died in 1956.

Beyond inclusiveness of the people who were already present by accidents of history at the founding moment, the Idere leadership went about deliberate community composition. A Yoruba town requires occupational specialists and devotees of òrìsà (spirits and gods). The original Idere population had too many of some kinds and none of others. Warriors and hunters, all devotees of Ogun, were over-represented. Eight of the fifty-seven compounds (out of a total of sixty-nine) whose histories were narrated in 1968 descended from warriors or hunters, although many retain only a name, a tradition of worship or a shrine site to indicate this. Only two compounds, Ile Ọlọdẹ and Ile Agẹdi, actively maintain the warrior tradition, Ile Ọlọdẹ being the custodian of the shrine to Ogun, the god of metallurgy, of hunting and of war. Early Idere also had three blacksmith compounds, only one of which, Ile Adiomẹwa, was actively working the trade in 1968. Some other occupations that people brought with them were inapplicable within the context of such a small town. The founders of Ile Bale Ṣango had been gatekeepers at Ọyọ, and the founders of Ile Asuamọn had been roof-makers to the palace, neither of which transposed into a small town context. By sheer good fortune two key skills were represented from the start: facial mark-making (Ile Olola) and the position of Alapinni to the Egungun cult (Ile Ogogo).

Before continuing with local history, the shape and importance of occupation demands exploration since it becomes a central theme, picked up in its organisational form of association in the following section. The linguistic form for occupations and expertise involves naming, and this is one of the most profoundly evocative processes in Yoruba culture (Barber 1991). Often it involves applying the prefix oní- or alá- to another word, which conveys the meaning of 'identification with' and 'animator of', or, more briefly if less accurately, 'owner of'. Every skill and every occupation can be expressed in this form: *oníṣẹ́* (owner of work) is a labourer; *aláàbáṣiṣẹ́* (owner of help with work) is a co-worker; *oníjó* (owner of dance) is a dancer. The prefix is applicable to just about any noun: skills such as dance or prayer, objects such as fish or money, features of character or physique,[7] status (a chairman is 'owner of the chair') and place (the Ibarapa ọbas are the Onidere of Idere and the Eleruwa of Eruwa), ramifying along inventive combinations for praise, profit and poking fun through puns and plays on words that seem endless.

Personal differences of occupation and expertise are neither dictated by group membership nor achieved exclusively by personal talent. In the past divination guided people's paths. People's life careers are individuated through the concept of *orí*, the choice made before birth, the religious concept identified with the inner head (*orí* being the ordinary word for head). Abimbola writes: 'Ori may be regarded as the greatest god of all. Every man's Ori is regarded as his personal god who is expected to be more interested in his personal affairs than the other gods who are regarded as belonging to everybody' (1976: 114). The wishes of Ori can only be discovered by consultation with Ifá; 'By doing so, every man would be able to tread the path already laid out for him in heaven ...' (Abimbola 1976: 115). Each person's life follows a trajectory of its own with respect to all the attributes that would affect social and economic decisions: the opportunity for success, the taboos and avoidances to be observed, the specific talents and expertise that one has. No one expects his or her life or talents to duplicate any other, and yet a person is also a reincarnation of an ancestor and a composite of all sixteen sides of his or her genealogy back as far as great-great-grandparents.

To my knowledge there is no comprehensive analysis of how Ori individuation and Ifa divination work in the economic domain as distinct from the religious life (for which see Lawal 1985). Clearly they do, since Yoruba philosophers have noted that the concept of individuation itself is not specific to a cultural domain, but rather presumes a basic moral composite (Akiwowo 1986; debated by Lawuyi and Taiwo 1990). Another conceptual angle on human difference is provided by different terms for kinds of personal power (Hallen and Sodipo 1986), and another by concepts of moral quality (Bascom 1951), both of which refer back to collectivity as well as forward to particularity.

The need to cultivate diversity, as a community, was clearly evident in Idere's foundational policies. With a small, haphazardly composed population, certain skills and sources of knowledge were not represented at all. For all of these, the ọba sent messengers to surrounding communities to recruit practitioners. There was no one who could fulfil the duties of Baba Mogba for the cult of Ṣango, and no one to be *babaláwo*, healer and worker of the Ifa oracle. In particular, Idere lacked certain types of drum essential for ceremonial life. Only *bàtá* came from Ọyọ. A drummer for *apèsìn*, Akinomi, founder of Ile Onimu, was invited from the neighbouring town of Igbo-Ọra. During the reign of Oyepami, well after the descent into the valley, a member of Ile Bale Ṣango, one Alade, learned to play *dùndún*, the drum for praise- and poetry-singing for the ọba, on a visit to his wife's kin in Ipaya. Both sexes of his descendants over two generations were taught to play in order to make up for their lack of numbers; the women only gave up when there were enough men to carry on. Gradually during the first forty years of its existence, Idere acquired drummers for several of the main Yoruba drums.

The masquerades for the political control association of Oro also had to be acquired from outside. The Oro cult was the community's sanction on royal conduct once the incumbent had been invested. This group held the ultimate power of criminal execution and deposition. The latter power has only been used once in Idere history,[8] but until very recently, the Oro festival was practised every year. By consensus, the Oro secrets came to Idere with the ancestors of two houses, Ile Olubuṣe and Ile Agunyan, who were linked to already-established compounds by marriage in the settlers' generation.[9] Oro was a novelty that did not come from the Ọyọ template of Yoruba constitution brought by the ọba and the majority of the people. It is more closely related to the populations towards whose area they were moving, the Egba and the Ijebu, than to Ọyọ, but its organisation was mapped over the quarter (*àdúgbò*) administrative structure of the town; each quarter has its own masquerader.[10] In principle, then, Oro was the ritual arm of the entire town, as a political collectivity distinct from and potentially opposed to a particular incumbent ọba, once the community had already become established by 'binding' itself together. Thus politically salient differentiation and opposition are not only based on the stories of pre-existing separate identity, even though these exist and are invoked for other purposes. They have also developed subsequent to the achievement of collective identity, and depend on the already-established structures of collective life.

ASSOCIATIONS

One of the pervasive themes of emergent collective life, for occupations as for the Oro and other cults, is association. Fadipe wrote of 'the genius of the Yoruba for organising associations' (1970: 243). The principle of *ẹgbẹ́* is recurrent and pervasive. *Ẹgbẹ́* of many kinds proliferate: age and occupational associations, religious groups and social clubs. Every person belongs to several and their social life is at least as predicated on these memberships as on descent and political hierarchy. In fact, although the term can be translated as a club or association, it applies to a wide and inclusive range of social forms that can include kinship and politics. Its original referent may have been to age sets and to occupational guilds (Eades 1980: 61), but this hardly

covers the depth of cultural resonance or the breadth of proliferation of the
ẹgbẹ́ kind of organisation. An organised descent group can be termed ẹgbẹ́,
and the war chiefs in the Idere hierarchy are known as Ẹgbẹ́ Balogun, the
association of the Balogun. Abraham indicates that an army is ẹgbẹ́ ogun
(1958: 178). It is even suggested that ẹgbẹ́ is the basic concept for the social
world itself (Drewal and Drewal 1983: 8). The primary emphasis accorded
in older descriptions to descent groups and town political hierarchies, about
which Peel expresses reservations (1983: 10), has relegated ẹgbẹ́ to the status
of a 'cross-cutting' organisation (e.g. Eades 1980: 61), whereas a case might
well be made that association is a key concept in all domains of social life.
Certainly the idea of differentiated occupations goes back to the beginnings,
and the foundation of a refugee town such as Idere evokes the deliberate
composition of a unit out of those different occupations.

Ẹgbẹ́ represent and perpetuate difference, and in fact contain it within a
certain model since, as Fadipe writes, 'no one was allowed to set up in any
trade unless he was the member of the appropriate guild', and each guild
had to represent itself to 'the authorities' of the town (1970: 254–5). The
moral authority of the town constitution remains important to the functioning of a greatly expanded associational life a century and a half after its
foundation. The bases of social diversity can change over time, from age
sets, to religious congregations, to occupations, and to political parties without the general principles altering very much. Even the titles from one kind
of ẹgbẹ́ can be borrowed and applied to another. For example, one of the
farmers in the study was pàràkòyí of the Muslim congregation, pàràkòyí being primarily a title in a traders' association in the market (Fadipe 1970:
255). The micro-dynamics of ẹgbẹ́ organisation depend on the process of
naming that has been mentioned already (see Barber 1991). Differentiation
by naming in this way is intrinsically an invocation of a potential for ẹgbẹ́
formation. The naming/ẹgbẹ́ mutual imbrication, that simultaneously
announces difference and connection, underlies far more of social life than
occupational specialisation alone.

KINSHIP AND COMPOUNDS

The compounds themelves were no less 'composed' than the communities
of which they constituted the basic administrative unit. While the ideology
of patrilineal descent has been replicated from Ọyọ, the actual genealogies
are a little more varied, especially in the founding generations. Patrilineal
descent groups may be spread over more than one compound.[11] Most compounds are more genealogically discrete, with other kinds of internal variety.
Some are divided into igún: sides, while others of no smaller size are not.[12]
Igún are usually identified by the personal careers of their founders, such as
religious injunctions given to their ancestors by the Ifa oracle, or a former
member's chieftaincy title, rather than by the complementary opposition of

classic descent group theory. A few compounds include lines descended through women.[13]

Possibly the variation in compound structure is due to differences in the traditions of origin that the settlers brought. After all, only thirty-five of the compound histories named Ọyọ as their place of origin. Two were even Nupe rather than Yoruba. But the variation is also consonant with other constitutional flexibilities, and reflects both the inventive nature of social life and the relative autonomy of the compounds to regulate their own membership. By virtue of the varying size of the foundational groups, fission and accretion, the size of compounds in 1968 varied very widely. According to the nominal roll book, which enumerated all men over the age of sixteen who were not full-time students, the average adult male compound membership was twenty. Eight compounds, however, had five or less adult male members while four, three of them important title-holding compounds, had over fifty.

The relative independence of the compounds, with their diverse histories of origin, occupational and religious affiliations, and their subsequent policies of internal division and accretion, is most strikingly manifest in the land system. Like the northern Yoruba towns, and unlike one of its Ibarapa neighbours, the town of Eruwa, Idere is collectively identified with surrounding land but its dispensation is entirely controlled by the compounds. Land ownership reflects the community's origin in hunting and warfare. Of the sixty-nine compounds listed in 1968, only about twenty were really landowners, onílẹ̀, and the areas owned bore no straight relationship to political power, demographic size or compound occupation. The largest landowner of all is the compound descended from Adanatu, the hunter, that is said to own a very large area corresponding to their former hunting territory. The royal family and the descendants of Jọoda also own land. But it is by virtue of being founders and early settlers that compounds claim both a political role and land; land itself gives no particular political privilege. Indeed in some isolated communities further north, such as Idiyan, it is the latecomers who own more land because they were told to go beyond the current boundaries, into territory that was in effect quite limitless at the time. By contrast, the limits of Idere land to the north, east and most importantly in the fertile area to the west, had been set in place by the claims of citizens of other Ibarapa towns. Latecomers were contained, and therefore simply had recourse to the ìṣákọ̀lẹ̀ system of tribute to the existing landowners rather than struggling to find land of their own. The area was sparsely populated, and the payments of oil and chickens annually in recognition of ownership were hardly onerous. As the classic Yoruba ilé-abúlé, dual residence system began to develop, probably in the early twentieth century, large numbers of Idere people settled in farming hamlets on land belonging to other compounds, some of them in other towns. A large part of the fertile land to the west of the town, for example, is owned by the titled compound of Ọdọmọfin at the neighbouring town of Aiyetẹ. So little was land ownership a factor of economic or political moment.

Before turning briefly to the rural–urban residence pattern, one needs to discuss 'membership', being a 'child' of a particular compound: ọmọ 'lé. There are sixteen sides (igún) to the person, each attributable to the descent line of one of sixteen great-great-grandparents, male and female, and marriage is not permitted within those lines. A person is therefore a child of all those lines of descent, traced through both males and females without discrimination. It is social organisation and not the conceptual basis of personhood that is patrilineal. Indeed it can be argued that gender is a quali-fier and not a foundational attribute in Yoruba philosophy (see Oyewumi n.d.), a point that will come up later with respect to the dynamics of gender and work. A woman never loses or even really attenuates her status as ọmọ 'lé, a child of the house, when she marries and moves into another compound. She has personal ritual obligations in her home compound throughout her life, and it is the fulfilment of these, rather than her subsistence duties as a mother, that have always made a personal income so imperative for married women. Many women used to return home after completion of childbear-ing, and even now it is a daughter rather than a daughter-in-law who is expected to drop everything else to take care of her parents in their final illness.

The children of those women are considered ọmọ 'lé of her compound, on principle. In fact, the word 'child' itself is gender-free, and has to be deliber-ately gendered by the addition of ọkùnrin, male, or obìnrin, female. It is awkward, and only attributed when asked, when the asker is too foreign to decipher the implied gender of a personal name, praise name or nickname. No one uses these composites routinely, and when they speak English many of the more marginally educated make random mistakes in the attribution of gender. As one man explained to me, 'it is an accident that a child is female'. When I was first in Idere in 1968 it was both rude and courting gross inaccuracy to ask a person how many children they had. They were literally countless, since they included every child of every person in all sixteen lines who could be referred to by one's direct descendants by the sibling terms of ẹ̀gbọ́n, senior sibling and àbúrò, junior sibling (both terms ungendered).

Occupationally, women clustered in processing and trade, pottery and cloth dyeing. In principle, however, a woman could aspire to be anything she wished and could be actively encouraged, like the duaghter of Akinomi the dùndún drummer, to take up unusual occupations if needed. As Barber writes, 'a woman becomes a babaláwo (Ifa priest) by choosing to be one; once she acts as a babaláwo she is one' (Barber 1991: 289; see also Matory 1994).

What all this meant in terms of land was that in principle anyone was free to farm, without tribute, on the land of any compound to which they could trace descent, in both male and female lines. Consequently there must be almost no one, in the entire town, who could not acquire farm land by descent rights if they wanted to. The fact that many have paid *iṣákọ̀lẹ̀* for generations reflects their preference for particular locations rather than their lack of access. The single and important situation where the patriline mattered in 1968 was in a case of extreme delict, when a compound head could say, effectively: 'We are dealing with the mother (who belongs to us) but not with you, her child.'[14]

It remains for later discussion how this basic framework is shifting under the pressures of provisions of the Land Use Act of 1978, requests for large areas by mid-scale and corporate farmers, the needs of women for farm land, and the vicissitudes of the *iṣákọ́lẹ̀* system. In 1968 and before that date, the very marked inequality of landownership had absolutely no implications for productive or commercial limitations. It was bound up in the foundational process of defining identity separately from and contributive to the new community. Every basis for land access was a story of arrival, acceptance and status, not a history of agriculture. The latter is a different history, not collected from compounds but largely from individuals, reflecting the importance of personal realisation in the living of a productive career.

Although most men farmed and most women processed agricultural goods, Idere was not an agricultural community during its foundational era. The site had not been chosen for reasons of production. The main principles on which it had been built had very little to do with the fertility of the environment, and the division of labour was as religious and political as it was productive. Complementarities of function referred as much to society – drummers, masqueraders, mark-makers, warriors – as to economy. It is only gradually and recently becoming an agricultural community, as occupations are added, as agriculture is expanded and the old occupational complementarities fall into decline. This process of re-composition, in a cultural context in which concepts and practices of differentiation and complementarity of function have very deep roots, is one of the main themes of later chapters.

FARMING

Settlement on the Land

In Yoruba ideology, to be a farmer is to practise a skill. A person is *àgbẹ̀*. All sources concur, almost without extensive justification, that farming was not just a general and obligatory means of staying alive, but a way of being a social person. The missionary William Clarke waxed lyrical about the farms he saw in the 1850s in the Ijaye region, already identified as a source of agricultural goods for the whole region: 'The natives are not so much interested in any department of labour as in the cultivation of the soil and consequently they lead no calling more honourable ... This is certainly a redeeming trait and confirms strongly the hope of the man who, in labouring for the generation of a lost people, beholds in their beautiful farms rendered doubly beautiful by nature's own scenery extended far and wide, oftentimes as far as the eye can reach, the elements of success and the foundation of whatever is permanent and durable' (1972: 260,262). A century later the urban population interviewed by Lloyd recognised that '(w)ealth from farming ... derives from the control not of land but of skills and labour. Farming is a skilled operation' (1974: 39).

Life in the *abúlé*, the farming hamlets, expresses the relative autonomy of productive careers most clearly. People only started to move out to the *abúlé* when the surroundings became peaceful enough to risk the great vulnerability of life in a small settlement in the open savanna. But they did not move out for lack of land, nor did they stay as close as possible to town. Some of the oldest Idere *abúlé* are far out in the savanna to the west, several hours' walk away, on land belonging to compounds in the neighboring town. And this in an era when there were hardly any cash crops, no transport except headloading and no bridge over the Ofiki River which became a dangerous torrent in the rainy season.

An elderly woman took me to the site of her grandfather's first *abúlé*, now abandoned but unmistakably marked by the shade trees and the bare, forked tree-trunk, richly glossed by the touch of countless hands, that had once supported the rafters of their house. As we approached she danced for the ancestors, with a look of such joy that one could momentarily imagine the child who had once loved the place. People moved out to the *abúlé* for a variety of reasons, but many of them were positive, coming down to the need for more leeway in life than the structures of the town afforded. Farm was less an exile or a necessity than it was a temporary and curative refuge, an alternative way of life. Members of a drumming compound did some of the teaching of their children at farm. Sufferers from certain diseases, such as epilepsy and mental illness, had to be taken care of at farm. And the *abúlé* housed eccentrics, both local and foreign.[15]

Although we gloss the word *abúlé* as farming hamlet or rural dwelling (as distinct from a house in town, which is always *ilé*), farming was probably not really their first function. The one thing the *abúlé* was not in those early days was a clearly superior place to farm. Certain areas did have specific advantages of soil type, natural vegetation or the presence of large flat rock outcrops that could be used for drying before there was concrete. But these advantages would emerge much later, with the improvement in transport and links to the market. Before then, cultivating large quantities of any crop in areas seven or so miles from town would mean headloading it in: a fairly massive task with only the labour force of the immediate family that formed the typical farm residential unit. It was difficult to return to town regularly during the season, and extremely demanding if someone died at farm and the body had to be headloaded back for burial. I saw this done in 1968: an extraordinary feat of strength that required a whole team of porters, taking short turns to carry the body, strapped to a bamboo stretcher. As a result of these transport limits, even in the 1960s well after the construction of the Ofiki River bridge and the establishment of rural wholesale markets served by lorries, the farms of men living in the *abúlé* were no bigger than those near to the town. Land access was clearly not the issue.

One possibility offered by the greater freedom and simpler authority structure was mobility. In the villages, and in farming in general, each person was then and still is now free to move as he or she pleases, within the framework of land access. In the past, no one was allocating or bounding people's space and generally no one could prevent anyone from coming and going. Compound membership in town is given by birth, but the location of work is entirely open; it is a temporary way-station, with no lasting significance. A person is working to realise him/herself, to fulfil obligations and to rise in status, to realise his *orí*, the spirit in his own head. Indeed, the marked attribute of farming in this highly structured community is the centrality of individual work and personal knowledge as the key resources.

Particular villages can then rise and fall with farmers' needs and fortunes in a way that the *de jure* town population does not. According to a population survey done from the Igbo-Qra Health Centre in the late 1970s, the Idere population residing in the farming villages was 2615 (almost exactly 25 per cent), with the other 75 per cent (8,143) in town (Brieger and Ramakrishna ms.). By the late 1980s some villages had already started to decline and others seemed to be growing as the prominence of market catchment areas shifted and as some farmers continued the search for suitable cocoa land to diversify their production. In general, however, the main areas of *abúlé* settlement have been quite stable for decades and although there have been surges of interest in life at farm there has been no very marked 'migration' out of the daily commutable hinterland of Idere that one might associate with serious land shortage in the town vicinity. As Richards writes of another Yoruba area, further south, '(d)ecisions about settlement are not to be explained solely in practical and utilitarian terms' (1992: 177).

The Idere Environment

The topography of Idere's land is first and foremost historical and religious. More areas are named than have current settlements: the site of an ancestor's pause on the journey, the location of a shrine, a place in the rocks where people hid during wars. The names usually reflect this history rather than any productive characteristics. Many are named for people, or events that gave a founder his personal nickname (Afuniẹ: we gave to eat), or simply the compound membership of the founder (Jagun). And like the names of people and compounds, they can change or acquire alternatives.

Major discriminations made about the productive capacities of the savanna are relatively simple. Apart from the rocks (òkè), rivers (odò), patches of forest (igbó) and river-bed land for cultivation in the dry season (àkùrò) the most important designations are by soil type. Ilẹ̀'dú (black soil) predominates in the area north and west of the town, and was thought particularly suitable for ẹ̀gúsí-melon cultivation. Ilẹ́ amòn (clay soil) is more characteristic of the area to the north and east of town, and is thought to be better for yam cultivation because it holds the heaps better. Ilẹ́ yanrìn (sandy soil) is not associated with particular crops, and is not highly desirable. Micro-ecologies are also recognised: the land under the rocks is thought to be particularly fertile; there are areas with more and less small tree cover, and land infested with ẹ̀ẹ̀kọn grass (imperata).

In scientific terms, however, the Ibarapa soils vary rather little, and the rainfall is so extremely variable from one year to the next that the small differences in soil are not relevant in consistent ways. By far the most relevant distinction is between land suitable for a tree crop farm (okó'gbó: oko igbó: a farm in the forest), and the open savanna suitable for arable crops (oko òdan: farm in the plain/savanna). When farmers developed plots in different locations in 1968, as some did, it was almost invariably to take advantage of such major distinctions rather than to exploit micro-ecologies dependent on slope or drainage or small differences in soil. Apart from the gallery forests and other patches of forest, the vegetation throughout the area is derived guinea-savanna, with scrub and small trees. All the soil has a moderate ferralitic content and has been described as 'moderately fertile' (Daly et al. 1981: 42).

As long as the land can be adequately fallowed for about eight years following four years of cultivation, and holding farming skill and attentiveness equal, most of the variation in production from one year to the next and even one place to the next, is seen by the farmers as a function of rainfall. The basic bi-modal pattern of rainfall has never been known to fail completely, and the diversity of crops puts Ibarapa farmers in a relatively secure subsistence position. Not everything will be equally dried up or washed out in any given very bad year. But the variability is great. Rainfall can be very localised, especially in the crucial early stages of the first growing season when farmers have to judge when to start planting. The fluctuation from year to year can be extreme. Let me illustrate by giving the rainfall figures for the two periods of field research, in the 1960s and 1980s, and then describing briefly farmers' response to the extremely unusual rains of 1987.

All figures come from the measurements taken at the Nigerian Tobacco Company station at Igbo-Ọra, and therefore relate as closely as possible to the actual area of research. In the 1960s, rainfall figures were only available for the crucial tobacco-growing months of April to September, so we have to work with that limitation. And it is a limitation since the March rains are very important for food crop planting. These data were added by the 1980s, but the comparisons can only be based on the April–September data, for the years 1966–68, and 1986–88.

There are three dimensions of variability. First, total rainfall: long-term averages make the area seem relatively favoured because the rains do not fail completely. There does seem to have been, however, a long term dessication and increase in instability over the twenty years. Taking the two three-year averages, the difference between the two decades shows a decline of about 12 per cent: for 1966–8, the average rainfall, April to September, was 928mm and for 1986–8 it was 813mm.[16] Regional rainfall data for the rest of West Africa show a similar decline, not only for the Sahel but for the humid areas. This must surely have effects on farmers' perceptions but the change was not clear enough at the time of field research for me to collect their commentaries on it. The overall decline may well be less important in their minds than the very striking changeability from year to year which they do see as more marked in the 1980s than the 1960s.

The variation from year to year was wide for both periods. The widest annual variation was well over 100 per cent, from 573mm to 1369 mm (April to September) for the successive years of 1967 and 1968, as represented in Figure 3.1.

Even more important for the farmers, however, than the absolute level of rainfall in any one year is the pattern of monthly variation. Although the

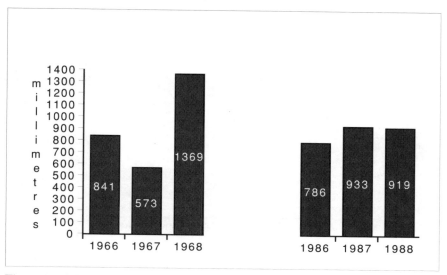

Figure 3.1 Annual Rainfall 1966–68 and 1986–88

total rainfall 1966–68 and 1986–88 is relatively similar, and the bi-modal pattern is followed in both, the 1980s showed a very much higher monthly fluctuation: the monthly coefficient of variation was two and a half times as high in the 1980s as for the 1960s. Figure 3.2 presents this in stark visual terms: in the 1980s the entire first season is almost a month later and the short dry season became deeper and sharper.

Finally, and most important of all, the monthly *sequence* from one year to the next can be very idiosyncratic, even when the totals are not. It is critical for farmers that the start of the rains in March be followed by steady rainfall in April. Failure in April cannot be made up for in May. In 1987 the April rains that generally follow the March first rains and planting period almost completely failed. Whereas the average April rainfall for all the other five years taken together was 111.2mm, in 1987 only 21mm fell, less than one fifth of the average, and the rainfall for every month from March to July of that year was the lowest recorded in any of the six years for which I have data. Crops planted in March shrivelled and had to be replanted, eventually yielding poorly. Then the deluge set in. August rains were three times the average for that month in the other five years. Fields were flooded out and the tractors could not prepare new land. A truly appalling year ended up with a total rainfall almost exactly on target with respect to the annual average.

Farmers have to try to anticipate and compensate, but with this unpredictable kind of variability to live with, they tend to anticipate either a typical rainfall pattern or the previous year's experience. For example, in 1969 the farmers in the diary sample planted their *ẹ̀gúsí* on the day of the first rains in

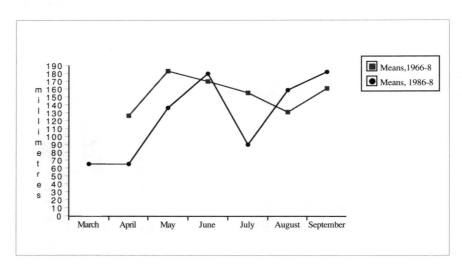

Figure 3.2 Monthly Rainfall Variation 1966–68 and 1986–88
Source: Records of Nigerian Tabacco Company, Igbo-Ora

their area, between 1 March and 10 March. Bare patches where the seeds had failed to germinate had been replanted by the end of the month. In 1988, by contrast, only one of the most skilful farmers planted *ẹ̀gúsí* in March (on 8 March), even though the rainfall distribution for that particular year was almost exactly the same as for the 1960s. They were working in part from the devastating experience of the previous year when the entire early planting had been lost due to the April drought.[17] Estimating the rainfall is risky, and increasingly so as the patterns seem to have become more unstable over time. By comparison with this unpredictability of the rain, the variation in savanna soil types and drainage must seem quite limited. For Ibarapa farmers, the weather is still, in their minds, the main determinant of production and of the difference between a good year and a bad year.

Their health, also, is a key unpredictable factor in production. Sickness leads to neglected fields, failure to open up new plots and drains on income. This is a guinea-worm endemic area, where the maximum rate of disability can go as high as 25 per cent, coinciding with the late dry season, just before the start of the new planting season (Brieger and Guyer 1990). There are also the usual vicissitudes of health and welfare: infections, accidents, childbirth, deaths in the family and the onset of serious disease. In fact, these two quite classic criteria marked all farmers' interpretations of year to year change: the state of the weather and the basic conditions of themselves and their families. I had to probe further to elicit commentary on prices and market conditions as determinants of a good or bad year, and political conditions hardly impinge at all on this level of explanation.

The Crops

Throughout the century, a substantial proportion of what was sold to the market did not derive from cultivation, but from hunting, gathering and processing, including bushmeat, palm products, locust bean, shea butter, and black soap. The crops available for cultivation in this area have changed over time. Yams come from the distant Yoruba past and are still the preferred staple. Because sorghum is used as a trellis for the yam vines, it too is an old cultigen. Egusi thrives in this area and was the first valuable cash crop for sale outside, being high-priced relative to the transport weight and bulk. Maize has been grown for a long time, mainly for local consumption. The present repertoire includes both old and new cultigens: cowpeas, pigeon peas, groundnuts, okra, indigenous tobacco, palms, citrus fruits, leaf vegetables, yams of several varieties, maize, guinea-corn, peppers of various varieties, egusi, teak, cocoa, commercial tobacco, tomatoes, and a ramifying set of cassava varieties.

Cassava is a special case. It seems to have come to Ibarapa from the Egba area, and greatly expanded and diversified over the twentieth century (Mabogunje and Gleave 1964). During World War II there was a push towards cassava starch production in Western Nigeria, in which the area north of Abeokuta was closely implicated (Falola 1989), and recently a new variety of cassava has been grown in plantation by Texaco on its farm just south of Igbo-Ọra. Otherwise, development has come from indigenous sources and has had wide ramifications, particularly for women. Cassava that is processed and sold to the outside, along with cooked food sold within the local community and to travellers, accounts in people's recollections for women's entry into independent marketing. Before cassava, women gained a cash income from harvesting labour, and from cloth dyeing, pot-making, oil preparation, soap-making, pito-beer preparation and shea-butter preparation. It appears to have been cassava, above all, that turned them into processors and traders to the regional market, probably towards the end of the colonial period.

CONCLUSION

Even though Idere is now so closely linked to the Ibadan and Lagos markets, farming is a quite minor and contingent theme in local history. The history of its social composition is an extended demonstration, in practice, of 'an axiom of this culture, expressed in other genres as well as *oriiki* (praise poetry), that the town's work is composed of a range of different specialisations, each of which has its own characteristic implements and techniques and each of which provides its practitioners with a separate path to success' (Barber 1991: 280). Its population is only now, in the last quarter of the twentieth century, pursuing agriculture in a broadly commercial sense. Local history has been highly eventful, but the dramas have been about politics rather than about economics. Even disputes over land were more about identity than about resources until very recently. This and other Yoruba communities have rehearsed and lived their history in inventive ways, structuring and restructuring relationships, commitments and activities, but economics was not the main issue at stake.

By the 1960s, there was probably far more expertise in organisation-building than in commercialisation to distant markets, but it would be unclear whether and how the one could be applied – and by whom, with what consequences – to the other. Over a century, particular goods had been moving one by one into commercial networks, with surges of organisation associated with each one. The growth that began after 1960 and intensified in the 1970s was more general, involving all resources, all crops and all categories of the community, all still working with the challenges of the humid savanna environment: the need for fallow, the importance of weeding in the labour profile, and the difficulties of the rainfall pattern. The next chapter begins the description of the agendas and activities of those who reshaped the commercial orientation of farming over the two main eras of the past thirty years: the late 1950s to the mid-1970s, and from then until the late 1980s.

Consonant with my emphasis here on the history of occupational specialisation, when I begin the analysis of local farming I start with the part-time farmers of 1968, who were farming mainly to feed their families. It is not their subsistence orientation that qualifies them for the beginning of the analysis, but rather the fact that their work in artisanship was the primary source of their income and social identity. As the town was founded by specialists (a hunter, a tollkeeper and a ruler), and the immediate concern was to fill out a roster of necessary specialist roles, it makes sense to frame the analysis of the growth of commercial farming as a development that stands on that foundation.

NOTES

1. The single exception was the kin of the one heroic casualty of the war, Ajayi, who built on the site of his grave. Even they retained their political membership in their quarter of origin, although they moved physically into the territory of another.
2. In fact, archaeological research would probably establish pre-existing settlements of autochthonous peoples from very much longer ago. The inselbergs and hills contain remains and signs of earlier habitation for which the present Yoruba population has no clear explanation, such as deep grooves cut in parallels or other patterns into the flat rock outcrops, and the remains of iron smelting. According to the Yoruba histories, however, the area was uninhabited at the time they moved in.
3. One Oṣinkọla, a younger prince from the royal line of Ọyọ-Ile, quarrelled with his senior siblings (or fled retribution from the people for the cruelty of his father in another version) and left, bringing his mother, Aye, with him. The small retinue and their descendants settled eventually at Ibona, about ten miles from the present site of Idere, which is still recognised in a certain sense as their home. Aye ('The World'), mother of the original settler, finally died on the site of the present town market (which is named after her), under the slopes of the rocks which she – being too old by then – could not climb. Another, non-royal, historian gave a version of the generations between the flight from Ọyọ and the settlement at Idere that was more in consonance with Aye's life span than with the four male generations of the official family history, so the length of time that the pre-constituted situation lasted must remain a question.
4. CMS Yoruba Mission Papers. CA2, O 35, 12. Journal of S. W. Doherty, January to March 1877. Quotation contributed by J. D. Y. Peel.
5. For example, the title of Baasin, which belongs to the inner group of kingmakers, the Afọbajẹ, came to Idere with the ancestors of Ile Gbongbon, but it appears only ever to have been held by them, as a kind of family property, until the colonial period. At that time the current Baasin was promoted to Jagun, and the position had to be filled, according to Idere custom, by an incumbent from a different compound; unlike other Yoruba towns, Idere seems always to have restricted compounds to one major title at a time, so there was a moment of lapse.
6. The history of royal rotation is as follows: a daughter's son of the ọba who had moved from Ibona (Ọlabosin, son of Olaṣewẹrẹ, daughter of Oyewọla) was invited to be ọba, a deviation from strict patrilineal succession that the kingmakers

thought would be a protection for the people against a single family's monopoly. When this incumbent, named Tẹyẹ, died early, the Afọbajẹ suspended the alternation rule and appointed another ọba from Ija, named Olunloye (also known as Awebeyabẹrẹ), in order to make the point clearly that alternation was now the rule. They had to defend it again from Ala after the very long reign of Laleye, who was from the Ala side, and reigned from before the beginning of the British presence – the court was established in Igbo-Ọra in 1917 – and 1942. His predecessor from Ija had been deposed in about 1900, so there seemed to be a possible opening for the Ala branch to try to rescind the whole alternation system, particularly since they now had their own incipient two-branch structure. The kingmakers fought off the claim, and incorporated the Ala subdivision, giving the double alternation pattern that now prevails: Ala (Baba Oloje) – Ija – Ala (Oyepami) – Ija – Ala (Baba Oloje), and so on. Although Ija comprises three compounds, in three different towns (Idere, Igbo-Ọra and Iseyin), they decide as a single group who to put forward as their candidate, without internal rotation. Competition may be fierce within the group, as it was for example in 1942 when Tẹyẹ's son Oyelami came from Iseyin to compete with Oyerogba who was brought up in Igbo-Ọra; but this does not directly concern the kingmakers. The kinglist that these rules and innovations have generated over the one-hundred-and-sixty years of Idere history is as follows:

Olufiji:	Ala	Approximately 1835
Oyepami:	Ala	Unknown dates
Tẹyẹ:	Ija	Reigned briefly
Olunloye:	Ija	Unknown dates
Ojo:	Ala (Baba Oloje)	Approx. 1860–1895
Gbamigboye:	Ija	Approx. 1895–1900 (deposed)
Olaleye:	Ala (Oyepami)	Approx. 1900–1942
Oyerogba:	Ija	1942–1956
Akintaro:	Ala (Baba Oloje)	1959–1973
Olunloye II:	Ija	1973–

7. One of Idere's compounds was known for a time as Ile Onimu, owner of the nose: perhaps in reference to its founder's physiognomy, or perhaps in reference to spirituality, the nose being 'the source of ventilation for the soul' (Lawal 1985). In fact, many of the names for compounds take this verbal form, referring either to founders or prominent members of the past or to characteristic occupations. Compounds are themselves, in a sense, associations of people that share characteristics.

8. In the early 1900s, Ọba Ggamigboye continually insulted his people, amongst other things calling them *ara oko*, literally 'people of the farm', or perhaps 'hicks' or 'country bumpkins'. He had been brought up in the neighbouring town of Igbo-Ọra, in his mother's compound, and found Idere rustic by comparison. For his arrogance he was first placed incommunicado by the chiefs, who failed to pay their daily respects and cut the palace off from all trade or other intercourse with the people. Then when he fled, the Oro Society came out at night with their drums and bullroarers and burned his house to the ground.

9. They brought the senior masquerader, Onikopa, with them from their origins in Ilugun, about fifty miles due east towards Ibadan. All agree that ultimately Orò comes from Ijebu to the south but no one was clear about the Ijebu-to-Ilugun link.

10. Onikopa for Apa, Adankuro for Oke Ọba, Ojolo for Onigbio and Kẹlokẹ for Koso. Adankuro and Ojolo are named for historical persons who were messengers of the most senior chief of the quarter, so one sees in the names themselves the

idea that the executive branch, in the literal sense, was the functionary of the senior administrative chiefs in the civilian hierarchy.

11. As is the case for the descendants of Mogaji, the husband of a woman from Jọoda's family, who now comprise Ile Ogbinte, Ile Dongo and Ile Aponbiede. One Baapa is said to be the father of Oyanaju, Baba Ibadan and Ile Oje compounds.

12. Ile Agbode, for example, had four acknowledged *igùn* in 1968, for a resident membership of the twenty-five adult men listed in the nominal roll book, plus wives and children. Ile Agunyan, however, with twenty-two taxable men, remained undivided.

13. In Ile Olode, for example, two out of eight successive compound heads have been daughters' sons of the male founder's line. Ile Balogun Apokun has two *igùn*, descended from two opposite sex siblings. One or two, such as Ile Asipa, Ile Bale Sango and Ile Aponbiede, include descendants of totally unrelated people whose origins and reasons for not developing their own compound are not always clear.

14. One farmer was put in this situation in 1968, when he failed to control the behaviour of his junior brother who had seduced the wife of a member of their mother's compound. He was put off the farm he had on that compound's land, in mid-season, with no recourse and no right to harvest the crop.

15. In 1968 one farm had taken in an itinerant Togolese bicycle repairer who eventually drifted on again. In 1988 one Idere village had become the semi-permanent home of both a young Igbo fundamentalist Christian, who preached diligently and loudly every evening to a group of rapt Yoruba children, and an older Hausa man who so preferred life in that corner of the world that he went back to the north to marry a wife and bring her back to start a family.

16. When we add March and October, as we can for the 1980s, the total rainfall is about 1,000–1,100mm.

17. Another possible factor in the four-to-five week delay in egusi planting could be the conditions for the newly-established tractor preparation of the fields. A little moisture is needed to make the soil more friable, and at that point there is a rush on tractor service, leading to a delay in planting. Also the mid-season crop of cow-peas has now been eliminated due to a disease specific to that crop, so that early planting of egusi is less crucial than it was in the 1960s. Of all these changes, more details will be given later. But farmers did also mention their fear of a repeat of the previous year's early drought, and simply waited until they were absolutely sure, in some cases until the middle or even the end of April.

PART II
NARRATIVES

4

NEWCOMERS AND NOVELTIES OF THE 1960s: MIGRANT LABOUR, CONTRACT FARMING AND OTHER INNOVATIONS

INTRODUCTION

Transport to western Ibarapa became somewhat regular and reliable in the late 1950s. The roads were graded, the Ofiki River Bridge was built, and the famous Bedford lorry was imported, starting in about 1948. Well before my initial study there had already been a motley collection of interventions by the food trade, government, corporate business, and the Fulani cattle traders, each one a vanguard for more intense engagements up to the present. The kind of hinterland that Ibarapa could become was already at issue: a general source of diverse (and changing) kinds of food grown by a peasantry for the urban provisioning of consumers, a specialist source of particular products for vertically integrated processing industry and business, or a holding-ground for the meat industry. The local farmers were already expanding production for the market. The Nigerian Tobacco Company was the early wedge for an agribusiness or vertical integration system that diversified in the 1980s to include the now-defunct Texaco farm, and presently includes Obasanjo Farms, the United Africa Company and the private farms of businessmen. Also the Fulani still control a determinedly expanding cattle business. Their view of Ibarapa's rolling grassland as essentially a pasture briefly coincided with the report of an American development consultant with expertise in ranching. Even to the present, all have been accommodated, although with increasingly nervous competition. That engagement began in earnest in the late 1950s.

This chapter sets the history of the various participants in motion. But it also introduces two interpretive themes: the coexistence at any one time of a jostling variety of different producers and activities, as would be expected in an expanding hinterland economy, and a form of change over time in which older rubrics were extended to new contexts. Some innovations helped to move the entire agricultural economy closer to the market: the development of migrant labour probably allowed some increase in farm size, and the extension of women's processing permitted the expansion of cassava production and a general rise in the variety and amount of rural goods that went into the market system. There were however many smaller novelties and even abject failures in the 1960s, that had lasting implications. Assimilating all these developments to hierarchical understandings of commoditisation, in terms of class, gender and state incorporation, is premature because it masks the lateral processes involved in market orientation: competition and accommodation between the different production regimes of agriculture and pastoralism, and crop shifts, occupational and institutional change within the agricultural population. It is worth reviewing the breadth of novelties, both to illustrate the multiplicity of endeavours out of which emerge the outlines of a regional market economy, and to show how – within agriculture – ideas were picked up and moved from one locus to another.

ACCESSIBILITY: A BRIEF HISTORY OF TRANSPORT

Eastern Ibarapa had been linked to Ibadan by rail since early in the century. In fact, the rail connection was the main reason that the seat of government was located at Eruwa. The road was extended to Igbo-Ora and then gradually as far as Tapa up to the 1950s, but there was very little wheeled transport on it. Even in the late 1940s people were transporting goods the 25 miles to Abeokuta by headload. The building of the Ofiki River Bridge in 1957 opened up an entire producing area to the market: the northernmost Ibarapa town of Igangan and the vast farming area to the west that extends all the way to the Benin border. No roads were built across the savanna until the 1980s, and even then they were not (of course) paved. By the early 1960s, just a few years after the bridge construction, there were already three wholesale farmers' markets in the area west of the road, linked to the main road by tracks that had simply been traced over the savanna, across rock outcrops and through small streams, by the small fleet of Bedford lorries that plied the route. Very quickly there was a wholesale market schedule, bàbá ọja (fathers of the market) to control order and decorum, pàràkòyi (bulkers and price mediators), and clientage relations between traders and lorry drivers. Farmers requisitioned wives and children to headload large baskets of goods on market day, often making more than one trip each over the two to three miles that separated some abúlé from the market. Enormous weights were regularly carried – calabashes of pitọ́ beer that women had prepared to sell in the marketplace, baskets of cassava flour – often requiring several people to hoist from the ground onto the bearer's head.

By the late 1960s, when large numbers of civilian vehicles had been requisitioned for the war and curfews on night travel into and out of cities limited drivers to one trip per day, the two regular market lorries that penetrated beyond the Ofiki River were overloaded almost beyond movement. Goats were tied to the roof, tins of palm oil to the sides, the tailgate was never even remotely closable and I once travelled in a lorry where there were eight people in the cab and hanging off the side doors, their movement even further cramped by baskets of tomatoes and peppers underfoot. The driver could hardly move the gear shift, and a combination of protective medicine, the prayers of world religions and the descent of several passengers was required to guarantee extraction from the stream beds we passed through. When it rained heavily the rocks could be slippery and the patches of sand a welcome respite from mud. In fact, the tendency of the soil to be lighter and sandier in this area probably contributed as much to the transport feasability as to the productive possibilities. Thus quickly did the farm area respond to the possibilities opened up by a single road and a single solid bridge.

Up to the late 1950s when transport began slowly to develop, it seems that there was little circulation between Western Ibapara and the urban centres of Southern Nigeria, except for tribute to Ibadan and headloading of a few goods to Abeokuta. The major axis of trade was the north–south trade routes, which are very old and in the twentieth century have been taken over by the cattle trade servicing the meat markets of the southern cities. A pastoral corridor of some antiquity runs through the western savanna, from whose fairly open grazing grounds it was only a few days' trek to the cities. Cattle brought down on foot from the north had to be fattened up a little and reconstituted before moving them on quickly to the auctions and slaughter-houses before the southern diseases started to take their toll. Ibarapa is along the southern and eastern border of the savanna as it approaches the coastal cities, ideally situated for accessibility and with the good pasturage produced by a relatively wet climate. The large herds of zebu cattle were already a frequent sight well before they became yet another of the navigational obstacles for the market lorries of the 1960s, as they struck out across the open savanna. By then there were already semi-permanent Fulani settlements whose leaders spoke Yoruba and mediated the very touchy diplomacy with local communities over trampled crops.

Regular wheeled transport encouraged other outsiders to venture in for economic purposes. The small patches of suitable cocoa land became accessible to the traders' lorries from Ibadan; government officials could plan the first of a series of rather modest schemes; corporate business could scan the commercial possibilities; and the workforce could be augmented by an annual influx of migrant labour from other areas of Nigeria.

NEWCOMERS
The Fulani Cattle Herders

The Fulani are the oldest newcomers in the regional economy, having started to use these areas at least by the beginning of the century, as soon as the urban meat market developed. In fact, Fulani communities have lived amongst the Yoruba for well over a hundred years.[1] In Igboho during the 1850s William Clarke noted 'a small collection of Fulani houses occupied by these native shepherds who are a people within a people, distinct and alone …' (1972: 70). Clearly the Fulani as cattle keepers were a deeply institutionalised presence in the South before colonial rule, distinguished in the local people's eyes by their occupation from the military Fulani from whom the

Yoruba were 'in continual expectation of an invasion' (Clarke 1972: 71) following the destruction of other northern Yoruba towns. This assimilation of ethnicity to occupation, in such a way as to attenuate the relevance of ethnicity alone, comes up several times in the history of ethnic relations in the hinterland. It could hardly be beter attested than by the Yoruba tolerance of Fulani herders during the time of Fulani–Yoruba warfare.

Areas such as Ibarapa are seen by the Fulani as part of their own map of long distance corridors linking accessible pastures, a map that is completely different from the Yoruba farmers' town–country plan of the same terrain, structured around ancestral landmarks with their radial convergences of pathways. In von Thünen's model, animal husbandry for meat and hides settles in the outer rings of the urban supply system, beyond the more intensive farming, and the animals are safely walked to market between hedgerows. In an ecology like the West African coastal regions, however, the live cattle are at serious risk of disease and weight loss once they cross a zonal threshold, so there is a solid logic to the inward pressure of the herds towards the point of consumption and to their owners' identification of the few suitable locales for holding prior to a final quick push into the urban market. Ibarapa falls squarely into that zone, even though it is also an agricultural area, ripe for intensification. Mutual accommodation has gone through two quite different phases.

The Ibarapa Fulani of the 1960s were residents of semi-permanent villages, acting as local mediators in the long-distance trade between North and South. Many of the wealthier Yoruba, and particularly chiefs, invested in cattle that were herded with the Fulani. Already in the 1960s the farmers saw conflicts of interest, because their chiefs were not necessarily loyal to their own people, or even neutral, when it came to antagonisms over crop destruction. But the Fulani women produced wàrà cheese to sell to the farmers, the manure was seen as useful, and everyone spoke Yoruba, socialised in the market-places, and generally behaved with deference and circumspection. The fact that the Fulani brought families, mixed freely and knew the local leadership quite well meant that there were no excuses for 'misunderstandings' about the location of the corridors and the obligations of the herders to steer clear of cultivated fields. Perhaps also well understood was their comparative wealth. A herd was capital beyond anything the local economy could muster, and it was obviously financed and organised on a larger scale than anything a local entrepreneur could compare with. While skirting the geographical periphery, and maintaining a low-key presence, the Fulani might well be seen as the most substantial component of regional wealth.

In the longer run, conditions have changed, and with them the behaviour of the herders and their ethnic designation by the farmers. To project forward in time, the 1970s saw greatly increased pressures on the southern pastures because of the Sahel drought. Cattle-breeding was moved into the middle belts of the savanna, and owners probably increased the number of cattle that they risked, and for longer periods, in the southernmost pastures close to the market. The farmers saw a dramatic change in the herders, and started to distinguish between the ordinary familiar Fulani and the 'Bororo', seen as volatile, quick to resort to violence, non-Yoruba-speaking and in general less 'civilised' (as English-speaking Yoruba put it) than their predecessors. People noted their filed teeth and more prominent weapons. Negotiation took non-verbal forms when the herdboys behaved as if they did not understand the angry shouting of a farmer trying to head off the steady march or the aimless meandering of a dozen cows right through his planted crops. People said that there were murders over cattle disputes, and farmers quickly discovered that the only effective way to drive the herders out of specific regions was surreptitiously to poison a cow or two.

These more aggressive 'Bororo' became permanently installed during the 1970s drought and did not return north.[2] There has been ongoing conflict between farmers and herders, to the point where a recent letter to me blamed the damage done by the Bororo for a shortage of cassava and a rise in its price. Relations seem more fraught than in the past. One prominent Yoruba chief had his entire Fulani-guarded herd of at least twenty head simply walked off one day along the trails into the more distant savannas. Regularly, the Yoruba-owned cattle in the herds meet with unfortunate 'accidents' such as snake-bites. And the Bororo, newly arrived in the 1970s, never did acquire a 'civilised' demeanour with the passage of time. The name Bororo and its conceptualisation by the farmers is almost a metaphor for the aggressive and unrelenting pressure they now feel from the cattle economy, a pressure more tangibly and intimately real to more of them than market forces or even the alienation of land to a few corporate enterprises and middle-class entrepreneurs, whom they see as ultimately more controllable.

Migrant Labourers from the Niger–Benue Confluence

The migration of the Idoma people, known by the Yoruba as Agatu, into Ibarapa began around 1960. Work for monetary remuneration is much older in the Yoruba economy than the employment of outsiders to do it. Most work was given or exchanged on a calculus of how much in area, by task, constituted a day's worth of work. The institution that crystallised these equivalences was debt pawning *(ìwòfà)*.[3] Where a pawn worked a certain number of days to pay off the debt, the idea of a day's work, by task and area, became standardised. Any farmer can give labour rates per *adé*, a unit of ten rows by twenty heaps: one *adé* of 200 heaps per man-day both to clear and heap ready for planting, two *adé* for clearing alone, and about three *adé* per man day to weed. These areas were given to me in the field in 1968, but they correspond fairly closely to rates of 160 yam heaps per day given by Fadipe (1970: 190) for *iwọfà* labour in the past, and 300 heaps per day of 'cleaning' given by Johnson (1921: 127) for the end of the nineteenth century. In fact, in the savanna environment, each of these tasks was about a long morning's work, as Johnson himself noted, and not at all up to the limits of physical possibility for a full day. The implicit definition of a day's work assumed people to be doing other tasks in life besides agriculture.

Because the calculus of task/area to work already existed it was a short step, after *iwọfà* was abolished and migrants became available, to measuring areas, days and tasks in term of a money wage. Falola (1995) cites a rate of 3d per 100 heaps as early as 1927, as the rule of thumb about the value of work. He also notes that *iwọfà* did not really die out until the 1940s, and in fact in 1968 one twenty-year-old told me that he remembered taking food out to the farm for his father's *iwọfà* when he was a child, presumably about ten years previously. So in the rural areas debt pawning and wage labour overlapped, allowing a certain continuity of the measurement and calculation component of the moral economy of work.

Wage labour was already institutionalised well before all the commercial changes of the 1970s and 1980s. By the time of my first study in 1968, probably only about eight years after the beginning of the migrant system in Ibarapa, many small farmers cleared new plots with hired labour. Labour payment was already part of the farm budget of money and time, and the workers came regularly every year. The diversion of a stream of Agatu from the cocoa belt to the food-farming districts only began in earnest in about 1960, perhaps initially due to the coincidence of the simultaneous downward slide in world cocoa prices in the early 1960s and the opening up of new urban food supply areas. Berry suggests the 1930s as the approximate onset of migrant farm labour in the cocoa belt (1975: 128), and certainly the system was well-organised by the time that the savanna started to tap into it. The Ibarapa farmers know that they are competing with other areas of the entire South for the available flow of annual migrants, and they anticipate that the labour supply may be unpredictable. The relatively advantageous conditions that they offer are seen as a necessary cost, and by the labourers as an improvement over areas such as the yam-fields of Iseyin, where it is said that the farmers are organised to control the wage.

From 1960 to the present the social organisation of the Agatu has been very similar, even though the age and career path of the workers has changed lately. They arrive in organised groups in March and go home late in the year, at the beginning of the dry season, when enough of the farmers' incomes are in that they can pay off their debts, and when the workers can be home in time for Christmas and other December/January celebrations. In the 1960s, all the labourers were young and unmarried, brought south under a crew-boss system. The organiser was an older man, who is known by the farmers by the Yoruba term ọ̀gá, which is used for the head of any instituted work team or workshop. He took charge of everything short of doing farm work itself: transport to the south, lodging, food, basic welfare, lining up jobs, negotiating rates, recording the amounts owed, calling in debts, calculating the workers' shares of the season's take, ensuring the profitability of the year and taking the crew home. Both in the past and at present, the crew boss is also the mediator and representative of the group in its relationship with the social life of the town or village where it takes up residence.

The division of income in the farm labour system involves extraordinarily complex mental accounting done by all concerned; being ọ̀gá to a work team is skilled work. A rate is agreed on for the task, which was almost exclusively confined to clearing and heaping new land in the 1960s. The task was assessed according to the size of the plot and the state of the natural vegetation; the denser, the higher the cost. Okó 'gbó (forest farms) are much costlier to clear than the savanna. But then a range of payment is put in place: if the job is paid off at once, the rate will be lower, whereas if it is left until the end of the season, which may be up to seven months away, an implicit interest/ risk rate is put in. What is actually paid is often something else again, depending on the the farmer's satisfaction with the job, his receipts from the crop, contributions he may have made to the workers' welfare during the year, and other contingencies. The payment might well be renegotiated at the time of debt-settlement. Even in the 1980s, the entire season's work – hundreds of jobs, each with its own complexities – was recorded as a feat of memory by the crew boss. There were amazingly few disputes.

A final word on the social position of workers: wage work is not necessarily, in and of itself, low status. Workers are onísẹ́ (oni-isẹ́: 'owners' of work) in the same linguistic construction by which owners of land are onílẹ̀ (oni-ilẹ̀). But as foreigners, as youth and as dependants of the crew boss, they were expected to keep their distance, particularly in relation to local women. When I returned in 1988, I was told highly disapprovingly of a labourer from Benin who had seduced a young woman and taken her home. It has been an innovation of the 1970s that some of the crews became mixed-sex, especially those coming from areas where women traditionally carry out farm tasks, and can therefore work in the fields as well as providing domestic services to the now-older work force. The fact that the story of the Beninois stood out, after over twenty-five years of migrant workers' regular presence for eight months of the year, is testimony to the power of the social model under which they have worked within the Ibarapa communities. The organisation of migrant labour places the workers in a hierarchy of authority and an array of recognised functions.

The Government

Although its cities were substantial (Mabogunje 1968), and rural areas such as Ibarapa already changing, Nigeria hardly had a food policy in the 1960s, as noted by critics such as Güsten (1968) and Olatunbosun (1975). In the era of marketing board control of the Nigerian export crops, government projects in the finance and control of food for domestic consumption were still largely on the drawing board. But some schemes were known to the farmers. The supply of the state-run Lafia canning factory with citrus and pineapples was a case discussed in the newspapers during the first months of my field research, where both plantations and peasant supply were mooted (*Daily Times* 30 October 1968). My own arrival in Idere 'to study farming' was initially understood as my search for a site to establish a pineapple plantation, so closely were people's ears to the ground for developments that might be coming their way.

Short-lived projects and plans go back several decades in the history of the Western Nigerian savanna. This area was encouraged to grow cassava for the starch export market during World War II, but the policy was abandoned in 1945 (Falola 1989). A settlement scheme for school leavers was established in 1960 to cope with the perennial and intractable problem of employment. One of the farms was at Eruwa. It closed within a few years and then reopened in the 1980s, in the next generation of concern about the future of educated youth. The River Basin Development Authority for the Ogun Basin passed this area by, and the World Bank Agricultural Development Project for Northern Oyo stopped at its northern border. One or two installations have stayed in place for several years, but their capacities fluctuate with government budgets. Examples are the AISU (Agricultural Input Service Unit), established by Oyo State after it became a state in 1976, which sells fertiliser and rents tractors, and the local government extension service which supplies seedlings for cocoa, teak and citrus trees.

The main efforts to connect government directly with the farmers have come through successive cooperative movements (see Beer 1976). The view from the grass-roots is that little has ever materialised. The Western State Farmers' Union was founded after national independence, and its main activity by the mid 1960s was to introduce new crops for the market. At a meeting of the Ibarapa branch that I attended on 11 May 1968, the organisers spoke of cotton, cashews, oranges, pineapples, palm trees, cocoa, cola, poultry and oil production, but the farmers complained bitterly of the failure to buy their cotton the previous year. The membership report given at that May meeting enumerated 176 card-carriers for the whole district. The number of twenty-one cardholders registered at Idere at that time is in the same range as the cooperative current again in the 1980s (about 20 members). These numbers are obviously minute compared with the 1,397 adult men enumerated in the nominal roll book in 1968.

The performance of the official cooperative has been even weaker than its numbers. The Kajọla Multipurpose Cooperative Society Ltd was founded in 1978 under another round of official enthusiasm about cooperative ventures. The official philosophy of that era is summarised in the writings of Idachaba and others (1980,1984) on 'Nigeria's Green Revolution'. The provision of inputs relied on 'farmers' cooperatives as primary outlets' and parastatals as the vanguard providers, eventually to be superceded by the private sector (Idachaba 1984: 84). Ibarapa was noted to have ninety-two group farms, the largest number for any administrative division of Ọyọ State (Idachaba 1980).

According to the Chairman of the Kajọla Cooperative at Idere, the first five years' income from their collective farm went into three activities: the costs of getting the cooperative legally registered (including dashes to functionaries) transport to central offices and (it was said) N1,000 for the certificate itself, the costs of attendance at regional meetings in places as far afield as Ilesha, Ondo and Oṣogbo. Membership contributions were used to pay for ploughing. The point of all this activity was to qualify for one of the loans or other services that seemed to have been opened up. In this particular case no loan ever materialised in any shape: as cash or as tractor access. By 1986 the members were discouraged and no longer held meetings, but they did still open up a farm together and they held onto all the paperwork, including the 'map', in case something turned up. After all, there had been lulls and revivals in official activity in the past. As long as official recognition as a constituted cooperative looks as if it may open up resources, this group is mobilisable at short notice even to consider doing such improbable activities as group farming that have abjectly failed in the past. It is often unclear exactly how or why very minor possibilities, such as cooperatives have always been, are maintained at all. But they clearly are, as if there were 'designated preservers', 'designated government brokers', and so on. As long as a practice might yield some benefit, someone in the community is likely to be keeping it going, albeit at a low level of investment.

Government surveillance of production in Ibarapa was also rather patchy. The agricultural sample surveys carried out in the 1970s offer some startling data with little explanation: very low total acreage under crops (Oyo State 1979:28), no area at all designated to egusi-melon (Oyo State 1979: 28) for which it was reported to produce half of the entire Oyo state production for 1976 (Oyo State 1976: 37), and a cassava flour price that is reported as less than one third of the mean for the twenty-one Local Government Areas in the State (Oyo State 1979: 52). The effect that these reports convey to the reader is of absent-mindedness, as if the record was created for other purposes and places, and half-heartedly extended to these outlying areas without much attention to particularities. There has never been, for example, a single mention of egusi-melon in any scheme as far as I know, whereas egusi

is Ibarapa's home crop. The main mention of egusi in any large-scale planning has been by the Nigerian Tobacco Company which developed 'crops of
maize, melon and cassava ... now grown on a commercial scale in rotation
with tobacco' (NTC Annual Report 1980: 70).

The point is that by the moment of commercial expansion, this maintenance of a low-grade involvement with government projects was already
well established through several rounds of local experience. By contrast with
government, the NTC has maintained an impressive consistency in its
engagement with the changing realities of the rural areas.

Corporate Agriculture: The Nigerian Tobacco Company

The NTC has been operating in Ibarapa for about thirty years, with one
fairly long interruption of several years when food crops became more profitable. In its first incarnation as British–American Tobacco the NTC established the first Nigerian cigarette factory in 1934, which was ncorporated in
1951 and became a public company in 1960. After the indigenisation decree
was passed, 40 per cent of the ownership became Nigerian. By the mid-
1970s it was working with 'several thousand' independent farmers (NTC
Annual Report 1976: 23).

The Idere Tobacco Growers' Association was founded in 1962. Initially
many people joined, but by the time the curing barn had been built it was
down to thirteen, mainly because of the cost involved in contributing to the
barn construction. Only one more member was added before I visited in
1968. At that time the farmers worked on one or two large fields,
prominently situated off the main road just before the entry to the town, on
land ceded by the royal compound. The fields were then divided up into
individual plots for cultivation. The company regulated and supervised
almost everything: it issued the seedlings, taught nursery techniques,
ploughed the land, regulated the acreage at one acre per farmer, applied the
fertiliser, supervised the harvest, tying and drying, and bought the crop. The
returns per unit area per year to the farmers I followed in detail were
considerably higher for NTC tobacco plus a second season crop than for any
other crop sequence available to them; almost 50 per cent higher than for
yams, cassava or the egusi-based rotations. But the costs had to be de-
ducted: labour, curing, and any inputs from the company. And the risks
were enormous, including leaves ruined by over-firing in the curing barn
and profits lost through inaccuracies in the book-keeping. It was entirely
predictable that if food crop prices rose, as they did in the 1970s, farmers
would abandon tobacco: 'kò pé!' , one farmer explained tersely,'It didn't
pay'.

Well before then, the NTC had cut down some of the risks by disbanding
the associations and dealing directly with families. This was made possible
by a technical innovation: the development of small-scale curing barns for

flue-cured tobacco. At one stroke, family barns eliminated the need for associational accounting, gave to the farmer complete responsibility for the curing, and accorded greater autonomy of decision making about field size and location and the planning of cultivation tasks (Kranendonk 1968). Other management decisions were decentralised. From 1966 onwards, the NTC increasingly started to hire private tractor owner-operators rather than using their own tractors and drivers (NTC Annual Report 1978), thus giving the farmers again more personal leeway in the timing of their activities. In fact, one father–son team of Idere tobacco farmers went into the tractor-hire business in the late 1970s, starting from an NTC contract. Tobacco provided the leading edge for what became a highly significant social innovation: the private ownership and hire of tractors.

In the late 1970s the NTC was caught between the provisions of the price control decree on cigarettes (NTC Annual Report 1978: 1) and the rising price of food crops to the farmers. Contract farming is eminently easy to abandon; hence NTC's innovations in combining extension work on food with its existing work on tobacco. But they failed to stave off a collapse of production in Ibarapa after 1978.[4] By 1984 the company was back again, working with a much smaller but educated and more highly motivated set of farmers, higher prices, more herbicides to cut down weeding and an emphasis on the complementarity of tobacco with food crops. By 1988 there were sixty-six tobacco farmers in Ibarapa as a whole. The NTC farmers of the 1980s are few and they have to be much more punctilious. The techniques of production are more difficult, the grades of tobacco more numerous (eleven as compared with three), and the financial conditions more complex.

The importance of the NTC is not in its own penetration of the cultivation system. The number of farmers involved is very small and even these can easily give up at the end of a season. It is rather that in the crucible of tobacco production, several practices of more general importance were either fostered or created for the first time: the extension of the female wage labour market in agriculture as women worked on the nursery-watering; the leaf-picking and the tying in bundles for curing; the experimentation with chemical fertilizer; the development of tractor hire; and the exposure of the farmers to the whole package of specialist disciplines that makes up scientific farming. All these had been applied to tobacco production a good ten to fifteen years before the sudden growth spurt in the food economy of the mid-to-late-1970s that forms the subject of later chapters.

NOVELTIES
Cocoa

The great cocoa boom of the 1950s had already passed by the time Ibarapa farmers started to cultivate the crop on their home territory. Most of the local land suitable for cocoa was to the west of the formidable Ofiki River, so before the bridge was completed any crop would have to be headloaded and ferried out. After 1957 the rush to colonise cocoa land was immediate and still intermittently continues.

The main expansion in the 1960s was around one of the *abúlé* in my study. The soil is *ilẹ̀ amọ̀n*, with a high clay content that retains water, encouraging the growth of a natural patch of dense woodland. The village had been founded by the fathers of the current adult generation, possibly as late as 1940. Several of the people already living there were timber cutters for housebuilding and carpentry before they went into cocoa farming. The masters ran apprenticeships in the sawyer's trade, and some of these apprentices were amongst the earliest cocoa farmers. A sudden expansion of the population made this by far the largest Idere *abúlé*, with thirty-four houses in 1968 (total population uncounted then), 151 people in 1981 (Brieger and Ramakrishna n.d.). The limits to cocoa farm expansion were quickly reached. In 1988 there were the same thirty-four houses, with 256 inhabitants, most of whom were dependants.

People already obviously knew of the course of cocoa development elsewhere in Southern Nigeria, because the landowning compound, Ile Jagun, rationed land from the start. They asked for an initial *iṣákọ́lẹ* in cash (e.g. £1:10:0, £2:10:0) for the right to clear. One member of the compound who was resident in the village, himself the largest cocoa farmer there, mediated all the acquisitions. Farmers gave dates such as 1958, 1959 and 1960 as the start of their cocoa farming careers, immediately after the bridge was built, and they had been selling for a couple of years by the time of my first study. The cocoa traders came in lorries all the way into the villages to buy during the season, and farmers became familiar with the names of the major Lebanese cocoa dealers working from Ibadan.

The expansive surge levelled off as the suitable land was used up. Many farmers have a patch or two, and a few are still on the lookout for new horizons. Some of the new planting is replacement, using seedlings provided by the extension services. But forest islands are a more vulnerable environment for orchard crops than full forest. Fire has proved a serious menace in terrain that is basically savanna, where people are accustomed to torching the grass for hunting and clearing out old vegetation before the new rains in March. Several cocoa farms have been incinerated by accidental fire. One of the most meticulous farmers has developed his entire food farm as a firebreak around the most vulnerable windward side of his cocoa farm.

So cocoa became a solid, but not extensive, component of the farming economy in the 1960s. It did, however, spearhead important social innovations: the mutation of *iṣákọ̀lẹ̀* to a cash payment, the greater control by landowning compounds of areas ceded out, the acquisition of seedlings from the newly established government services, direct ties to the big operators in the Southern Nigerian economy, and wheeled transport all the way into the *abúlé*. Social innovations that later became much more generally applicable were first fostered by this crop change, in a style that I have argued may be classic of the social-technical development of the humid savannas. Even a fairly minor crop can provide the crucible for organisational change.

The Extension of Women's Harvesting Labour

Women's paid labour also predates the commercial expansion of the 1970s, but the cultural and organisational framework has always differed from that applied to male migrants; there is no concept of 'wage work' in general, that comprises both. Women are designated by the task they do, and the template for all women's harvest labour is the egusi harvest.

Whether for consumption or sale, egusi has to be harvested and prepared for storage on a tight schedule, otherwise the seeds germinate. First the fruit on the now-withered vines are gathered into small heaps and beaten with sticks by teams of men, to bruise them enough to allow a certain level of rot to take place in the flesh. After a few days, teams of women come into the field to extract the seed, carry them to the river for washing in perforated calabashes, and spread them out on mats or rocks to dry. The women's work should be done as quickly as possible, over a day or so at maximum. Farmers in the same vicinity calculate the timing of their harvests so that the teams can move in rotation from one farm to another.

From too long ago for people to remember its inception, there has been a system of payment for the women who carry out this work. They are paid one *olódó* (market measure) of egusi per woman/day of work. The accepted rate of pay has remained the same over a very long period of time, but work-ers can bargain over how full the measure is. There are differing terms for a level *olódó*, a heaping *olódó* and an *olódó* augmented by an arm placed around the rim (*olódó fọwọ́kọ́*). By 1968 all women were paid one *olódó fọwọ́kọ́* as payment. In 1968 cowpeas were also harvested by teams of women, who kept a certain proportion – half it was said – of what they picked. Women prefer payment in kind at standard levels because it offers each woman the possibility of following her own plan: to keep the crop for consumption, shell the egusi and sell at a higher price, keep it for sale during the off-season when the price rises or give it as a gift.

Women's long experience in paid work for harvesting was reinforced in the early phases of commercialisation because egusi and cowpeas were high value savanna crops in regular demand in the southern cities. All the bases for expansion – means of recruitment, organisation of work, techniques, and wage levels – already existed in the small-scale domestic and village level cooperative groups of the past.

Women's Processing

Women's processing and trade for the regional market developed relatively late at the western edge of Ibarapa, by comparison with other places. About twenty-five miles away, Abeokuta was the closest substantial consumer market and the only one that was feasible for the staple food trade until the era of lorry transport in the 1950s. Because of the head start that Egba women had in the food trade supplying their own city, the women who were based in the small towns took up processing and local sale rather than long distance trade.

Apart from egusi, which was simply dried rather than processed, possibly the earliest product devoted to the market was èlùbọ́ iṣu, yam flour. Yams have always been high value, and even the tubers themselves were some-times headloaded to Abeokuta for sale. By the 1960s a significant proportion of the yams produced were boiled, dried to a pale nutmeg colour and pounded into a flour that had fairly good qualities of preservation. The real basis for making a living in food processing, however, was cassava flour (láfún). The oldest cassava processing techniques in Ibarapa involve simply drying the cut tubers very slowly in the sun during the dry season, often on the roof of the farm shelter. They turn brown and take on a characteristic flavour that many old people still prefer to the technique that produces láfún. The new technique was introduced expressly for the market. Obviously, slow drying is a technique that can only be used for very limited quantities and on a seasonal basis. By contrast, peeling, soaking for three days and spreading out in very small pieces to dry in the sun took up to a week and could be done year round. In the 1960s, before much capital was put into processing, there was a premium on access to the large flat rock outcrops that dot the local landscape, whose deep indentations and crevices could be filled with water, the whole site making a natural soaking pit and drying platform. Farmers within easy reach of these sites, like those in one of the villages studied, could prepare láfún on an almost continuous basis, year round, harvesting a row or two at a time. For those more distant from suit-able soaking and drying areas, the best alternative to home production was to sell the cassava in the field to women who then took over the harvest, porterage and processing.

Local women were already processing and selling láfún in this way in the 1960s. The practice of buying crops in the field that became much more important later was first institutionalised with the growth of láfún prepara-tion, possibly on the model of agreements between the harvester-processor and the tree owner over palm nuts for the making of palm oil, a practice that predates the regional market by a very long time.

Women's work in processing was reinforced during the Civil War, when almost everything had to be dried or processed. So few were the market lorries and so strict the town curfews, that market trade had to be streamlined[5] and backed up by contingency plans for goods not sold on a particular day or unable to be transported. Local preservation was at a premium: it diminished bulk, lightened weight and hedged against all the contingencies. In 1968, almost everything could be prepared in preserved form. Maize was left on the cob in the field to dry. Guinea-corn, being more vulnerable to the birds, was threshed and stored. Cowpeas and oilseed were simply dried. Yam and cassava were made into flour. Indigenous tobacco was sundried in large bunches and packed into cone-shaped bundles. Bushmeat was smoked. Locust-bean and shea butter were processed. Peppers were dried in the sun, and even okra was cut into pieces for drying.

On the eve of market expansion, local women had consolidated a set of skills and relationships that would launch them into new opportunities, but which were also in sectors that would come under strong competitive pressures.

CONCLUSION

I saw the production of the 1960s in Ibarapa as 'traditional'. People farmed but the population was only just becoming an urban provisioning community. The Yoruba division of labour was still in place, whereby drummers, tailors, blacksmiths and religious functionaries all farmed, but without thinking of themselves as *àgbẹ̀*, farmers, and without necessarily orienting their farming to the market. But the building of the Ofiki Bridge ten years before my fieldwork was the means and symbol of a new integration into regional supply networks. As the area moved structurally from being in the remote hinterland, a provider of specialty goods that were mainly hunted and gathered, and into the peripheral hinterland for cultivated products, new people and new functions immediately started to move in, in small but growing numbers: Fulani cattle herders, Ibadan cocoa traders, lorry drivers, Idoma labourers, government officials and NTC experts. Local women started to manoeuvre into new positions in the regional economy.

While it makes sense, from the urban hinterland perspective, to aggregate all these effects into a spatial understanding of expanding commercialisation, from the perspective of an understanding of dynamics in the humid savannas the most tangible effects were the diversification of participants in the rural economy and changes in the crops and techniques of the Yoruba farmers. From the perspective of Yoruba social history, each of the new crops, new situations and new techniques created space for small scale social innovation or adaptation. Developments of the more distant past, such as the land/labour measurement of the *ìwọ̀fà* labour pawn system, became the basis for the calculations on which wage labour depended when it came in about 1960. Egusi nurtured a template for women's harvest labour, while tobacco was the context in which a much less highly paid, monetary wage was paid to women for certain agricultural tasks such as watering and plucking. Cocoa was the crucible for innovations in land payments, tobacco for tractor rental. Women's processing laid groundwork for selling crops in the field. In this respect then, the innovations of the 1950s and 1960s were critical even though the overall commercial involvement was very much lower than it would later become and the quantitative contribution they made to the economy was limited. Multiplicity fostered the creation of a repertoire of alternative and complementary social and technical resources, no one element of which has swept away the others.

In the 1960s all of these developments were still grafted onto the older Yoruba division of labour in ways that they ceased to be by the late 1980s. The next chapter describes in some detail the central tendency of Idere farming, as it was practised by the male small scale farmers, in 1968–69.

NOTES

1. Adebayo (1996) offers the most comprehensive review to date of Fulani pastoral populations in the south.
2. I do not know how the groups that the Yoruba call 'Bororo' relate to the Fulani of the 1960s: whether they were in competition with one another, or so tied into the large networks of the trade that they had essentially been redeployed from the centres of power and wealth. Whatever the process or the reason, these less cooperative Bororo did not return north at the end of the drought.
3. See Austin (1993) for a review of West African credit, including pawning.
4. The NTC employee who related the history of the 1970s to me did so with graphic dramatisations. He said that the farmers were unreliable, took the supplies and the ploughing services and then did not grow tobacco; 'We had to go to the farmers and beg "Do you want me to lose my job?"'. They paid little attention to the crop; one farmer had gone to Lagos for his son's freedom (from apprenticeship) ceremony and had stayed two weeks in full harvesting season instead of coming back after the weekend. They did not care to learn; they simply asked for consideration when criticised: 'Ògá, please. Ògá, please.' In a classic mix of scorn for the indiscipline of those on the periphery of intense economic life and recognition of the freedom and incontravertible logic they brought to their choices, he compared the Ibarapa farmers unfavourably with those of other areas closer to major towns.
5. In war-time there was a premium on speed of negotiation in the market. In 1968, the wholesale markets were dominated by mediators of the price between farmers and traders. Known by the Hausa term pàràkòyí they were appointed by the bàbá ọja for all products. Individual farmers brought in baskets of, for example, peppers, which were bulked, bargained over in large lots and sold by the pàràkòyí who then repaid the farmers according to the amount they had brought in. Only yams have been predominantly a male domain in the market. For other crops the entire financial success for both farmers and traders depended on the acumen of these women. Styles of bargaining, the standardisation of measures and regular price expectations all developed as the wholesale markets became established, and they were particularly intensely lived and institutionalised under the pressures of the war.

5

FARMING IN THE PERIPHERAL HINTERLAND, 1968

By the year 1968 the violence of the Nigerian Civil War had been contained within the old Eastern Region, and indeed the rural Yoruba areas of the old Western Region saw limited hostilities during the war, concentrated on its eastern border. The indirect effects of wartime conditions were still considerable: on urban demand, on the transport infrastructure and the national economy more generally. In their situation in the periphery, the farmers had to come several steps to meet the market to develop the commercial side of their activities.

There was some leeway for growth of production, but the incentives for any particular food-crop farmer to expand or change his farming were insubstantial. The population fell quite far short of the hypothetical carrying capacity of the land under four years of cultivation and eight years of fallow, and no one discussed land shortage or changing rotations. The two growing seasons per year more or less ensured that basic needs would be covered. Few people migrated out in search of a different living. Members of a team of researchers in the 1970s observed that formal education had almost lapsed in Ibarapa (Daly et al. 1981). It was a conservative moment in the food system. Only in certain ways were the small-scale farmers orienting their agriculture to the urban market or their social lives to the larger region.

FARMERS AND THE FARMING REPERTOIRE IN 1968–69

In 1968 I was working with two life cyclical models. Although neither was adequate to an interpretation, they both encouraged a methodological orientation towards diversity. The present analysis does use the mean values of major variables, but only to block out some baseline parameters. It then moves on to the shapes of technical and social diversity as far as I can reconstruct them.

Three main characteristics of farming in 1968 need exploration: the difference that existed in 1968, but no longer exists in 1988, between full and part-time food farmers; the agro-ecological variation that existed then, and still exists although with a changed crop repertoire, from one micro-ecology to another; and finally, and least important in the long run, the variable I gave most interpretive stress to in 1968, namely the social status of the farmers within the Yoruba administrative and kinship hierarchies.

Growing Periods of Selected Crops

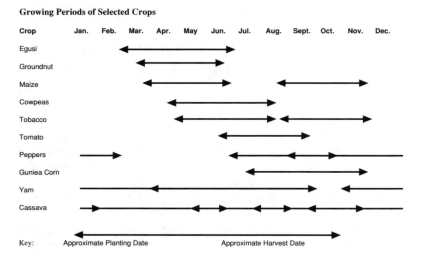

Figure 5.1 Growing Periods of Selected Crops, Idere

Farming as a technique and a career is described below for each of these three characteristics. Figure 5.1 (from Guyer 1972: 51) summarises the annual cropping cycle that applied to all farmers' enterprises, to show the basic agro-ecological synchronies (see Figure 3.2, p. 48 for corresponding rainfall).

Part- and Full-time Farmers

In 1968 some people were full-time food crop farmers, producing for the market; others farmed part-time and largely for the family food supply; and a third category did not farm at all. In this last group were most women and a few of the artisans: weavers and blacksmiths, for example. The women were almost entirely devoted to all the ancillary activities that made food-marketing possible: harvesting, processing, headloading and trading.[1] Very few women had farms of their own in those days and some of the few only worked tiny dry season plots in the stream bed behind the town. The two women in my sample who were farming the open savanna in 1968 fit perfectly into the category of full-time farmers, so little did gender *per se* seem to affect their aspirations or possibilities.

The pattern of activity I termed 'part-time' farming seems logically and historically primary, with the present pattern of activity in 'full-time' farming as a later commercialised development. Some part-timers were traditional artisans, such as embroiderer and blacksmith, who saw their occupational status in terms of both the expertise of the job and the socio-ritual responsibilities of the identity. Farming was a secondary activity. In 1968 this system of identification, and a range of local crafts from palm-fruit cutting to brewing, was still perceptible even though the expansion of Islam, Christianity and the agricultural market had secularised work and turned many other specialists into farmers. It was no longer possible to make any considerable income from drumming, praise-singing, dancing or mark-making in the circumscribed arena of a small town within six miles of a considerably larger one, although several of the farmers who were highly skilled artists still honoured the obligation to meet their ceremonial expectations. For example, one of the young men working on his father's farm was a virtuoso dancer who was in regular demand for celebrations. Some of these artists represented and honoured an older conception of work and identity while nevertheless defining themselves as farmers and falling into the 'full-time' sample. Other parttimers were part of the commercial economy in rural goods, such as cocoa farmers and timber-cutters, or salaried employees such as teachers, workers for the local council and religious functionaries.

There is some overlap in farm size and organisation between the low end of the full-time size range and the high end of the part-time range, but for the most part the two size categories were quite distinct, and there were corresponding differences in plot numbers and crop diversity. The mean farm size for the entire sample of the fifty-seven farms for which measurements were taken was 2.9 acres. For the full-time food farmers ($N = 38$) it was 3.7 acres and for the part-timers ($N = 19$) it was only 1.4 acres.

There were two key differences between the farms of part- and full-time farmers: part-time farms are much smaller and, on the average, more diversified in cropping pattern than full-time farms. Table 5.1 summarises the differences for the second growing season of 1968, and the following text explains how the part-time pattern relates to the domestic provisioning goals that were its main purpose.

The presentation of crop diversity requires some prior explanation, because it can be done in different ways for different purposes. For simplicity of comparison I eliminate intercropping altogether by simply dividing in half the area devoted to the two major intercropped staples in a field, and adding the result to the single-crop acreage for each crop.[2] Another aspect of crop combination that is relevant for the present analysis is the seasonal sequencing.[3] I will draw out inferences about the differing sequencing plans of part- and full-time farmers after presenting their cropping patterns for 1968, second season.

Part-time farms were only a little over one-third of the size of full-time farms. Their cropping pattern, however, was quite similar, differing in only having proportionally less maize and more 'other crops' (tomatoes, vegetables, peppers, indigenous tobacco). Maize was the most important commercialised second season crop in 1968, so the part-timers' limited maize reflects their limited engagement in the market. Their relatively high investment in perishable garden crops ('other'), which was up to two-thirds of the

Table 5.1: Size in Acres and Cropping Pattern of Part- and Full-time Farmers, September–December Season, 1968.

Main Crops	Part-time Farms ($N = 19$)		Full-time farms ($N = 38$)	
	Mean Acres	Per Cent Area	Mean Acres	Per Cent Area
Maize	0.37	26	1.31	35
Cassava	0.27	19	0.77	21
Yams	0.17	12	0.44	12
Guinea-corn	0.11	8	0.56	15
Total major staples	0.91	64	3.08	83
Other crops	0.36	25	0.58	16
No accurate info.	0.14	10	0.06	1
Total	1.42	100	3.72	100

absolute acreage devoted to these crops by the full-timers, reflects their ori-entation towards the diet. So the part-time farmers kept, on average, diver-sified and balanced farms: all staples were substantially and quite equitably represented, and a high proportion of the farm was given to ancillary crops and soup ingredients.

The size of part-time farms corresponded quite closely to a calculation made from the vantage point of daily needs: 'During the intensive study the farmers kept a rough record of the amount of staple food which they pro-vided for their own consumption from the farm. In general a farmer takes the equivalent of 2–3 rows (40–60 heaps) of cassava, yam and soup ingredi-ents from his farm each week. Cassava and yam are both crops which require a whole year to mature, so the main subsistence sector of the farm has only one harvest per year. So the area needed to provide subsistence is 52 x 40 (60) = 2,080 (3,120) heaps' (Guyer 1972: 97).

At the rate of conversion of heaps into acres of 3200, this is almost exactly an acre. The extra 0.4 acres per farmer beyond the subsistence minimum in staple crops that was measured for the part-time sample can be accounted for by soup ingredients and W. Allan's 'normal surplus' (1965: 38), that is, the difference between the average needs and the worst productive scenarios that farmers envisage. The crop diversity and balance of these part-timers is consistent with the subsistence aims of a population whose income and therefore status come from other occupations. These are not *àgbè* in the occupational sense, but men who farm.

The part-timers' pattern of production gives a somewhat solid basis from which to understand the full-timers' initial frontiers of expansion into the regional food market. This expansion covered the entire spectrum of crops, maintaining an extraordinary balance. It is almost as if the full-time farm was simply a larger scale model of the part-time farm. It had over half again the number of plots (eight versus five), and each plot was over half again the size (0.5 acres versus 0.3 acres). The two exceptions to proportional growth are complementary: full-time farmers disproportionately expanded maize

Table 5.2: Cropping Pattern on Full-time Farms, September–December Season, 1968 ($N = 38$), and March–August 1969 ($N = 12$).

Main Crops	Sept–Dec ($N = 38$) Per Cent of Total Area	March–August ($N = 12$) Per Cent of Total Area
Egusi	0	41
Maize	35	8
Cassava	21	27
Yams	12	19
Guinea-corn	15	0
Other crops	16	5
No accurate info.	1	0
Total	100	100

acreage, and they kept 'other' crops (most of which are perishable) relatively limited. The leader into the market appears from these data to have been maize.

In fact, the seasonality of the data for the complete sample over-empha-sises maize because the plots devoted to maize in the second season are likely to be given to egusi-melon in the following March. In the 1960s maize was very much a second-best commercial crop in terms of returns; it was planted mainly because there were few good alternatives for the sequential farming of egusi, then an exclusively first season crop (March to July). Maize was planted on newly cleared land in the second season, to prepare the plot for egusi, which was never planted on fresh land. To see the place of different crops more accurately, as they were leading farmers deeper into the food market, we need to look at the first season as well. As mentioned, I only collected the first season cropping patterns for the smaller diary sample, but these data for the first season of 1969 give some indication of the sequential relationship between the egusi and maize crops, and support the inference that it is really the egusi/maize *sequence* that leads into the market, not maize alone.

Essentially, the cassava and the yam/guinea-corn rotations continued over the year, taking about 25 per cent and 15 per cent of the land respec-tively. Egusi took over in March the acreage that had been in maize in Sep-tember, for a total of 35–40 per cent of cultivated acreage.

Egusi was the real high-value crop, and maize primarily its low-return complement in the rotation pattern. Much logic supports egusi as the mar-ket-leader amongst the food crops. It has a high value per unit volume, in the interests of the traders with their high transport costs. And for the farmers, I calculated the one-year rotation of egusi/cowpeas/maize (or guinea-corn) as yielding almost the same income per unit area as yams and cassava (14 shil-lings per *adé* of 10 rows by 20 heaps, by comparison with 15 shillings for yams or cassava). Yams, however, were awkward to transport in those days of headloading, and cassava demanded labour intensive processing before it

could be sold at all. The entire routine of the egusi harvest was institutionalised, which could obviate the potential bottlenecks of rapid expansion.

One of the logics of receptivity to new crops and varieties is worth noting
here. There can be 'gaps' in the rotation, where farmers know that the crop
they are growing – in this case maize – is not ideal. When better transport
allowed them to grow perishable crops, second-season maize declined in
favour of tomatoes, as one would have predicted from the calculated returns
in 1968.

To return to farming in 1968: one can see from this schematic comparison that the Ibarapa farmers protected their subsistence base, expanded
across the board and started to specialise, all at the same time and without
any new technical inputs. Subsistence, expansion and specialisation were
complementary processes, not competitive ones, as men began to cut down
on other occupations. Possibly also the process had already begun whereby
the rhythms of social life associated with old occupational identitites and
ceremonial and political commitment were becoming streamlined, a process
that picked up greater momentum later. Even so, full-time farmers spent
substantial time on social and ceremonial obligations. They would take a
week or more to attend a funeral, days here and there to attend naming
ceremonies, time to entertain visitors, trips to visit kin elsewhere, and so on.
A third of the diary sample's days were spent in activities other than farming.

Although the comparison of part- and full-time farmers draws attention
to the growth of full-time farms, it more than likely understates past differentiation in farm size because the rich of the past could support debt pawns.
Ìwòfà seems to have died quietly, if very late, in this area, but has left a large
'negative space'. It is a powerful absence in farmers' strategies, as holders of
cash can no longer invest it securely in a reliable source of farm labour. Ìwòfà
offers the beneficiary partial exemption from the need to control workers
under competitive conditions. In 1968, labour limited growth.

As the previous chapter suggests, migrant labourers became available
around 1960. By 1968 the majority of the farmers had most of their new
plots cleared and heaped by hired labour, superceding the group exchange
labour called àárò and any iwòfà they had been able to afford. Expanded
clearing by hired labour then also raised the demand for weeding. Àárò
labour moved into weeding and various collaborative harvesting activities,
and some of the extra labour did come from within domestic groups. But it
was also very marked in 1968 how many young men worked for their
seniors. I only designated six of the sixty farms as 'joint' farms,[4] but the
contributions of youth were very substantial. In fact, it is hard to imagine a
chief or elder with unexpected ceremonial obligations ever managing to
maintain a large farm, so often and for so long were they called away to
attend a funeral, hear a court case, attend to a dispute. On the three joint
farms of the diary study, two of the juniors spent more days at farm than

their elders, and the elders' contribution to farming dropped to about half their days instead of two-thirds. In the other case, the son was also his father's apprentice in drumming and dancing, the traditional family occupation, so he was still working under authority even when he was not farming. In return for labour support each of the juniors fully expected to have bridewealth paid for them out of farm proceeds and each also had their own field, *àbùṣe*, that they worked in the afternoons to make a small personal income to pay the costs of *egbé* membership and start into their own career in town social life.

Junior labour was probably most relevant for two purposes: the flexibility of schedule that it offered to elders, whose intense social life was particularly exacting after the decline of *iwòfà*, and the insistent challenge of weeding a larger farm before new sources of labour became available for that task. Farm size was not related in mechanical ways to the number of people who were theoretically available from amongst the junior members of the family, because the amount of work put in by individual men was a function of their motivation and health as well as their time availability.

From the work diaries kept for the six months of March to August 1969 one can present a general argument about labour thresholds and farm size. Full-time farmers worked on the farm an average of two-thirds of all available days during the first growing season, half of them in weeding (sixty days). It was their single most time-consuming and demanding activity. Most fields were weeded at least twice during the study period of six months, so we can assume a minimum of 7.5 acres-equivalent of weeding and probably closer to 9–10. This range of weeding rates, between six and eight days per acre, corresponds closely to Phillips' calculated standard rates for Nigeria: 4–5 days for light weed growth and 8–10 for heavy growth (1964: 174). A larger farm, a crop requiring more weeding or a change in the weed growth, would place pressure on either the one-third of days devoted to non-agricultural activities such as ceremonial and social obligations, to housebuilding, religious observance and illness, or on the time devoted to other agricultural work. I concluded that about four acres would be the upper limit of farm size by hand cultivation for the hypothetical average farmer. The sample of full-time farmers was just under that, at 3.7 acres. Hence my inference that junior labour was a flexibility factor rather than predominantly a contributor to the sheer size of the enterprise.

The correspondence between measured farm size and the logic of labour (for the full-time farmers) and the logic of subsistence (for the part-timers) was therefore quite close: four acres for the first and just above one acre for the second. In the days of equilibrium theory such coherences between principle and empirical findings were foregrounded at the expense of the approximations and spaces for change that a historicised approach would privilege. Equilibrium theories define growth in terms of the mitigation of major bottlenecks and the crossing of thresholds, whereas theories of construction and emergence, through practice, allow for incremental creation of new configurations. In retrospect the capacity to reconfigure through small changes of various kinds has been far more striking in this system than breach of major bottlenecks and transformations, so one looks back for the specific areas where life presented gaps, struggles and breachable limitations: second-season maize, which was not an optimal crop but was the only commercialisable crop that fit into the rotations; an unpredictable socio-political life, that presented enormous challenges to a more highly commercial farming; the kinds of dependant labour, that were diminishing while farmers were not yet able or willing to hire labour for all the tasks formerly covered by juniors and debt pawns, particularly weeding; and the limits of conjugal negotiation, that were being actively tested over wives' free porterage services to the markets. That these areas of dissatisfaction and contention might be foci of creative change, of negotiation that eventually finds resolutions, is very difficult to perceive at the time but their subsequent importance validates taking 'struggles' seriously as crucibles for the small-scale innovation that accounts for much of the growth.

Agro-ecological Variations

In the original study, the sample was chosen to capture differences the farmers said existed in the soil quality and in market access. The small *abùlé* of Afunije has black soil, in the remotest area by foot from Idere. Jagun is a cocoa village, distant by lorry but less far from Idere by foot. Onilẹka has more clay soil and is on a well served road within easy trekking distance. People said that more yams were grown at Onilẹka, more cassava and egusi at Afunijẹ, and somewhat less variety at Jagun because cocoa was the main crop. Idere's immediate environs had no particular ecological advantages but the location on the road did spare the farmers from severe transport limitations. In an economy with no locational differences in access to land or labour, there was clearly an interest in exploring the bases and implications of such variations in reputation about styles of production.

To my discouragement – since travelling from one *abùlé* to the other every week for the six months of the diary study had been one of the most demanding aspects of the entire research design – there seemed to be absolutely no economic or social differences from one to the other. Incomes and even returns to labour by crop-sequence were very similar. Everyone worked in comparable ways. This, of course, makes sense where rural residence is entirely optative. If people in the distant *abùlé* really were earning considerably less income they could easily leave.

Even so, the cropping differences were quite marked. Farmers in Onilẹka were, as their reputation suggested, devoting more acreage to the yam/guinea-corn sequence than those in Afunijẹ: about 40 per cent of the farm in

Onilẹka in 1968, compared with only 10 per cent in Afunijẹ. And Afunijẹ grew considerably more maize and egusi: 48 per cent per cent maize, in comparison with 22 per cent in Onilẹka, and 50 per cent egusi compared with 30 per cent in Onilẹka. Cassava and 'other crops' were more similar in the proportions of land devoted to them at all four sites, but they still varied, with Afunijẹ leading the investment in 'other crops'. With only one year of data to go on, one could interpret these patterns as variations in micro-ecological adaptation, but it is certainly more complex than this, involving the development of local traditions of expertise that attract reputation and therefore interested traders. Even with such an individuated farming system, where every farmer is free to take his own decisions, the shared emphasis of farmers in the same villages is striking. I will show later that the villages still differ from each other, but in somewhat different ways than in 1968. Name and reputation seem to be collective as well as individual assets in the search for a place in the market.

Variation by Age

In the original study, I struggled with the life cycle. Too many different dynamics were relevant for any single relationship to stand out starkly. First, and most important, people could have recourse to the market and to extensive kin networks for food, so at the individual level there was no necessity for a strict relationship between family size and farm size for subsistence. The part-timers, who were primarily farming for home provisions, showed no relationship at all between age and farm size. Second, people were so highly mobile from one house to another that the idea of 'dependancy' was impractical to study. What I did expect, and did argue for in the end, was a relationship between the farmer's status and his economic activities. The most active farms, however, were not those of elders who could mobilise junior labour, but of men who were still building a career, in the mid-years, and especially those in senior positions within their sibling groups who could legitimately work towards stature and influence. Although the overall curve of farm size with age follows the expected physical maturational pattern, I argued then and still argue now that we make a mistake to assume that either physical strength or demographic dynamics must account for that. Cash earnings were quite largely devoted to social life, so it was the parameters of social life that one needed to explain agricultural patterns. In 1968 gifts and ceremonial expenditure accounted for one-third (35 per cent) of all cash outflow. The only other categories that came close to demanding even 10 per cent of cash outflow were subsistence needs (salt, meat, oil) at 9 per cent, clothes at 10 per cent and housebuilding at 10 per cent (Guyer 1972: 132).

A man could start modestly, maintaining a relatively small farm up to the age of about 30. Full social independence was achieved quite slowly. Farm size grew above all with the assumption of obligations and aspirations in ẹgbẹ́, religious congregations, kinship and ceremonial life. From the age of 30, men built up quickly to a peak of social investment. People knew within broad limits what their own personal social investment would have to be (naming ceremonies for children, for example), what their familial obligations would be, and what they wanted to build in the way of interpersonal networks. Ambitious men contributed often and generously to the ceremonials of others: namings, funerals, personal support and the entertainment of álèjó, strangers. Interpersonal reciprocity was highly formalised. The amount of a contribution varied with status and was proportional to the previous gifts in the relationship, so that each and every dyadic relationship had its own history and expectation of support, down to a detailed level of commitment. At any time an adult person could list off their outstanding relationships and the cash involved. For each major ceremony at which the entire descent segment needed to be represented, such as a funeral or a chieftaincy installation, junior siblings (of both sexes) contributed to their oldest sibling; he (or she) in turn contributed their collective cash to the next higher generation, which then pooled the entire proceeds with its own senior sibling. The collective contribution was then made by the senior person for the entire group. For ceremonies involving ẹgbẹ́, each member made a contribution to a single gift.

Men varied markedly in the complexity of their networks, the amounts they contributed and the frequency with which they participated. From the small sample I studied in detail, it seemed clear that the men in mid-career who stood likely to move into influential positions were those who maintained the largest networks as well as working the largest farms. It was far more this dimension of economic life – its sources in marketed produce and its destinations in personal investment in cash – that shaped the life cycle of farm work. The decline in farm size in old age reflects not just a decline in subsistence obligations and in physical strength, but also an increasing ability to tap the cash income, as distinct from the farm labour, of one's juniors for social expenditures that were in collective interests.

Understanding the life cycle of farm size is a clear example of the importance of not imposing known models with too great alacrity. The fact that surface behavioural patterns in a new case look familiar from a known case is simply a testimony to the history of the discipline, not to the dynamics of the cases. The 'familiar' life cycle pattern in farm size is, in this case, a reflection of the cash economy and not the subsistence economy, and of social/ceremonial aspirations not consumption needs. Although I agree with Berry (1989) that many of these expenditures have the quality of investment, with a feedback into productive life and resource mobilisation, they are also more than this. Idere farmers were not under pressure for basic resources. Sociopolitical identity was a fundamental justification for their economic life. It gave meaning and direction to ambition.

CONCLUSION

Idere's farm economy was beginning to be commercially oriented in 1968. Subsistence coverage accounts for only a proportion of productive activity. Farmers were expanding production in ways entirely consonant with market theories: they were expanding in non-perishable crops, with high value for both producers and transporters, while keeping the basic food supply system intact. They rarely purchased foods that could be cultivated, as would be predicted for a farming community located at the distant end of the market networks. The basic rotation of four years cultivation and eight years fallow was easily within reach of a population still below the carrying capacity of the land, so the extent of expansion was largely a function of labour organisation and the demand for a cash income. Farm work was individuated and much more egalitarian than the political status system to which many aspired and devoted substantial proportions of their income.

The consonances with market theory predictions, however, do not mean that generic 'rationality' explains them. Expansion depended on new institutions and had to be consonant with social conceptions. An adult man could not give up food provision for his family, nor tie himself down to a rigid rhythm of work, without erosion of status obligations. As long as the ceremonial structure was in place, there would be literally no purpose to production if, in order to expand it, farmers undermined their capacity to benefit from it in the way that was most meaningful to them. If work rhythms are to be intensified, attendant on commercial involvement or population growth, then the demands of socio-political life have to change as well.

In 1968 the social framework was already slowly shifting. The late 1960s were an uneasy period. Political incorporation had entailed the decline of *ìwòfà* and its unique capacity to support status differentiation that had a solid, reproducible economic base. At the same time, incorporation into the peripheral hinterland was undermining old occupational specialties. The range of means and pathways for carving out career paths became relatively narrow, even though cash incomes were probably rising. Most Yoruba specialists now described themselves as farmers even though they still practised their expertise. As full-time farmers they did not have very solid resources in the crop repertoire to pursue individually diverse patterns of farming, even though all decisions were entirely individuated. They differed from one another more in farm size than in the range of crops grown. It was the sudden extension of the transport system and the surge in urban demand in the years after the war ended in 1970 that brought the farming economy into the sphere of regular, daily accessibility.

NOTES

1. All women's activities were directly or indirectly monetarily remunerated, with some activities such as headloading during the civil war years hovering precariously and with great disputation on the brink between the indirect payment of conjugality and the direct payment of contract/task work. In 1968 there was a bitter struggle brewing over porterage. The male farmers were so extremely dependent on women's transport labour that they explicitly insisted on the assimilation of headloading to the indirectly rewarded domestic duties and organised to resist the attempt by one or two men to hire headloaders for wages on a regular basis.

2. All crops were intercropped at some stage in the cultivation cycle in 1968: maize intercropped with new cassava was very common in the second growing season; many plots had some peppers interspersed, or a pineapple border, or rows of cassava planted at regular intervals, a technique known as *ilàkọ*. The simple calculation used here means that the category 'maize' is made up of monocropped acreage, plus half of the acreage for 'maize and cassava' and 'maize and yams', etc. Complex intercropped fields of vegetables, okro, tomatoes, peppers, pigeon peas and the whole list of cultigens are simply grouped as 'other', even if they did contain a few stands of the major staple crops. At issue here are the broad contours of difference rather than subtleties of agricultural performance.

3. The cropping pattern for any one season is really a function of the longer sequence to which that season belongs. Two of Western Nigeria's major crops, cassava and yams, occupy the fields for an entire year, or longer in the case of cassava. Guinea-corn planted in the second season is usually a precursor to yams that are planted in November or December against trellises of the remaining bent-over stems of the harvested guinea-corn crop. Farmers will only plant cassava or guinea-corn in the second season if they are planning to devote that field to an all-year crop for the following year, either yams or cassava. By planting single season crops they leave the plot free, particularly for egusi, to be planted in the main growing season starting in March.

4. In which both men were adult even if they were of different generations. Most of the middle-aged and older farmers mentioned intermittent help from sons, sons-in-law (who still bore the expectation of significant work for their fathers-in-law), grandchildren, junior siblings and so on.

6

THE OIL BOOM: TRANSPORTERS, TRACTORS AND NEW SOURCES OF HIRED LABOUR

In 1968 Ibadan was sub-Saharan Africa's largest city. Although it was the administrative capital of one of the four Nigerian regions, the site of several major educational and research institutions, a major market in consumption goods and the largest Yoruba polity, it had little industry and business by comparison with Lagos. At the end of the 1960s it was artificially quiet due to the war, its population reduced by the exodus of Igbo back to the East. By 1988 the boundaries were several miles further out, the population had at least tripled, and people had poured in from all over West Africa. Some of the foreigners had been repatriated in the official expulsions of the early and mid-1980s, but the population was a cosmopolitan mix of people from all over Nigeria and beyond. The immediate rural hinterland had become residential land, and in some directions the spreading suburbs began to approach the adjacent independent settlements. With the old farm land of the indigenes increasingly taken up and the population growing from distant inmigration, the proportion of food consumers must have risen even faster than the absolute numbers of urban residents.

The urban growth of Lagos and Ibadan really took off in the mid-1970s, as national oil revenues expanded. Its effect on the food supply hinterlands was twofold, with contrary implications: they became stimulants to rural production but also destinations for rural out-migration. Just as the hinterlands had already started to attract outsiders from beyond the periphery – the Fulani cattle herders and the Idoma farm labourers – the cities now started to draw off the youth of the hinterland itself into the urban wage labour market and the professions. While specific locations were moving structurally closer one notch at a time, parts of their populations were leapfrogging towards the centre. The possibility of becoming a kind of modest yeomanry or at least a commercial small-farm sector began to emerge for the rural farmers, with a reliable market, dependable transportation, the solid status of indigenes, access to incoming wage labour and realistic educational ambitions for their children. This scenario would however be possible only on condition that more resources could be tapped to expand production and the encroaching outsiders could be kept under control. Furthermore the category of outsiders began to include not only greater numbers of cattle herders but also corporate agribusiness. Add to these a local middle class of returned and retired professionals, and other groups responding to market possibilities in food production, and the potential for pressures began to build. If these newcomers prevailed, the local population would be increasingly squeezed and possibly even partially dispossessed, as has happened in the late 1980s in parts of Eastern Nigeria (Omeje 1992). A contentious and politically indeterminate situation began to develop, with new and old elements competing for space, and not under the solidly progressive political and economic conditions that are associated with the expansion of a yeomanry, but rather amid all the volatility of post-Civil War boom and bust, military and civilian rule. The urban population continued to grow after 1984, but in the context of economic crisis.

The period between 1968 and 1988 is therefore not one of slow and continuous growth in the institutions of the food economy, that parallels the demographic growth of the centres of urban demand. The oil boom, from about 1975 to 1983, deeply marked the rural economy in ways that continued to affect it in the era of structural adjustment that followed. Amidst all the criticism of the conduct of the oil boom in Nigeria, which includes a venal failure/refusal to invest in rural production, a space needs to be kept for examination of the nature of the 'trickle down' that did take place (see Watts 1987 for a nuanced view). The Ibarapa economy did grow during the oil boom years. Indeed, it would have been extraordinary if it had not, given its location. Some new resources became available, primarily transport, tractors and increased farm labour.

TRANSPORT[1]

As national income soared, the insatiable Nigerian demand for cheap and convenient mobility could begin to be met. There arose a scramble of competition for a piece of the lucrative import business, an increased number of automobile dealerships located in more cities, a greater variety of types of vehicle, and changed conditions of purchase, so that even relatively poor farmers at the end of the capillaries of distribution found that they could afford a motorcycle or at least a style of life that dramatically reduced their headloading and trekking. The famous Datsun pick-up (1500 or 1600 series) – nicknamed in Yoruba the *jálukere*: 'let's go into the pot-holes' – was the vehicle that most altered the rural areas, so I use the import figures for new 'dual purpose passenger motor vehicles' (entry 732.16 in the *Nigerian Trade Summary*) to illustrate the spectacular increase in the transport fleet of the country during the later 1970s and early 1980s, and its equally spectacular collapse in the era of economic crisis and structural adjustment.

During the civil war about 1500 of this kind of vehicle were imported per year, hardly any of them Japanese. The year of extremely rapid increase was 1975, when imports almost tripled from 6419 in the previous year to to 19,170. By 1977, the annual imports were at almost 31,000, a peak only

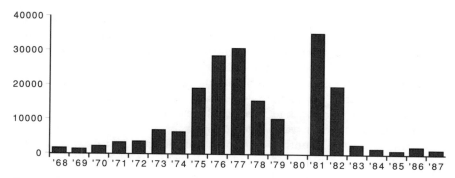

Figure 6.1 Imports of Dual Purpose Vehicles, 1968–87   *Note:* 1980, no data

surpassed in 1981, when 35,000 came into the country, almost twenty-five times as many as ten years previously. Thereafter the decline was precipitous. By 1984 annual imports were back to the same level as during the war and were still at this level in the year before my research, 1987. Figure 6.1 summarises the import statistics for dual purpose vehicles.

The Japanese share of the market for dual purpose vehicles follows the growth curve for the total market. Vehicles from Japan only started to creep up on German, French and British imports in 1972 when they accounted for 13 per cent of imports, but in 1977 Japan controlled 49 per cent of the import market. From then until 1981, the peak before the rapid decline, Japanese vehicles accounted for over 40 per cent of imports, after which its share fell to 30 per cent or below. Although the trade statistics give 439 as the number of Japanese dual purpose vehicles imported in 1987, one driver said he had not seen a new one since 'about two years after the Second Republic', (i.e. 1985). Two drivers explicitly linked vehicle imports to civilian government: there would be more 'when things will be normal again'. The sense in the late 1980s that the growth period represented the 'normal' condition of things, and that the high prices of structural adjustment were a passing aberration associated with the stringencies of military government, sustained people's consistent investment in the rural conditions put in place in the oil boom era.

In view of structural adjustment conditions which set in with force in 1985, the period of rural transport growth in Nigeria seems a rather brief moment of about six years: 1975 to 1981. Thereafter, people have been managing with repairs, recycled engines imported from abroad under special conditions,[2] spare parts increasingly produced in Eastern Nigeria, parts from wrecks, and pieces scavenged over an ever-increasing radius, all reassembled through imaginative tinkering on a scale and at a level of expertise for which the wartime experience was probably the only training adequate to the challenge. Nigerian mechanics give new meaning to the concept of bricolage. Up to 1988 the fleet was more or less maintained, although passengers increasingly travelled in vehicles whose doors only opened from the outside, whose seats were torn and showing the springs, whose tyres were bald, whose visors were stuffed full of spare copies of official paperwork in case of harassment or confiscation, and whose windshields were eclectically decorated with the talismans of various new and old religious movements that the passenger suspected were needed for safety almost as much as the screwdriver was needed to open the door.

Petrol subsidy was another component of the transport expansion, and understandably became a key populist political issue of some complexity. The price of petrol has been kept low throughout the entire period; petrol and kerosense followed a much lower curve of price increase over the twenty years than all other items. From 1975 to 1984 the petrol price fluctuated but started and ended the decade at the same nominal level, a period over which the palm oil price doubled or tripled.

It was not only the number of vehicles and the subsidy on petrol that mattered for the growth of the small-scale sector, but also the kind of vehicle. The Datsun pickup is extraordinarily suited to rural Nigerian conditions. It is said by the drivers to be very strong: a necessity for driving on rural tracks and into farms. Spare parts were always available: an absolute requirement for drivers outside of main town centres who have to keep the vehicle on the road to make a living. The design also fit Nigerian requirements. Unlike many pickups of the time, one popular Datsun model had two rows of seats in the cabin, so a substantial number of passengers could be carried in far greater comfort than in the Bedford lorry that had served the rural areas for twenty years. The back was open, so that the loads could be piled up, or failing that, people could sit or stand there. Local carpenters fitted wooden barriers to allow higher loading, and – thus modified – the back of the Datsun pickup became a standard measure in the price–volume bargaining system for agricultural goods. Jùjú and later fuji music accompanied journeys. Decoration with proverbs and aphoristic philosophical comments on trade, life and love had been the main mode of aesthetic domestication of the lorry. Now there was music. The pickup became a social institution: taxi, crop transporter, source of entertainment and unoffical measure of amounts of produce small enough for the transporter to deal directly with the producer.

The pickup could hardly have differed more in its versatility from the cumbersome, uncomfortable, high volume, utilitarian market lorry that had mediated the original growth of urban food supply. Apart from the obvious fact that the pickup was more affordable and there could simply be many more of them, the rural areas had never been served by a vehicle whose capacity was commensurate with their own levels of production. The lorry system depended entirely on the bulking and bargaining institutions of the periodic markets. With pickups a buyer could also go straight to the *abúlé* and buy directly from the farmer, as long as the tracks were passable.

The oil boom years were halcyon days for the aspiring small purchaser of vehicles. Dealerships even offered hire purchase (purchase on credit). Several farmers or produce buyers in a town as small as Idere were able to buy pickups, either for cash or on credit, and go into the transport business. A tomato farmer profited from windfall prices in 1978 and bought a pickup for N10,000 cash. Ordinary farmers in a family might put their money together and buy a vehicle either new or second-hand for cash. Enough vehicles were on the road, and enough of their owners were local, that for the first time, people could plan, book and bargain on the doorstep, rather than wait for whatever turned up.

Transport also generated employment for local people: drivers, apprentices, loaders and of course all the support services at petrol stations and mechanics' workshops. As in all Yoruba occupations, the 'owners' are organised into their own *ẹgbẹ́*, by town and for the Local Government Area as a whole, meeting every two weeks to set prices and discuss policies.

Motorcycles were the complementary component of a newly localised transport system. A farmer with a motorcycle could cultivate in several different places, transport small amounts of produce quickly from farm to *abúlé*, or *abúlé* to market, and feel confident in his ability to get home to the town quickly in case of ceremonial, political or health needs. In town, motor cycles could be used as personal taxis. In a year such as 1981 when cassava prices were unusually high and vehicle prices were still reachable due to the 'overvalued naira', even the most ordinary of farmers was able to afford a motor cycle if he wished.

The trade statistics for motor cycles show a similar pattern of growth to those for dual-purpose passenger vehicles (and an even higher level of domination by Japanese producers). The year of spectacular growth was 1975, when the slow development from under 10,000 per year during the war to double that in 1974 suddenly hit 71,000 in 1975, and by 1977 reached over 215,000. The quasi-totality of this market from 1973 onwards – over 80 per cent, and in some years all but 100 per cent – was dominated by Japanese vehicles.

Small-scale vehicle ownership however, for all its impact on farming and trade, is difficult work. The daily frustrations of wear and tear on the vehicle, coping with the state of the roads in all weathers, dealing with challenges from the police, vehicle inspectors and tax collectors, packing endlessly varied loads, managing a motley set of crises from people falling out to petrol being unavailable, and often keeping up an endless stream of conversation all day, makes transport an exhausting occupation. Because of the farming calendar, the vehicles are in greater demand during the rainy season, exactly

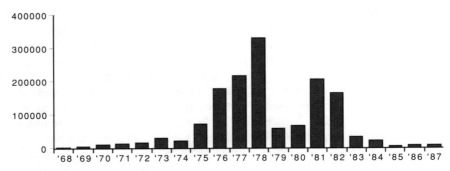

Figure 6.2 Motor Cycle Imports, 1968–87

at the moment when the roads are in their worst condition. Owners who did not drive were spared the stress but usually sacrificed the vehicle. Drivers are paid in relation to the daily income, so they have every incentive to overload, rush, work long hours and generally squeeze as much as possible from the vehicle. The life of those vehicles was short, and in fact the only *jálukere* left working from Idere itself in the late 1980s were owner-driven. This seemed to work well, since the regular passengers of a much reduced fleet were more clearly aware of the costs and quite often chipped in to help out, whether to intercede with the police or contribute to a repair. The need for repair is a constant problem. Most of the functioning pickups were bought around 1982 or 1983, and have been on the road continuously, in all seasons, since then.

It would be difficult to exaggerate the importance of a sudden influx of vehicles into an economy poised in the outer ring of a commercial food system, already oriented towards the food markets. The pickups immediately forged out into the countryside, well before the roads and tracks were adequate. Hence the name 'let's go into the pot-holes.' The *jálukere* owners became a lobby for road improvement by jacking up the fares explicitly to cope with damage caused by the potholes. Public outcry about transport prices became one of the classic modes of complaint about government. In fact, transport problems became far more amenable to direct linkage in people's minds to the capacities and policies of local and national government than agriculture itself could ever be, given the diffuse relationship between policy and farmgate prices and the ever-present influence of the weather on production. The condition of the roads, the availability and prices of vehicles and spare parts, and the cost of petrol – all conveyed with rhetorical flourish to the captive audience wedged into the two rows of *jálukere* seats beside and behind the driver – were directly attributable to the actions of government.

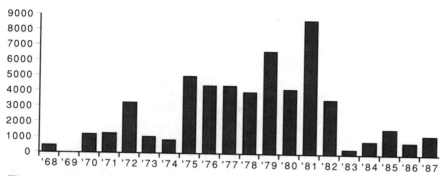

Figure 6.3 Tractor Imports, 1968–87

The effects of the *jálukere* on agriculture ramified in several directions, but they stemmed from two capacities: the ability to sell from the farm or *abúlé* rather than bulking through the periodic market sytem, and the sudden feasability of selling fresh produce. For the women who had mediated the paid and unpaid linkages between farm and market there was both a reprieve – from headloading – and the threat of intensified competition – to their control of processing. Even highly-perishable fresh cassava, the backbone of the year-round artisanal processing industry, could now be sold directly from the field to the trader, to be processed in bulk by mechanised methods, closer to the consumer markets. Farmers turned fields over to perishable crops such as tomatoes and peppers, and the whole panoply of preservation methods for other crops, such as the preparation of yam flour or the drying of okro or the making of millet-beer, went into sharp dcline. It was only the overall expansion of production, the sheer variety of goods demanded, and the slow growth of local demand for food items, that allowed local women who processed and sold goods on a very small scale to stay in the market.

Farmers, on the other hand, could only benefit, since an entire component of the marketing system had been so radically simplified. The question for them was how to go about expanding a production system in which weeding labour was a major constraint and family labour was less and less controllable. Two pieces of the answer were provided by innovations that flowed as directly from the oil boom as the transport situation: the availability of tractors, and the changed supply of farm labour. Both, however, also stimulated the mid-scale and agri-business concerns that would move in on the land frontier.

TRACTORS

Tractor imports describe a much slower growth than passenger vehicles. The rise is not so steady after 1975, and 1981 was the peak year, with only about seven times as many as in 1970, the year that saw the end of the Civil War. Japan was never a factor in this market; the USA, Britain, Italy, Roumania and Germany all contributed. Even at the local level it was readily apparent that tractors were not the first investment on people's minds, and it came as something of a surprise as structural adjustment set in for people to see how deeply tractor cultivation had become entrenched in the rural economy and how relatively lucrative tractor ownership could be. Tractor availability did however expand during the oil boom years, and they did make their way out to places like Ibarapa where most of the farming was done on a small scale.

Tractors came first to Idere through the Nigerian Tobacco Company in the mid-to-late 1960s. They were entirely restricted to the tobacco plots, but several of the present tractor owners started out learning about mechanisation while they were contract farmers for NTC. Oral history has it that the kind of private tractor hire that developed in the 1980s was introduced in the mid-1970s by the Irish Catholic missionary at Igbo-Ọra. Father McCabe owned three tractors, it is said, which he hired out and drove himself, at least in the beginning. For him, renting tractors was an aspect of community relations, not a business, so the price was not set by economic considerations. The earliest local owner bought a second-hand tractor in 1976 for N2,000. Four others that I know of bought in the early 1980s, on hire purchase, at the peak of supply and before the rapid rise in prices that set in after 1985. About this time tractor ownership for hire to the farmers became one of the occupations of retired military and professional personnel. One famous case at Igo-Ọra is a military man who in 1988 owned six tractors and two buses, all for public use.

The brief moment at which tractors could be bought on credit was critical to the development of the private renting system that seems so unusual in sub-Saharan Africa that Pingali et al. (1987) explicitly eliminate it from their study of mechanisation. The use to which tractors are put in Southern Nigeria, namely field preparation alone, already militates against private ownership and exclusive use. The attachments are limited to ploughs and there are no carts. Hence there is no year-round or even multi-seasonal use for a privately owned tractor unless it is rented out for other farmers' field preparation. But several owners explicitly mentioned that even though they originally had in mind a private owner/private use plan, the credit conditions made it impossible to observe. One of Idere's most diligent larger farmers bought on credit in 1982 for N17,000 plus N2,000 for the plough, with a cash down-payment of N4,000. The rest was paid off by 1985, through the income generated from renting, not primarily through the income generated from his farm. One or two very large farmers did try to keep their tractors out of the rental market, particularly those who bought in cash after the price rises of structural adjustment in the latter half of the 1980s. They worried about the wear and tear on the vehicle, and about the relatively sluggish response of the hiring prices to the dramatically changed conditions of purchase. By this time however it was difficult to keep their tractors out of popular use.

By the time hire purchase became impossible due to the instability of the currency, the institutions and expectations of a renting system had already set in and tractor use was imbricated in the entire egbe organisation of occupations. The demands on tractor owners were particularly acute because the local supply has always been limited relative to the demand for services, and one cannot go further afield to bring new services in simply because of the enormous cost of driving tractors uselessly around the roads. However, once the local tractor owners were organised into an association the link between specialist and market deviated sharply from the daily auction it might otherwise have been. Predictable terms of access were set. Any resentment of tractor-owners on the part of farmers was not due to the wealth differentials of private ownership, and they were remarkably patient with all manner of difficulties. They always paid cash for their tractor clearing and they submitted to the regular price rises of structural adjustment with only short-lived complaint. It was total monopoly of use that was intolerable; if a machine existed it should be available at some price or other to those who needed its services, rather than sitting in a shed. As a result, even when the owners prohibited it, the drivers of privately- or state-owned tractors hired them out surreptitiously by doing an acre here and there 'as we were passing'. They had to be watched like hawks to prevent them from developing their own businesses on the side, and maintaining such vigilance was outside the capacity or the willingness of anyone wealthy enough to buy the tractor in the first place. They had other things to do than constantly check up on the activities of a group of youths. The local élite themselves tapped into available resources in the same way.[3]

The tractor owners' association was formed in 1977, with the main purpose of setting the rental price per acre for the season. Prices are thereby uniform for the whole district at any one time, and only rise on agreement among the owners, who announce the price for the season after their meetings. In the late 1970s an acre could be ploughed once for N10. By early 1987, it cost N30. The owners' association tried to raise it to N40 later in the same year but could not succeed until the new season in 1988. Mid-1988 saw a successful mid-year raise to N50. A letter in 1993 told me that it now cost N240 to plough an acre, a steep rise probably due to the inability of the owners to partially insulate themselves from structural adjustment prices for spare parts any longer.

Even so, discipline within the association on the agreed and announced price is usually very strict and members do not deviate from it in obvious ways. The deviations that do occur follow classic Yoruba bargaining patterns: one changes the size of an 'acre' rather than changing the nominal price. Tractor-owners will not work a plot of less than an 'acre'. The farmers say that a measured acre corresponds almost exactly to fifteen *adé*, the traditional measure of 200 heaps. They can eye-ball this area with ease. In principle the tractor operators are supposed to measure by rope on demand, but they do not. So the acre ploughed is the result of a bargain over what exactly an acre is in this particular case, under these particular conditions, by two experienced assessors. I had expected the variation in the farm 'acres' I measured to be quite significant as a result, similar to the variation in the volume of cassava flour or egusi in the standard *olódó* market measure. A very few people were indeed either cheated or naive. But the mean acreage actually ploughed turned out to be extraordinarily close to the 'acreage' bargained over, and farmers were just as likely to have a little extra done as a little less. People can complain about bargaining and loop-holing, but in fact the discipline maintained by the association is remarkable in the face of ever-changing circumstances and the acumen of the customers.

So strong is the price agreement that restricted tractor availability has been met by tightening the booking conditions rather than raising the nominal price. Farmers pay in advance and book the time, rather than making the usual payment in full and in cash at the time the work is done. In some cases where an expensive repair has to be done to a tractor, a group of farmers will club together and pay for it, as an advance on, and guarantee of, later services. Some tractor owners have developed a kind of reciprocity with farmers, whereby the latter keep guard over and perhaps even work on the former's farm in one of the more distant villages, in return for guarantee of tractor services. The losses from these developments are mainly felt by villages that in easier times could be sure that a tractor would randomly pass by some time during the season, so that they could flag it down to serve their needs. The more that tractors are booked by organised groups, the less will they be available to the passing customer.

The price of ploughing by tractor has risen steadily under structural adjustment but probably more slowly than the rise in price of new tyres and spare parts. During the later 1980s, the owners scavenged the dealers in several states in the weeks before the first ploughing season in a search for second-hand and cannibalised spare parts that had become something of an annual nightmare. In February 1988, one of the longest-standing owner-operators of a by-now very old vehicle needed a new rear tyre (at N700) and a new plough disc (at N185). He expected to have to visit parts dealers in several major cities to find the right one at an affordable price, but was currently prevented from starting on the quest by a serious attack of guinea-worm. It is this kind of search despite its vicissitudes that keeps an ageing tractor fleet in business at all.

The effects of tractor clearing on farming will be addressed in each of the chapters on the different categories of farmer. Suffice it here to note two things: first, because of private renting the use of tractors did penetrate to the smallest farms during the period when they were relatively inexpensive and available. Use of tractors was clearly widespread, both socially and geographically, by 1988. For the forty-nine male small-scale farmers in the sample, 52 per cent of the total land cultivated for food crops had been initially cleared by tractor, and 59 per cent of the farmers had at least one tractor-cleared plot. For the forty women's farms the proportions were not much lower: 42 per cent of the land was tractor cleared and 42 per cent of the farmers had hired tractors. All the villages, even those in quite distant places, had tractor-cleared plots, albeit in lower proportions than Idere and places closer to the main roads. So although tractors did let loose the ambitions of the larger scale farmers as I will describe in following chapters, their use was deeply popularised during the early and mid-1980s.

Second, however, it is still unclear to anyone whether such widespread tractor clearing is ecologically desirable in the open savanna, with lateritic soils. The numerous small trees that used to be pollarded, burned and kept in place as trellises for yam vines are now completely uprooted for tractor-clearing of selected land. The remote sensing data clearly showed the sharp boundaries of tractor-cleared fields because of the complete removal of other vegetation. A few conservation techniques are used against the harmattan winds and torrential rains. For example, some farmers leave the weed cover to become heavy at the end of the second season, to remain in place over the dry season, and I found that tractor-cleared fields are more often chemically fertilised than hand-cleared fields. But in terms of effects on soil structure, the farmers themselves do not know yet whether there will be long-run effects of total clearing and planting on the flat instead of on heaps.

In a system dominated by the demands of weeding, tractors could never be a complete answer to farm expansion. They could not even be the complete solution to land preparation because of the need for heaps. Just as the overvalued naira and the immense amount of money flowing into the Nigerian economy during the oil boom stimulated the vehicle revolution, so also did they generate new sources of farm labour for hire. Most important was the influx of foreigners from francophone West Africa, followed by modest changes in wage labour by local women and youth, and in annual migration by the Agatu.

FARM LABOUR

There had been a three-way differentiation of the relatively limited wage labour market in 1968 into women harvesters, local youth for a variety of tasks, and Agatu for clearing and heaping. These were not interchangeable categories to any great extent. Women had a complete lock on harvesting work for egusi and cowpeas. It was their right and their obligation, and they were already organised to defend their access to it and to protect the level of remuneration from erosion. Local youth were the only people ever hired to do cultivation and tending of crops. They were paid at a higher rate than the migrants and expected to be punctilious up to local standards. The migrant Agatu cleared and heaped new land.

By the 1980s there were more categories of farmer with their own specific needs, and more categories of worker. As they moved into the newly opened economy, all the foreigners had to learn some Yoruba, and the farmers had to figure out how to get on with them on a fairly intimate basis: to know which workers were adamant about observance of the Muslim evening prayer in the mosque and therefore could not be kept late at farm, to understand which wives came from female farming traditions and were therefore willing to do field work, to set up living arrangements for them, accommodate their own kind of social life in the evening and develop means of dispute settlement over everything from unpaid wages to social confrontations and life-threatening accidents. During the farming season the rural areas became microcosms of West Africa. On a July evening in 1988 in one of the villages a Fulani woman from the cattle herders was selling white cheese, a settled Hausa family was bringing home crops from their own farm, a group of young Agatu had already washed and changed into city clothes and sunglasses and were sitting around waiting for the evening meal, and an Igbo youth was holding an animated evangelical prayer meeting in Yoruba with the farmers' children.

At the beginning of growth in the mid-1970s, the farmers did not actively recruit workers from far afield. They suddenly found that new conditions were possible to negotiate with the people who flooded in from across the border, where economic conditions were less favourable. In the event, the old conditions of work held their own quite substantially in those areas of the economy that already had bases for labour hire: the women's harvest and Agatu clearing and heaping. Change came as novelty. Nothing was replaced. There were new workers, new tasks and new conditions of work.

Women

Women's work on the egusi harvest is probably the oldest form of paid task work in the Yoruba economy. Carried out by organised work groups, paid in kind at one heaping *olódó* of egusi per day of work and comprising a daily meal cooked by the farmer, the women's egusi harvest work is an annual institution to which most women devoted about three weeks a year in 1968.

It was remarkable in 1988 that the level of payment in kind had hardly budged at all over the twenty years of change, in spite of the downward pressures exerted by agribusiness and the occasional upward pressure exerted by women using brinksmanship in their bargaining.[4] Table 6.1 summarises the comparison between rates of pay on small- and mid-scale local

Table 6.1: Female Egusi Harvest Wages by Mode of Farming, August 1988

Mode	Value (Naira) of Food per Woman/Day	Percentage of Farmer's Crop Paid in Kind	Total Naira Value per Woman/Day
Mid-scale (N = 5)	0.61	13.4	8.61
Small-scale (N = 16)	0.97	16.1	8.97
Female Farmers (N = 3)	1.19	17.6	9.19

farms in 1988, translated into a naira minimum by using the current egusi market price of 8 naira per *olódó*.[5]

The local mid-scale farmers had managed to save a little on the harvest by comparison with the small-scale farmers, but only to the extent of shaving off 30 kobo's worth per day from the cooked food budget and such a small amount of egusi as to be unnoticeable.[6] The stability of women's wages and working conditions in the egusi harvest is the precipitate not of custom alone but of constant testing as conditions shift. The women's economy has itself diversified, so that fewer women take on the egusi harvest as seasonal work than did in the past. But those who do are now more emphatically identified as *elégúsí*, more organised in stable groups and more determined about the wage. In 1988 one group even tried, unsuccessfully, to alter the size of container used to measure the egusi, from *olódó*, the metal market measure, to *iki*, a particular size of plastic bowl.

Most local farmers are resigned to this system, but as the marketing of other crops becomes more convenient and less expensive I heard other farmers use the *wàhálà* (grief) of brinksmanship, including bargaining over food quality and expense of the harvest, as reasons not to grow egusi at all. As the crop data for 1988 show, the total acreage devoted to egusi by small-scale farmers has fallen over the twenty years, and the proportion of men growing it has fallen even more.

This increasing specialisation of egusi cultivation to certain farmers, working under certain conditons, which will be explored as agricultural practice later, has implications for the women workers. The fewer but larger plots require groups of harvesters that are larger, more carefully synchronised and more disciplined since more is at stake and losses are more possible. In 1988, sixteen small-scale farmers needed an average of 14 woman/days of harvest labour each to bring in the harvest, and the harvesters worked mainly in staggered one-day stints in teams of six to eight women. The mid-scale local farmers, however, needed an average of 102 woman/days of harvest work, again staggered, but using teams of fifteen or more, about twice the size of groups used on the small-scale farms. Once this size is reached, the *ẹgbẹ́* form of organisation replaces the informal kin/neighbour

form of the small-scale sector. One woman will be designated as the re-
cruiter and organiser of the labour for all the farms in one vicinity. Concomitant, then, with the greater specialisation of crop cultivation has gone the
professionalisation of labour organisation for that crop. In the case of egusi,
the old wage relationship has been maintained at the same level throughout
this process, as Table 6.1 shows.

The female wage has only been altered in the context of new crops, activities and types of farm. In the small-scale sector, women and youth tend to be
paid the same for tasks such as nursery-watering, and at a rate much lower
than the egusi harvest. The corporate farms in eastern Ibarapa employ
women harvesters for maize and cowpeas, at up to three hundred women at
a time, but as a new form of oganisation they can try to set their own conditions. Unable to take care of food provision and unwilling to pay in kind,
corporate business deals entirely in cash. Some harvesting is piecework and
some is day-wage. In 1988 the daily wage was N5.25, though farm managers
said that very fast piece-workers could earn up to N11. This compares unfavourably with the value of the in-kind payment, at a minimum of N9, in
the small-scale sector. These opportunities tend to recruit from different
categories of women, such as those whose husbands are poor or ill,
especially under the stringent conditions of structural adjustment, and – as
conditions worsen – schoolgirls trying to pay for uniforms and books.

Innovation in the wage sector for women, therefore, involves two processes:
consolidation of pre-existing conditions in the old sectors and creation of
new task/wage conditions in the new sectors. In spite of high demand, the
wage conditions in the new sectors are on the whole, for both men and
women, inferior to those in the established sectors, due to two factors exerting
downward pressure. In local conceptions, it is increasingly the lower-return
tasks that are being commercialised at present. The corporate sector is
bound to be trying to reduce the costs of production by keeping wages low.
Due to the opportunities and higher wages in the trade and small-scale sectors,
the corporate farms are not usually in direct competition for the same labour
force, but when they are, the small-scale sector has clear advantages.

Agatu

With much competitive jostle and experimentation over terms and payments, the ethnic–regional categories of workers have tended in the longer
run to settle into different niches in the economy. The Agatu men still come
in work crews, and have maintained their steady hold on seasonal clearing
and heaping, which is paid at a higher rate than weeding and tending. The
Ṣaabẹ men – a term used to refer to everyone from beyond the Benin border
– stayed longer, sometimes came with their womenfolk, and were more
likely than Agatu to work under long-term arrangements with particular
larger-scale farmers or settle in particular villages and carry out a range of

tasks for the local farmers at varied rates of pay. Hausa men sometimes come from the urban areas, usually individually, and hire themselves out on a day labour basis. Yoruba youth tend to specialise in weeding. So although all hired workers are referred to as *oníṣé*, in the male labour market heterogeneity is ethnically identified. In fact, closer familiarity reveals that there are people of a variety of origins in a category such as Agatu or Ṣaabẹ. The term Agatu is used not only for the migrant workers from Benue State, but for all workers who specialise in clearing and heaping.

Very substantial areas of farm land are still opened up each year by hand labour. About one half of the land under cultivation on men's farms in 1988 had been cleared by tractor and one half by hand labour. Of the latter, two-thirds – or one-third of the total area – was opened up by hired labour while the remaining one-sixth was cleared by the farmers themselves. On the women's farms the proportion cleared by hired labour was much higher, at two-thirds of the total acreage, because women used tractors somewhat less, never cleared their own farm land and hardly ever had it cleared for them by male kin or husbands. Almost every farmer who opened up new land called on hired labour for some of the work, but women were particularly dependent.

More of the farmers' income is being devoted to wages but also more labourers are being hired for more tasks. The single unambiguous wage increase for clearing and heaping over the twenty years has not been in the value of the cash wage, which has been remarkably stable (see below). Rather, an increase in the number of daily meals given from two to three, and the occasional commutation of the meal budget to cash, has been a very successful and calculated competitive strategy of the small-scale sector to maintain the labour supply against other regions and the large-scale enterprises. The highly specialised small-scale sector elsewhere in the south cannot easily supply food since the farmers do not grow as much, and agribusiness does not have the capacity to cook and serve meals.

The sources that I have on the cash component of wages cover one set of tasks, only: the clearing and heaping that was done throughout this period by the Agatu. As described already, the rate for a particular piece of work is bargained for by the crew boss on the basis of the area to be cleared, the natural vegetation cover, whether payment is immediate or at the end of the season and of course the bargaining skills and relative needs of the two parties. Personal considerations may also enter: for example, that the farmer renders some service to the crew boss, such as according him a small plot of land, or contributing more to the food. A price is agreed on, but as in the past it may still change over the year until final payment in October. Every piece of work is carried out under its own bargain, on its own time frame. The deal is not final until the end of the year when the Agatu return home.

The rates of pay given below are taken from the plot histories, from the farmers' reports of the number of workers, days worked, and amount paid in

Table 6.2: Costs for Land Preparation by Hired Labour by Year, Male Farmers Only, 1980–88

Year	No. of plots	Total Acres	Naira/Acre	Naira/Man/Day	Man/Days/Acre
1980[a]	6	3.50	188.00	8.50	22
1981[a]	1	1.50	200.00	17.00	12
1982[a]	7	2.60	96.00	2.83	34
1983[a]	2	1.10	270.00	11.25	24
1984	6	5.20	148.00	10.59	14
1985	22	12.70	175.00	11.65	15
1986	18	11.80	165.00	9.16	18
1987	51	27.60	186.41	10.97	17
Total	113	66.00			
1988	24	20.64	244.13	20.53	11

[a] Years poorly represented by either numbers of plots of number of farmers reporting, and for 1980, probably memory.

cash (i.e. not including the food component), calculated against the measured size of the plot, and reported for total land preparation (the two operations of clearing and heaping). The farmers could define these amounts exactly for most plots, given that all the payments up to 1987 had already been finalised. The data cover 113 plots prepared by hired labour between 1980 and 1987, and 24 plots prepared by hired labour in 1988.[7] Although the numbers are small, for the period 1985–88 they are fairly complete, and the calculations involve enough data points (plot area, total cost, number of workers, number of days) that I do have some confidence that the apparent relative stability is not an artefact. The data are reported for male farmers only, since the acreages for women are very low until 1985. Table 6.2 summarises the results in naira.

The mean of between N10 and N12 per day for the past three years is exactly what farmers suggested the daily wage rate should be, even though they never calculate the work nor pay for it on a daily basis. In fact, the reason they remember the number of days worked is because of the food provision, not the cash payment. Again, one goes through detailed calculations of numerous cases, only to come up with exactly what the farmers suggested the outcome would be: relatively stable work conditions at N10 per day and about N170–180 per acre.

It is worth at this point asking whether there is any evidence that labour costs per unit area or days worked have substantially altered over the much longer time period from 1968–88. I have only case material to go on, but the following case is very similar to all those on which I have records for 1968–69. One farmer paid six labourers, for one day, £2 pounds to clear and heap half an acre in the open savanna. At 16 kobo to the penny (taken from the food price index for the two years, 1968 and 1988, see Appendix B) this is equivalent to N153 per acre and N12.75 per day – almost exactly the same as in the period 1985–87. The quality of work has also been stable. Looking back to examples from 1968, I find cases of labourers working in very open savanna at the rate of about 1.3 *adé* of land cleared and heaped per man/day of work, which calculates to twelve days per acre. Farmers themselves worked considerably more slowly, at 1 *adé* per man/day of totally prepared land, or fifteen man/days per acre. Both rates are within the range calculated for the labourers for the years 1985–87. Again the stabilities behind all the enormous fluctuations and variations are uncanny, and not easy to explain without a theory of community and culture whereby there is an orientation to persistence along certain measures despite, or perhaps in order for there to be, rapid growth and change in others.

The figure for 1988 suggests that new forces are at work, when there was a surge of new clearing. The workers raised their daily wages, but proportionally more by rushing and botching the work than by altering the rate for the task-and-area unit on which bargains are struck. Again, the qualitative shifts are more marked than the shifts in the cash that changed hands for the job. I myself saw newly cleared plots where the clumps of savanna grass had simply been turned into the soil, complete with roots. Farmers complain bitterly because a plot cleared poorly shifts some of the cost back to the farmer in increased weeding, and using these grounds they may bargain down the final payment to the crewboss at the end of the season.

These manoeuvres around quality may be the first effects of the influx of unemployed young urbanites into the agricultural wage labour force. Some of these young men have not worked on a farm for a decade and are not committed to it. At the same time, farmers themselves are trying to narrow down on their own clearing and heaping to specific situations, as shown by their very high labour rates, at twenty-four days to the acre, when they do report it. In fact this number probably reflects the fact that they are only clearing small fields, for fractions of days at a time. So a set of new processes may be at work in the late 1980s, leading to more intense engagement and recrimination, not over the wage *per se* but over quality deviations from accepted standards at a time when farmers have become accustomed to concentrating their own clearing work into a very narrow range of their own work portfolios.

The figures suggest another reason why the 1988 labour situation began to look different and more contentious. The conditions probably favored the crew bosses pushing their own advantage on the rates of pay, as well as consolidating the advantage they had earned already in getting access to cultivate their own plots on Ibarapa land, as a concession to the farmers' interests in them continuing to return. An unprecedented price volatility had begun to set in, due to bad weather conditions and the continued plunge of the naira. Although they were in short supply, food crops were being exported to the surrounding CFA economies – 'smuggled' as the official commentary went – thus driving up the consumer price in the great cities. A situation that shifts away from the norm, especially for a relatively high value service such as clearing labour, benefits the intermediaries (in this case the crew bosses) more than anyone else because there is always a better margin to be made in unstable competitive conditions than when long-term stability (short of the appearance of monopoly) has rendered the margins transparent to everyone.

The cost of labour for weeding illustrates how advantageous it was for the organised crews of Agatu to remain as far as possible in clearing and heaping work, rather than moving into the weeding that farmers were increasingly contracting out. In 1968, no farmer paid to have someone else weed his farm. In 1987, weeding only paid on the average N5 per day by comparison with double that for clearing and heaping. The lower-status late-comers, such as the Ṣaabẹ, and younger workers, such as the Yoruba teenagers working for school fees, gravitated into weeding.

The stability I found in this sector of wage labour is not a simple function of a continuity in the identity of the participants. I talked informally to about twenty labourers. It turns out that they are not, in fact, either ethnically or occupationally homogeneous. The men I talked to were from at least three different ethnic origins in Benoue State: Idoma, Egede and Igala. Their work backgrounds were quite different from one another. Several had professional or apprenticeship training: a tailor, a typist, a graduate of a three-year electrician's apprenticeship, a graduate of commercial school, an eleven-year army veteran. These men were working alongside school leavers and non-educated men who migrated for the same reasons as their predecessors in the past: no land of their own or remoteness from the market. In 1988 all of them worked together, under the annual migration system run by a crew boss, which is by now a solid institution of the rural economy.

Ṣaabẹ

People use this term to cover all the workers who came into the area, mainly from francophone West Africa, on a more open-ended, less organised basis and to a context where they were newcomers in an established system. 'Ṣaabẹ' has referred to people of various origins: the 'Abassa', Togolese and Ghanaians, as well as people from just beyond the border.

These workers were a boon to the large-scale farmers because they were much more flexible about conditions than the Agatu and could be hired more or less on contract. Agribusiness used them for its small permanent labour force. Many of the 200-or-so women living in Igbo-Qra who were on the daily roster for cassava peeling at the Texaco plantation were foreigners. They alone could be on regular daily call.

The most important niche that the Ṣaabẹ fill is as a regular labour force for the larger local farmers, who need more work done and greater security of access to workers than the local labour market otherwise offers. One only has to watch a mid-scale farmer trying to recruit someone – anyone – to carry out a week's worth of tending or weeding to realise the vast advantages of semi-tied labour to this category of farmer. The economy simply does not have a dependable casual day labour force willing to work for low wages. A local farmer may be in need of ready cash, but will look the other way and say he cannot get to the hired job until the end of the week; the school children are only available in the vicinity of the schools; women do not do weeding; the Agatu are working on clearing contracts.

One of Idere's largest farmers who is also a transporter, recruits, pays the transport and provides the housing for about ten or fifteeen labourers from Benin a year. Their only obligation is to work for him first whenever he needs them. Otherwise they are free to work for others. Both sides honour the going labour rates, so the security of work and residence benefits both worker and farmer. It gives the farmer the security of access he needs, at the cost of the capital investment for housing and an annual transport fee. Within limits, it is an ingenious system for both parties, since the farmer is not responsible for the workers' total income, but he does get access to very substantial labour on request and at the going rate.

Another large farmer had a regular Ṣaabẹ worker who worked exclusively for him, while the farmer himself also did substantial work, along with his children. Even so, he decided to loosen up the mutual commitment for the following year because it proved difficult to know how much to pay as all the local wage rubrics are by the task.

In 1988 a final possibility for labour control was developing: the granting of a small patch of land to the worker. Several individual workers had their sights set on this. If they could get a small toehold into farming then they might gradually control a larger part of their income by providing their own food, first of all, and then eventually becoming more substantial commercial farmers. The great advantage for a village of granting the oníṣẹ́ or the crew boss some land is that they are now likely to stay in one place and be predictably available to the local farmers. No one envisages that they could ever completely give up farm labour because they are strangers, so no one predicted the situation that is gradually developing, where some of the labourers have shifted their emphasis to work on their own account. For example, two Ṣaabẹ brothers who had been living in one of the villages for several years, were planning to plant egusi, tomato and maize on their patch of three acres. Slowly they are developing a farming style that demands the same level of attention and the same seasonal demands as the local farmers. In the late 1980s land cessions met everyone's needs perfectly, but it is not difficult to imagine a scenario in which the labourers have enlarged the ranks of the farmers rather than enlarging the farms of those already established.

Hired labour – its sources, deployment and social conditions of work – is one of the most important and volatile frontiers of change as the hinterland savanna begins to fill up with new activities and new actors.

CONCLUSION

Vehicle ownership and wage labour fit into different categories in a western perspective, since each controls a different resource of the land/labour/capital trio of resources. In this local arena, where very few owners have more than one vehicle, where the Yoruba terminology dignifies both sets of people as '*oni-*', 'owners' of, and where the moment in history is experimental and expansive in both cases, the difference between the two is considerably narrowed. Vehicles are ephemera under Nigerian conditions: not just because of the wear and tear of constant use at a hundred per cent capacity on marginal roads in all weathers, but because of the instability of the exchange rate. No small owner could have saved enough from profits during the oil boom years to replace a terminally decrepit tractor or *jálukere* during the bust, when prices quintupled in about three years and then continued a dizzying upward trajectory. Apart from the local bus- and tractor-owner, who is a military retiree and for whom this was a real profession, all the rest of the vehicle owners I knew were like small artisans. They were certainly not necessarily the wealthy of the community, and the farmers knew this full well, as evidenced by their willingness to pitch in, help out and provide support as if these services were a collective resource, which indeed they are. Several larger farmers knew this from their own failed experiences: a *jálukere* wrecked by a careless driver, a tractor finally sold for spare parts. Under present Nigerian conditions, then, vehicle owners are a volatile occupational category, not an established social stratum.

The *oníṣẹ́* also form a changing and diversifying category, albeit at a lower status level than the farmers and vehicle owners. Firmly wedged into their stable situation are the *elégúsí*, the female egusi harvesters. The Agatu also have built up a system, a set of institutions, and price guidelines in clearing and heaping. Into the new spaces opened up by the demand for wage labour to take over other tasks have moved other kinds of workers, named and understood as their own separate category: the Ṣaabẹ on long-term contracts, the Hausa in independent and individual day labour, Yoruba youth in weeding, and so on. All are also quite volatile in social membership over time, although the categories themselves seem to stabilise.

The expected processes of closer urban incorporation apply: increased inputs into the rural sector, the increased presence of mechanised inputs, and the extension of wage labour. The social composition of the local economy, however, reflects lateral diversification and small incremental steps of ordinal differentiation because novelties have added to the repertoire of named occupations rather than substituting or reordering the elements into broad classes that would correspond to workers, peasants or capitalists. The particularism has been diligently worked over. Negotiations have followed the lines of a moral economy of association: a conception of the competitive market economy that I argue in the following chapters has been rigorously applied by the local people to the mid-scale and corporate farmers, even though they themselves have been trying to dance to a different drummer and to use agriculture not as an occupation but a means to improved returns to investment.

NOTES

1. Parts of the information in this section, including the interviews with drivers, were collected by Dr William Brieger, who is gratefully acknowledged.
2. For example, one importer described buying up Japanese engines that have become obsolete due to changes in the emissions standards. They were sold more or less as scrap, by the pound, but crated intact for import and sale in Nigeria as working engines.
3. A group of large farmers, for example, contracted together to hire a tractor belonging to the neighbouring state government. In principle its use was supposed to be limited to citizens of that state, but the limits were there to be overcome through market forces: if the driver was offered enough he should cross state lines and deliver the service. Once the *ẹgbẹ́* structure had been imposed, private ownership was not private use, and tractors that owners wanted to keep for themselves alone had to be locked up.
4. By threatening to postpone their arrival in a farm where the fruit has already been bruised and the seeds are likely to germinate if left.
5. By 'minimum' I mean the current market price of the payment in kind. If a woman kept her egusi until the off-season when prices rise she might earn more than twice this rate.
6. It is interesting perhaps to note that the three female egusi farmers whose harvests I could track tended to pay their workers at a higher rate. But women tend not to grow much egusi yet, so the question of a specific women's style of employment is still open.
7. My own confidence in these rates as a price series is diminished for the years before 1985 because of the low number of plots; the four-year rotation system had taken much of the land cleared earlier out of cultivation to put into fallow. The figures for the years 1980 to 1984 therefore reflect the idiosyncrasy of special cases and of memory to a much greater degree than the years 1985–87. The year 1982 is particularly problematic since five of the seven plots cleared in that year were cleared for the same farmer and the amounts paid are very low. Possibly he had a personal arrangement with the worker. I do, however report the 1980–84 figures, not because they can be representative of each year's labour bill but for two useful purposes: to illustrate the variability of labour costs; and to suggest quite forcefully that, taken together, agricultural wage rates for the years of the 1980s – like the tractor-clearing rates – do not show a rapid and commensurate response to the dramatic changes in the value of the naira which set in in 1985. The wage rate and cost per acre reported for 1987 are almost the same in nominal terms as the rates for 1980.

7

THE MID-SCALE FARMERS

Large-scale farming is not new in Africa, but with non-industrial technology it was only possible with large-scale labour control. Wealthy Yoruba of the nineteenth century extended their farms through the deployment of debt pawns and slaves, but when all kinds of servitude were outlawed during the colonial period the dilemmas of the aspirant larger-scale farmer became acute. The costs of keeping youth and other dependants in line has been so striking a problem that entire theories of kinship and religious institutions have been developed around the functions they fulfil in mediating the labour control problem. The functional arguments for ideological control (cf. Meillassoux 1978) seem highly plausible as one stands in a vast stretch of unweeded maize surrounded by the independent small farms of the people who might otherwise be weeders, or accompanies a larger farmer on his quest – rapidly sliding into a plea – for workers to fulfil an urgent task, or bargains for a particular service to find that it cannot be done until the week after next and only then if nothing else happens to postpone it. Building labour relations in an environment where there is a land frontier and every-one has free status is a daily challenge.

Farming in the 20–100 acres range developed in Ibarapa at the same time as the corporate farming described in the next chapter, starting in the late 1970s. It is a genre of its own, well beyond the upper size limit of ten acres in the small-scale sector, and far below the hundreds of acres of the cor-porate farms. Unlike the other two sectors, this mid-scale farming did not respond to a discrete segment of urban demand, although its proponents certainly tried to find one amongst the buyers in the food processing and bulk provisioning industries such as feed mills, hospitals and cafeterias. Rather it responded to two new conditions on the production side: increased investable cash in the hands of rural residents and the availability of tractors. Everything else remained to be worked out: viable cropping strategies, land and labour access, crop storage and transport, markets, strategies to mitigate risk, in fact, the entire technical and economic framework for realising returns to scale in the humid savanna environment surrounded by success-ful small-scale farming.

Far from dominating the local agricultural scene by virtue of superior resources, the mid-scale farms that sprang up like mushrooms from the late

1970s were still experimental in the late 1980s. Farmers who have been in business for many years are working their way towards various solutions, albeit with many costly mistakes and a more heightened sense of difficulty than they started out with. Mistakes and even total failures are inevitable and the economic conditions are unpredictable. For example, the cost of tractors and parts quintupled between 1985 and 1988 due to the devaluation attendant on structural adjustment; sales to feed-processing plants and breweries were unstable due to changes in import restrictions on competing cereals and the privatisation of state enterprises; rainfall variation is more threatening to monocropped than diversified farms; mid-scale farmers have been dependent on private contracts for transport, which turned out to be expensive; and so on. Where institutionalisation is so weak the risks are correspondingly high, especially by comparison with the local and regional nexus that supports the small-scale sector and with the corporate context for agribusiness. Given the relentless economic and agricultural challenges, mid-scale farming can only be understood in the context of the broader political economy of Yoruba and southern Nigerian society.

In an area with a land frontier and within reach of a dependable market which occasionally provides windfall prices, food crops seem worth trying for someone looking for relatively small investment possibilities. A farm is unlikely to be a total catastrophe. In the short run it does not seem to demand much specialist knowledge or social organisation beyond what anyone brought up in the rural areas could easily master. The use of fertiliser promises, probably mistakenly, to solve the long fallow problem. The fixed start-up costs that are sunk into a farm are relatively limited by comparison with enterprises in the manufacturing sector. There is no fencing, drainage, irrigation, farm buildings, planting of permanent crops and so on that might necessitate bank credit on a serious scale. One needs only the legal and negotiating costs of establishing some kind of land title if necessary (as for outsiders to communities), the cost of stumping the land for tractor cultivation and sometimes the purchase of a tractor. For absentee farmers, a farm manager has to be employed. As a result a farm can be expanded and contracted at will in relation to personal resources. In fact, it is personal resources that in most cases dictate the farm strategy; they provide the cash, the insurance against failure, the market network and the other sources of income that balance out the seasonality of sales and the risks of price fluctuations. Only one mid-scale farmer whom I knew really made the majority of his income from the farm, and he alone worked at it with as great or greater application than the small-scale farmers.

Most of the men who went into mechanised farming on a larger scale belonged to a new social category that grew out of the expansion of the Nigerian civil service after 1945 and into the nationalist era. They were the first substantial generation of middle-aged retirees from government employment.

The Udoji Commission's revisions of the terms of service for civil servants in 1974 gave relatively generous pensions to government employees such as teachers, civil servants and military personnel, and at the same time mandated retirement after thirty years' service (see Forrest 1995: 143–4). Someone whose professional training (starting as young as 16) counted as part of their service, could be retired before the age of fifty. Many of them had no settled home in the urban areas, having moved around from place to place throughout their careers as teachers, post office employees, military men and administrative officials, so in retirement they wanted to return to their home areas, to pick up local political careers as heads of families, chiefs and local notables. Farming by tractor was a feasible local investment to make and it also inserted them as active participants into the growing debates about 'development' in general and land tenure in particular.

MID-SCALE FARMS

Beyond the commonalities outlined already, the mid-scale farms are quite varied because they reflect the farmers' longer-term purposes in life. Current patterns of production are probably somewhat ephemeral, so I describe the dilemmas farmers have faced over the decade or so that they have been in business, using the examples of five in Idere, plus the farm of the Onidere, and the special case of the farm of the Eleruwa, the ọba of the neighbouring Ibarapa town of Eruwa.

Two of Idere's mid-scale farmers, Ogunjobi and Okeyale (since deceased), have retained aspects of small-scale farming in that their farms are at the small end of the spectrum and highly diversified. They both worked full time on the farm in 1988, although both started up with resources from other work: Ogunjobi is a retiree from a local government council job, and Okeyale was a cocoa buyer.

Ogunjobi retired in the 1970s, established a small food farm and bought a shop. In 1981, when the NTC was picking up again, he started contract farming of tobacco and became chairman of the Tobacco-Growers' Association. Once he had access to a tractor he enlarged the food farm as well, using the classic small-farm crops and combinations. In 1982 he bought a tractor on hire purchase which he rents out as well as using on his own farm. He had tried buying a taxi first, when vehicle prices were low, but lost money on it and abandoned the whole transport sector. By owning a tractor he ensures his own access and makes a dependable income as well by hiring it out. In case of problems he always has the backup of the NTC which has its own tractor hire service. He spoke at length, however, of the difficulties of managing the tractor operators and preventing them from 'doing whatever they like': underworking and wasting time or overworking and ruining the machine. His tractor repairs for the previous year cost N4,000, which he attributed to the carelessness of the operator. In the past he paid their wages by the month, but by 1988 has arrived at a system whereby he pays by the acre ploughed, at one-eighth of the total charge to the farmer. The plan instils in the operator an incentive to find plenty of customers while also taking minimal care of the machine to keep it running.

Ogunjobi grows an acre of tobacco per season, and then all the local crops – egusi, maize, yams, tomatoes and vegetables – with an emphasis on maize. In 1988 his egusi amounted to forty-two bags. He has built a very large cement soaking-pit and drying platform for preparing cassava flour from his own harvested cassava. He says that he has about fifty acres in total, in two different places. To work the farm he makes use of every different kind of labour arrangement: female harvesters for tobacco, maize and egusi; male workers for weeding and heaping; in-kind exchange with farmers who work his farm in return for tractor clearing; and he himself works very hard, above all when the work has to be punctilious during the tobacco harvest and curing period. For the maize harvest he has extended the egusi-payment rubric to female maize harvesters: they receive one olódó (market measure) of dried maize per day worked.

In the evenings and for ceremonial occasions he still works in the bar he built in town but he expresses diminishing interest in the profitable potential of drinks, or perhaps less devotion to preventing what he refers to as 'giving it away' to the odd friend and relative in the daily traffic of casual customers. Income from drinks is made more dependably from the bulk transactions for parties than from the daily passers-by.

The diversity of enterprises, crops and labour sources, and the solid basis of all these in local institutions makes the kind of farming that Ogunjobi does quite viable, as long as he himself can work on it. Like the small-scale farms, it is an entirely personal enterprise that will have no necessary longevity beyond his capacity to be directly involved.

Okeyale's farm is very similar in all respects: an enormously imaginative enterprise with complementarities within its crop and field repertoire and beyond the farm in his other occupations, by a farmer who has no major further aspirations in life than to be locally established. His farm in 1988 was about seventeen acres in the savanna and about fifteen acres in the slopes and crevices of one of Idere's historic rocky outcrops. Within a short climb of his farm are the remains of house-walls from pre-colonial retreats to defensible sites, and a broad flat rock slab high up in the place from which messages were sounded out on bamboo sticks, to carry across the valley. He made use of every micro-ecology that the rocks offered. Differences of slope, moisture, shade and sun were all taken into account for yam fields, cocoa groves, nurseries for citrus and cashew trees, oil palms, pineapples and vegetables of every kind. Every small plot had a different combination of crops.

Okeyale turned this farm over to food crops in 1983. It had been his father's cocoa grove, but a savanna fire destroyed everything and he decided against replacing it entirely with cocoa. By this time he had already expanded into mid-scale farming of food crops. 1980 was the turning point. He had always been a farmer, but added cocoa buying when he was able to buy a motor cycle. The combination of farm and produce buying gave him enough income in the windfall year for cassava farmers of 1981. He started to invest in the transport business when vehicle prices were still low, eventually owning two *jálukere* and a bus. One of the vehicles he drove himself for a while, but found the whole venture unprofitable. One *jálukere* was ceded to the son of his senior brother and the other vehicles were sold. He said that it did not occur to him to buy a tractor because a regular customer relationship with one of the tractor owners gave him reliable access for his own needs. His main challenge was labour for the fifteen acres in and around the rocks that could not be worked by tractor. Okeyale is one of the few farmers who has experimented with recruiting labour from the workers' home area, and then basically employing them full time. In 1987 he had two full-time workers from the Benin Republic. The whole arrangement was still in the experimental stage when he died, but the direction he was going was towards more flexibility and less daily commitment.

One of the most interesting aspects of Okeyale's life as a successful full-time farmer and multi-careerist was the sheer difficulty of finding productive outlets for his cash income. Vehicle-ownership and the working assets for cocoa-buying are two possibilities that he tried and eventually kept going at a low level. The cocoa-sales took him to Cotonou, where the price was better than in Nigeria in the early 1970s. Using the money he made from cocoa he bought eight cows from the Fulani, who continued to herd them in the savanna pastures around Idere. In the kind of story I heard many times from different people, the Fulani drove them off with their own herds, told him his own cattle had died and, when they were eventually located in Abeokuta, offered to pay back the purchase price for only six of them. The farmers are in a weak if not indefensible position *vis-à-vis* the Fulani herders, which makes cattle investments extremely high risk. On another occasion, Okeyale joined a credit union whose members contributed N200 each – a very substantial sum at that time – to build a shop for rental so that there would be an income into the union in addition to the interest paid by the borrowers. The failure of some members to repay their loans put the whole endeavour into an imbroglio from which it had not yet recovered. Okeyale also married three wives, had twelve children whom he has educated, apprenticed and supplied with occupational equipment. He has built a house and established an active career in town social life. In 1988 he was thinking of expanding his cocoa-buying and wanted to buy a new hunting rifle.

Taken as a whole, his life shows both the possibilities and also the constraints for the 'enterprising peasant' (Tiffen 1976) who is trying to build a diversified income portfolio in the rural areas. It is hard work, there are hardly any formal sector benefits to be tapped, and viability depends entirely on the farmer's own acumen. The long-term effects are largely inter-generational, and largely restricted to the education and training of children, as Berry (1985) has described for the cocoa belt.

Alhaji Orelope's farm is part of a much more ambitious enterprise with a regional reach. At one time he had four lorries and one *jálukere* which he used for transport and commercial haulage. His history is a little unusual in that he first expanded the farm on the basis of migrant labour, before tractors became available. Migrants started to come into Nigeria from the franco-phone countries as soon as the oil wealth started to circulate, some time in the early-to-mid-1970s. Alhaji says that a group known as Abassa started to come in about 1973, and it was on the basis of these new labour sources that he was able to expand his farm far beyond the usual size range. As noted in the previous chapter, the Agatu only did clearing and heaping, which then left weeding, tending, harvesting and a range of other tasks to be covered in other ways. With workers who would take care of these low-return tasks, the farm could grow, even before tractors offered new possibilities. It was in-come from the farm that gave him a start on his purchase of vehicles.

For many years Alhaji has had at least five or six regular workers resident in a village house he built for them, who come to his farm whenever neces-sary in return for transport and housing. He has customer relations with up to ten more. He now finances the transport of as many as ten Ṣaabẹ coming from Benin. Up to a few years ago he could bring as many as twenty. He does occasionally lose someone who fails to honour the agreement, but he emphasised that Ṣaabẹ workers were particularly reliable and competent.

The farm covers sixty acres, now that tractors have permitted a second phase of major expansion. He grows mainly egusi and maize, that is, field crops grown on the flat rather than the full range of crops grown on the more diversified farms. Alhaji's farm organisation resembles commercial mono-cropping and is much more like a business than Ogunjobi's or Okeyale's. He talks about it in terms of the cash input and cash output of the entire farm for the whole season, not the returns plot by plot or crop by crop. He gives an example of putting in *àpò mẹ́wàá*: 'ten bags', that is 10 x N200, or N2,000 in cash, and realising a net return after everyone has been paid off at the end of the season. He knows exactly what the margin of earnings has been for any one season, keeping the accounts in his head.

Alhaji is a patron, dealing in fairly large numbers and spin-off projects. Three of his six wives and four of his fifteen children have farms of their own, for which he negotiates the tractor arrangements. They use his transport and employ his labourers, even though they pay for everything themselves. He himself does not work as often on the farm as Ogunjobi and Okeyale, possibly because he is somewhat older, but this also gives a sense of a commercial purpose rather than a career of agricultural experimentation. In brief, although he is local and relatively unschooled in the formal education system, Alhaji exemplifies a more specialised and commercial style, and it is this style that particularly characterises the farms of the educated retirees.

Retirees generally lead a life that makes it impossible to be committed to a daily routine of farm work. They are often occupied in local politics, organisations, small business and maintaining far-flung networks of relationships beyond the local arena. Even more basic than meeting the demands of the work itself is the challenge of getting out to the farm in the first place. Farm land situated conveniently on the roads may be difficult to acquire, and even plots fairly close in to town require transport to get there unless the farmer is willing to travel on foot. In some cases the land they found is far from home, and in the opposite direction from most of the traffic. Time constraints, status considerations and the weather militate against trekking on a regular basis, and the cost of taxis adds up. A personal car or motor-cycle is really a necessity for this category of farmer, but it is not always affordable. They need, then, to have someone on the spot, in the local village, who will keep an eye on things. Theft of crops is not unknown, and workers have to be supervised. For reasons of interest, knowledge and convenience, the retirees would prefer to work with a farm manager and simply supply the cash, plan the crops and supervise the sales themselves.

Local retirees usually have land rights based on kinship and political relationships, and rely on kin for farm supervision, whereas absentee farmers hire farm managers. The styles of farming, however, are not dissimilar and neither are the difficulties. In both cases, these farmers are generously accommodated by the population, at least in part because of their activities in larger regional networks which are in the community's interest to foster. They do get some well-situated land, in extensive acreages, even if it means that the landholding compound has to move a few other small-scale farmers to other plots. They do not necessarily however use the land to the same degree from one year to the next. The areas cleared by the retirees whom I know bear closer resemblance to their financial means at the moment than to a specific economic or agricultural plan. If they lack the funds to hire a tractor the entire farm may lie unworked for a season or more. Since they are working with a complex portfolio of activities and commitments they may not be able to make up for unpredicted problems. If the early rains fail, for example, farms may have to be replanted. It takes either work or funds to recuperate, but by then the retiree farmer may have moved on to other planned commitments.

The result is farm histories that are much more erratic than for committed mid-scale farmers such as Ogunjobi, Okeyale and Alhaji. The farm is founded with a large expenditure of energy and money, rather than from smaller endeavours that then grow up from early successes. One absentee retiree, a former administrator, was able to get a minimally secured bank loan to open up about 350 acres, at a cost of N60,000 to bulldoze the land and N40,000 to buy a tractor. The task was enormous: he needed twenty-five workers just to plant the farm, and had a constant problem of recruiting weeding labour. The volume of the harvest presents problems of both labour recruitment and sale. The farmer needs to get the entire harvesting and drying process finished and the crop sold in bulk, in order to obviate storage and transport costs. The work needs to be done expeditiously in August so that the land can be reploughed in time for second season planting, and this at a time when the entire local farming economy is at the limits of its capacity for work. The task of management falls on a resident farm manager who earns a monthly salary during the farming year, a man who has his own local farm to tend. In sum, the whole enterprise is over-ambitious. It is economically, logistically and agro-ecologically problematic. The occasional gain from opportunistic response to market fluctuations must surely be cancelled out by the difficulty of maintaining a tenuously organised enterprise over the inevitable vicissitudes of agriculture in the tropical savanna. In the first season of 1988, only four years into its life, this last retiree's farm was completely unplanted and its owner pursuing other commercial possibilities in trade. At some point, however, he may well make a come-back.

Retirees working in their own communities are usually more committed than this to making a go of some kind of home-based enterprise. The extreme case however does illustrate a real difference between the full-time mid-scale farmers for whom farming is a career and a category of farmer who is using agriculture as a financial investment that might bring windfall profits or as a way of keeping a foot in the local social arena. The former keep their farms within the range of fifty acres or less; the cropping plan is diversified, even if it focuses on egusi and maize; the farm is never abandoned; and its on-going viability is based on complexly orchestrated labour relations. The latter may be investing in agriculture but they are not really farming.

My last cases of mid-scale farmers form a unique category: they are the two ọbas of Ibarapa towns, the Eleruwa of Eruwa, and the Onidere of Idere. Both have been quite dedicated farmers, although the Eleruwa is a case apart, not only in Ibarapa but in Southern Nigeria. He had been experimenting, innovating, and collecting inspirations about agriculture on his many foreign travels – including to Israel, Canada and Britain – for at least forty years. In 1988, he was using small machines rather than teams of labourers to hull his maize, and asked me about the technologies that might adapt to egusi-drying. He saw farming as one of his major careers and was essentially his own farm manager for an enterprise that covered several hundred acres and a great many crops: egusi, maize, cowpeas, cassava, tobacco and poultry. He was always trying new possibilities: soybeans was the new crop in 1988. Over his career, starting well before he was installed as ọba in 1972, he grew more or less everything that can grow in the Ibarapa savanna, and tried every way of running a farm. He grew cotton and developed a poultry farm in the 1960s; he had been a tobacco farmer for the NTC and a cocoa buyer; he had invested in cattle and developed ancillary industrial interests at various times in construction and gravel production; and he knew about mechanics and types of agricultural machinery. During the season he spent most of every day at the farm, carrying out in the evening all the many administrative and ceremonial duties that could not be delegated to someone else. Once a year he went on vacation to London, to take an intensive period of rest and recuperation.

The Onidere, by comparison, has not considered farming to be such a major part of his career. He took it up when he became ọba, and works together with his brothers and a son. He does, however, take the farm very seriously. He plans, works in the fields and sells for himself. He has land belonging to the compound, close to town, on the road to Igbo-Ọra, so within easy accessibility, given that he has his own transport. The farm is about twenty acres in this location and ten acres in another, and yields a considerable income that adds to his government salary. His farm is, like Ogunjobi's and Okeyale's, a smaller farm writ large, with its tractor-cleared plot devoted to egusi and maize, and diversity of other crops. He, like them, takes great interest in new varieties. He was one of the first to experiment with a new variety of cassava brought in by the Agatu very recently, so his experience, and any supply of stem cuttings he makes available, will diffuse the innovation. He sells to the local wholesale market, after unappealing experiences with bulk sales to mediators for industrial processors. He prefers to rent his own vehicle and deal with the traders.

People of high status in the traditional hierarchies may enjoy some advantages when it comes to credit, contacts and land access, but no farming can succeed without adequate labour. Neither of the ọbas can mobilise labour by authority alone. Each has to recruit, remunerate and supervise their workers with exactly the same vigilance as any other mid-scale farmer. The occasional unusual possibility may turn up: a very capable, non-local man willing to be an all-purpose client, or an organised group of women willing to work their ọba's harvest first. But no matter what the initial avenue of access, the terms have to be adequate or the source will dry up. From his long and varied years of experience, the Eleruwa was convinced that he needed to be at the farm almost every day to adjust conditions and deal directly with the workers.

CONCLUSION

There are both unifying principles and variety in the new mid-scale farming. It is a recent development, unprotected by formal sector frameworks, and without an obvious place in the growing food market. The only institution within the food market itself that favours the development of mid-scale farming is the industrialised processing sector, mainly the feed mills and breweries. Their demand for raw materials is constant and fairly high compared to the capacities of the small-scale farmers, so the mid-scale farmers make convenient customers. On the other hand, the bulking and wholesale aspects of the small-scale sector are developing apace, and may soon be well-organised enough logistically to meet the demands of large processing concerns, as long as these are not looking for the kind of uniform product that is only produced by scientific farming. Wholesale food prices on the open market will always, however, be a problem for larger farmers because the prices cannot be predicted more than a few days in advance, so the space for mid-scale farming in the market of grains for industrial processing is tenuous.

Production conditions favour mid-scale farming even less than marketing conditions. For a hundred acres of commercial farm it is inconceivable to leave two thirds of it under fallow at any one time, as the local fallow regime would demand. The costs of stumping large acreages of land for tractor ploughing make it unattractive to leave the land after four years for a fallow of eight. All the mid-scale farmers use fertiliser, but none had yet pushed the potentials of the land to their limit. Indeed, no one seemed to know where the agro-ecological limits might be.

It could be that this kind of farm tends to collapse for economic reasons before it collapses for ecological reasons, or to shrink to more manageable size. Locally-based farmers have more of a stake than absentees in resolving the problems. The institutional and technical tinkering that they do may be their long-term importance to the productive economy, rather than the proportion of the total market they ever account for. Neither the market logic nor the ecological logic favour mid-scale farming in its present form, and the social profile to qualify as a niche in the local economy has not yet developed.

8

THE FOOTHOLD OF CORPORATE AGRIBUSINESS[1]

The literature on African agriculture in the 1980s implied that corporate agribusiness was steadily growing (Mkandawire and Bourenane 1987). Andrae and Beckman argued that the creation of backward linkages into farming by the manufacturing sector in Nigeria was 'a process of major significance' (1987: 6). Declining oil revenues for the purchase of inputs and political pressure on foreign firms to invest in Nigeria both contributed to a changed set of forces that fostered a development that they termed 'Industry Goes Farming'. Certainly more corporate farms sprang up than existed in the past, but whether the conditions that favoured their development will also sustain their survival and allow their institutionalisation is more doubtful, as Andrae and Beckman pointed out at the time. Although this chapter refers to the general Nigerian context in which companies went into farming, it does not cover the larger national situation. It simply describes the agribusiness farms that have been established in Ibarapa during the 1970s and 1980s, and the ways in which they are co-existing with the small-scale farming sector.

It seemed unlikely for large-scale farming to develop in an economic environment such as Nigeria in the 1970s. The urban food supply system was functioning, the large-scale traders were making profits in food importing, and specific crops that required substantial capital, such as wheat (Andrae and Beckman 1985) and rice, were benefiting from state subsidies. The official policy that was embodied in the World Bank Agricultural Development Projects was to promote small and perhaps mid-scale farm development by individual farmers. There was no obvious place for corporate production for the domestic market, unless it was to mitigate the technical problem of product uniformity for industrial processing.

Three innovations of the later 1970s and 1980s made agriculture more attractive to investors who deal in the national and international capital markets. First, the indigenisation decrees of 1972 and 1977 (Biersteker 1987) gave foreign firms the obligation to develop local shareholding. Particularly under the Obasanjo military regime of 1976–79, the enacted policies were accompanied by exhortations and the positive requirement that large firms invest in Nigerian basic production. The oil companies were under special pressure to put some of their profits into agriculture. The Texaco farm near to Igbo-Ọra, just over the state border into Ogun state, dates from this period.

The same regime passed the Land Use Act in 1978 to try to free up land from inherited and often collective ownership under customary law, and to make it attractive to investors. The land was nationalised and a long-lease system put in place that allowed 'rights of occupancy' to be ceded by the 'customary occupants' for a period of ninety-nine years. The contract usually had to be mediated by a lawyer and the 'certificate of occupancy' had to be registered with the state government. The functioning of this law underlies all corporate farming in Ibarapa and elsewhere.

These two conditions made corporate farming possible and politically favoured, but they did not create an obvious economic function. A market for the crops produced by agribusiness developed much later. Under structural adjustment conditions after 1985, an embargo was imposed on the import of certain grains, including wheat, barley and other ingredients for brewing and for animal and poultry feed. Smuggled imports were unreliable, so firms in both these industries began to develop backward linkages into local agriculture. The problem posed to manufacturers under the conditions of the 1980s was which agriculture to link into to meet industrial demand. Nigeria had no commodities exchange for futures trading that in fully capitalist agriculture mediates the market for industrial processors of agricultural products. A committee to establish a Commodity Exchange Market, with spot and futures transactions, was set up in 1989, more than a decade after the passage of the Land Use Act.[2] General Obasanjo himself experimented with supplying his brewery from women traders who dealt with small-scale farmers, but the story of his encounter with them was told as if the arrangement was a tentative experiment.[3] Total dependence on the volatile market for consumer grains, in the hands of a myriad of relatively small traders, is an awkward proposition for any capitalist business that has to work from predictions and accounts.

For most firms it was managerially and economically less complicated to develop their own farms, through vertical integration, than to depend on the market.[4] Large breweries and well-known food concerns such as the United Africa Company and Leventis, took advantage of the political and economic moment to establish their own farming ventures, for the twin purposes of claiming public-spiritedness and sourcing their own inputs. Advertisements for the companies' products began to include photographs of farms and tractors, accompanied by captions about development. In the long run then, neither the *raison d'être* nor the ultimate fate of the corporate farms depends on local conditions. Nevertheless they do constitute a local presence. They depend for land and labour on the regional economy and they affect the local conditions for all the other farmers who function outside the formal sector.

Texaco was the first company to open up a farm in the area, as an investment for oil profits in 1975.[5] Explaining the decision thirteen years later, the
chairman of Texagri said, 'As good corporate citizens operating in Nigeria
for over half a century, we have committed ourselves to contributing to the
government's ambitious programme to feed the nation from its own resources' (quoted in Lawrence 1988: 21). Two thousand five hundred acres
were acquired at the main site on the Igbo-Ora–Abeokuta Road, and a
further area of 486 hectares near to Igbo-Ora to make a total of 3,886 acres
by the time the farm closed in 1987. The Texagri farm became a regional
landmark over its thirteen years of operation. It was the key site for the first
experiments with bio-control of the cassava mealy-bug which threatened to
devastate the entire African cassava stock in the early 1980s: a catastrophe to
compare with the Irish potato famine. A new variety of cassava, developed
by the International Institute of Tropical Agriculture, was planted at the
Texagri farm and disseminated into the local economy from their stem
cuttings, hence its local name of 'Texaco'. A Nigerian popular novel was
written about scientists working at the site. In demise it may become a prec-
edent-setting case for the devolution of land rights when agribusiness pulls
out.

The land contract for this vast area was complex. It was carefully mediated by a dignitary who held both a southern Nigerian chieftaincy title and a
US business degree. Villages stayed where they were and retained certain
lands. Farmers from the eighteen villages who wished to meet the conditions
laid down by the company could be organised into semi-autonomous
groups to become the equivalent of contract farmers to the business and
part-share-holders (15 per cent equity in the company). The farm cultivated
cassava exclusively. A gari-factory was built on the premises and operated
year-round. The largest single group of workers was for cassava peeling, by
hand, before industrial processing took over the next stages of processing
and packaging. The farm kept a roster of 200 women, employed on a daily
basis (about 140 per day), who were paid a piece rate of N1 per 100 kg,
making a daily wage rate of N4 to N6. This gross total was docked, according to local information, the 25K per person that it cost the company to
transport the workers from town to the farm.

According to the British manager of the farm from 1981–87,[6] it was
always difficult to run at a profit. Local farmers could bid up the price of
field labour by including more meals in the workers' daily pay package and
offer work closer to home. Then the price of gari was volatile on the consumer market. At first, most of the gari was used for purposes internal to the
company, and then sold in small retail outlets at petrol stations. Once their
product was launched into the public market, the company found the competition over taste and price very difficult to survive. The peoples of the
different regions of the country favoured slightly different tastes and colours,

so that a uniform product could not compete. The final straw in the profitability struggle was the long-term currency devaluation that set in in 1986, which made the imported inputs for mechanised cultivation prohibitively expensive for a product that was sold exclusively on the domestic market. Devaluation of the naira also dried up the most reliable source of low-cost female labour, namely the migrants from the franc zone.

The final collapse was acrimonious. At the time that Texaco sold its 60 per cent share it also alleged Nigerian mismanagement, and the Nigerian partner alleged rifling of the assets by unknown parties prior to liquidation or sale (Lawrence 1988: 20–1). In 1988, the Texaco shares were sold to the Nigerian partner at a concessional price, partly, according to Lawrence, to avoid litigation over the already-advanced liquidation of movable assets such as the crop itself, tractors and vehicles. The electric generator had also been damaged. Eventually the farm, now under another name, was closed and the search began for a way of liquidating the fixed assets, including houses, an underwater dam and the factory. At the time of writing I know only that the solution of outright sale was challenged by the local customary occupants of the land on the grounds that they, as presumed holders of reversionary rights, must therefore be party to subsequent transactions. The law does not cover such an eventuality with any clarity, so how it plays out, in or out of court, will be exemplary of the fate of agribusiness investment, and perhaps a profoundly cautionary tale for both sides.

The demise of the Texagri experiment is certainly due to more complex causes than conditions on the local labour and consumer markets, but it does illustrate the local logistics that all corporate business must face. They need a much larger labour force than local organisations have had to generate in the past, and if they plan to make a profit they have to make those workers maximally productive. The interests of the local and small-scale farmers with whom they compete for labour do not necessarily lie in chiselling down the returns to their own women-folk or in extending the working day for their labourers. The remarkable stability of the cash segment of local labour rates reflects, I have argued, an institutionalised competitive culture that differs markedly from that of corporate business. Whereas the corporate farms compete over the relatively short-run profit margin on capital investments, the local economy competes over long-term spaces for different producers in the market for goods and services. A hard-working, self-employed, multi-occupational peasantry, which has its own rubrics for wage labour and produces for a market characterised by volatile prices, must be one of the most difficult in which to try to compete for an enterprise that depends on capitalist labour relations and short-term profits (cf. Chayanov 1966).

Neither did the experiment in local shareholding work out well. The local shareholder-farmers never produced much for the factory. Lawrence writes that 150 of them were sent to the Odeda Farm Institute in Ogun State to be trained, and only six of them actually contracted to grow the ten acre plots that the company stipulated. Ten acres is far too large an area for a small-scale farmer to put under monocropped cassava. The local people also came to dislike producing the Texaco variety, in spite of its advantages in yield and disease resistance. The tubers were more watery than was convenient for their own processing techniques and the large diameter of the tubers made peeling difficult; a woman could hardly hold a tuber in one hand and peel with the other. When difficulties of production and market compounded one another they generated a non-viable situation.

Both of the other corporations running farms in Ibarapa, the United Africa Company at Maya and Obasanjo Farms (Nig.) Ltd, are vertically integrated into primary processing and marketing of food products. In fact, the company's market drives the form of their backward linkage into farming, rather than vice versa. A part of the land on which the the UAC farm was located was still (in 1988) owned by Chief Bola Marquis (a former Texaco employee) who had mediated the land acquisition.[7] According to the roadside sign, the enterprise is planned from Britain and the farm manager in 1988 was British. Like the Texaco farm, the UAC farm was sometimes used for experiments by scientists from research institutions. The long-range plan in 1988 was the completely integrated production of pork sausages for the retail outlets of Kingsway supermarkets and Rendezvous snack bars, also owned by the company. A farm of about 718 hectacres produced the field crops (primarily maize) to support the home production of animal feed for the 2,500 pigs bred by artifical insemination from Hungarian stock. A slaughterhouse and sausage-making plant were planned in 1988. The pigs are cared for by a graduate veterinarian. Strict rules of hygiene are followed, the piggery is designed and built according to exacting standards, and the farm is fenced and guarded at the gate. In 1988 the arable farm was about 500 hectares, devoted to maize, soybeans, cowpeas, sorghum, melon (egusi), groundnuts, some tobacco and experimental sunflower. Surpluses above the needs of the feed mill were sold into the UAC network of companies, for example the Nigerian Brewery.

Provision of inputs for beer has been a major impetus behind large-scale farming. The demand for industrially-manufactured beer in Nigeria has risen greatly over twenty years. The price has remained very low in real terms by comparison with the CPI for other consumer products,[8] and the number of breweries has proliferated, some of them as public investments under state government parastatals and in joint government–private ventures.

Obasanjo Farms had two enterprises in Ibarapa by the late 1980s: a predominantly arable and livestock farm at Lanlaṭẹ and a poultry farm at Igbo-Ọra. At one time, all of Obasanjo's several farms came under a single integrated plan as Temperance Enterprises, but in 1988 the structure was altered back to independent accounting on the part of each farm. Nevertheless their activities were linked. Poultry breeding under tropical conditions is very risky, so the component processes are kept physically separate from one another. The Lanlatẹ Farm, which controlled up to 2,000 hectares but in 1988 only cultivated about half of this area, was devoted to arable crops, livestock and the grandparent poultry stock for the parent stock which was kept at Igbo-Ọra.

The vertical integration of these farms means that they are enclaves in the rural areas. They acquire land and employ labour but otherwise engage little with the local economy. Their core of year-round workers have to be specialists, so the main axis of interdependence with the people is for peak period labour. This is critically important; the UAC farm may need as many as 300 casual labourers a day for the maize harvest, for which they have to compete on the local labour market. As described already, the established market for male labour is structured in such a way that the daily wage that business wants to pay for fertiliser spreading, weeding or harvesting – about N4, or as high as N11 for a very fast piece-worker, in 1988 – is inferior to the wage a worker could make from clearing and heaping in the peasant sector (N10–12, plus meals). Women's wages in egusi-harvesting amounted to at least N8 per day plus meals. Only the youth, earning about N5 per day for weeding in the small-scale sector, earned within the range that agribusiness was willing to pay its workers. The result is that farm labour for corporate business comes from a fairly narrow band of women and youth.

People said that working the harvest primarily devolved on women in middle age whose financial resources were particularly low relative to the needs of a set of still-dependent children. Their plight might be due to a husband's illness or death, a failure of business, or a sudden need for a quick and sure income. Very quickly these women have established their own institutions for disseminating information about work availability and labour recruitment, with networks of mediators who deal with the farms and send out word to the potential labour pool when work is needed. These larger organisations which deal with the large farms were not yet ẹgbẹ́ in any formal sense. There was no authority structure, no right of the leadership to bargain on conditions for the membership and no sanctions, but it could be that these networks are gradually moving in the direction of formal organisation, like the groups of women who do the mid-scale and small-scale farmers' harvests in the local economy.

For the moment, the labour system was still insecure enough to threaten the corporate farmer with failure, especially at the time of year when the entire small-scale sector was itself gearing up for the harvest season. Farm managers could find themselves in danger of being unable to raise a harvest labour force, forced to think about approaching local chiefs or even going into the city to bring in casual day labour. Corporate farms have had recourse to both of these panic, stopgap methods.

The deteriorated economic conditions for some people during structural adjustment clearly provided the corporate farms with a new pool of candidates for relatively cheap labour. Women and youth who needed cash urgently to cover the rising costs of school uniforms, books and medicine moved into the agribusiness labour pool. They needed the opportunity to tide over a difficult patch or make a particular purchase, although the level of the wage and the number of days available for harvest work made it a relatively small contributor to the cost of living once prices began to rise. At N6 per day it would take two to four days to earn the money for a school development levy, buy a book, take the bus to Ibadan or buy a single medication. It might take as much as forty or fifty days' work to pay the initial fee to begin an apprenticeship for a child, or seventy to eighty days' work to cover the costs of a major illness. No worker could be guaranteed this many days of work, so the harvest is a very short-term, emergency measure in the difficult day-to-day task – for women with children to take care of and little support from husbands – of providing a routine, year-round cash income.

Some resentment has been expressed towards the corporate farms but by 1988 there was no organised local opposition that I know of. It was said that some of the land payments had been far too low, and at least one local politician opposed a particular agreement. The recurrent abolition of democratic representation at the local level means that there are no obvious fora in which such disputes can be settled openly, and without careful detective work on the part of the researcher it is impossible to identify the processes at issue. There has been the odd act of sabotage at the corporate farms, such as the murder of a security guard, token killing of livestock, burning of a residence, theft of chickens, attack on one of the Nigerian owners. But it is not clear whether local people were involved with any of these incidents. They could have resulted from commercial or political motives, or been part of the generally rising level of crime in the country at large.

As long as there is a land frontier, local complaint is more about the terms of engagement than about the presence of outsiders in the first place. Local leaders do want what they still see as 'development'. Many see the large farms in these terms because they draw prominence to the area. After the price inflation of structural adjustment, a substantial number of local citizens need the jobs that agribusiness offers. Even so, the farms hover on the brink of tolerance, not embedded in their local communities by much except land agreements and labour employment. Yoruba rural society has its own model for commercial dealings, in which enclaves are suspicious.

CONCLUSION

Agribusiness both compares and contrasts with the other commercialised innovations in the farming economy of Ibarapa. It is less vulnerable than mid-scale farming because it is vertically integrated and thereby ensures its own markets. It also has the political clout to defend itself and promote its own interests effectively on a national level. Even so, it has still to make structural links to a local economy that is rapidly commercialising in its own style. Like the mid-scale farmers, agribusiness has had to experiment: with products, with the local ecology, with the various modes of labour recruitment and payment, and with the price fluctuations of the food market. For example, the decline in demand for high-end goods during the early phase of structural adjustment led UAC to close Kingsway supermarkets, which was one of its outlets for the sausages made at the Maya farm. In the complex mix of conditions that makes corporate agribusiness work when the national economics and politics are as unstable as they have been in Nigeria, relations with local producing communities must surely loom quite large.

NOTES

1. This chapter is based on work by myself and by Olukemi Idowu (see Guyer and Idowu 1991; Idowu and Guyer 1991). Sections of the chapter are taken from Idowu and Guyer (1991).
2. *Sunday Times* 12 March 1989, p. 18. Article by Ngozi Ikeano, 'A boost for the nation's agric'.
3. Personal communication, Akin Mabogunje 1989.
4. Contract farming was tried for some crops, with limited success (Little and Watts 1994).
5. Parts of this story come from a detailed article by Ben Lawrence entitled 'Texaco's Gari Dream Shattered', *The President*, 3 July 1988: 20–1.
6. Interview with Gilbert Heys, 14 March 1988.
7. Interview with Chief Bola Marquis, 25 January 1988.
8. For the CPI and the price of beer over twenty years, see Appendix B.

9

WOMEN'S ENTRY INTO FARMING

INTRODUCTION

Johnson's classic decription of Yoruba occupations designates certain kinds of production and certain techniques as male, and others as female: 'The principle occupations of men are: agriculture, commerce, weaving, iron-smelting, smithing, tanning and leather, carving on wood and calabashes, music, medicine, barbing and other minor employments'. Women seed cotton and spin thread, shell palm nuts, tend small livestock, dye cloth, make palm oil, brew beer, manufacture beads, make pots and dress hair. He adds an acute summary comment that perhaps also reflects a Christian reformer's perspective. Men's and women's work follows different rhythms: 'On the whole the women seem to be far more industrious than the men, for whereas the men always contrive to have leisure hours and off days from work, the women seem to have none. Boys and young men certainly have more idle hours than the girls. The care of children also devolves almost entirely upon their mother, an inevitable result of polygamy' (Johnson 1921: 117–25).

Early colonial Christian visions for a new African gender division of labour focused on the development of monogamy and domesticity (Hansen 1992), patterned on the agricultural and artisanal household of Europe. Springing from similar roots, analytical works suggested a similar development: from female to male farming, extensive to intensive agriculture, root crops to cereals, individual to household labour, women's farming to women's processing within a household model (Baumann 1928: Boserup 1970). The course of change in conjugality and women's work in Africa has been a topic of debate, so at variance – and varied – does it seem from expectations. The evolution of a peasant household model of complementary occupations, under male control, has seemed to me implausible for Africa (Guyer 1981). By contrast Netting (1968; 1993) and Stone et al. (1995), argue from their work amongst Kofyar farmers on the Jos Plateau, that the household is still the most useful approximate concept for the full participation of women in small-scale, intensive, commercial joint farming with their husbands. Pathways and possibilities of change are clearly nuanced, conditioned by crops, culture and conversion (Linares 1992), and constantly subjected to the forces of the macro-economy and politics.

None of the standard projections prepared me for the eventuality in Ibarapa that women who were already specialised in processing and trade would move decisively into farming, not in a household model but on their own account, and not in a style that was exclusively and markedly their own but in a manner that had some characteristics in common with the men. Over the ten years between 1976 and 1986, the proportion of women having their own farm went from around 10 per cent to 67 per cent, as the female artisans and traders in a society often cited as *the* example of male farming/female processing in West Africa surged into agriculture, without major social dramas, alongside their own male family members who were also expanding and experimenting.

Ten miles from Idere and three miles of narrow footpaths from a wholesale market lies the village that in 1968 housed the only two women I knew of who were farming the standard arable rotations on their own account. They were sisters, daughters of one of the village founders, both at the beginning of middle age, each with her own small residence. One also made a living outside farming by retail trading in kerosene, oil, salt and dried fish to the surrounding farming community. Her farm was small, at 1.8 acres, but it was oriented towards family food supply and sale of *láfún* (cassava flour). Her sister was also middle-aged, living separately from her husband. She produced food for herself and one child, prepared and sold cassava flour, and grew egusi which she sold after laborious shelling, an activity she combined day in and day out with conversation, stirring the cooking pot and resting in the shade at midday. In Idere, a few women had taken up dry season cultivation of onions in the àkùrò, the river-bed behind the village. Esther was then a very energetic young mother, who earned money from her onion garden and in various other ways: a little trade, various day-labour jobs such as planting, watering the nursery and plucking on the NTC tobacco farms cultivated by her brothers.

In 1968 these women were unusual. Some women were full-time in one aspect or another of trade. The majority made an income from a seasonally-changing sequence of tasks in the farming economy – such as working the cowpea and egusi harvests, collecting shea nuts for preparation into butter, preparing locust bean, shelling egusi, preparing palm oil, manufacturing black soap, cooking and selling guinea-corn beer (*pitọ*) – while also cooking, helping to prepare *láfún* and other crops for market, and headloading from farm to village and from village to market in the context of the domestic economy.

Twenty years later the two sisters were still farming in the same village. Now in their late sixties, definitively terminated in their marital careers but with children and grandchildren living with them in new village houses, they had expanded their farms considerably as the wholesale market became more frequented, the footpaths were widened into vehicle tracks, and the tracks were graded to become laterite roads. The growth in Esther's farming career has been more dramatic. After widowhood she moved back to her natal family compound with her seven children, and decided to support them herself by farming and eventually by running a bar as well. Since she had experience as a worker for the NTC, and both of her brothers had been members of the tobacco growers' association, she applied to become a tobacco farmer on land ceded by her natal compound. The NTC stumped two acres of land for her and she cultivated tobacco for two years. At that time, in the early 1980s, many farmers were abandoning commercial tobacco and she too left it after the two years to grow egusi and cassava for the buoyant food market. In 1985 the junior brother of her mother gave her another three acres adjacent to the first plot when he 'saw her struggling' to support her children in school. By 1988 she had a farm considerably larger than the mean farm size for male small-holder farmers, that was regularly prepared each season by hired tractor. A complex of concrete soaking pits built next to a natural rock outcrop completed the *láfún* production enterprise that provided her main source of livelihood. She owned a small beer and soft drinks parlour in town that was run on a daily basis by her high-school-age daughter, to whose educational costs the proceeds were entirely devoted.

Yet more striking, however, than either of these patterns of growth and change for Idere's few women farmers since the end of the 1960s has been the veritable surge of other women, the non-farmers of 1968, into farming. In July 1988 a sample of Idere women was interviewed to establish the scale and pattern of growth of this phenomenon. Of the 222 women interviewed,[1] 153 (69 per cent) had farms of their own. The growth of women's own-account participation in farming had started from apparently negligible levels in the late 1960s to reach over two-thirds in the late 1980s.

When we understand this 'growth' from several angles, it appears far more as a process of reconfiguration than as a revolution. By looking at the whole breadth of women's activities in 1968 and again in 1988, it seems rather that farming has taken on a new prominence in the repertoire than that it has been a complete innovation, a replacement for women's former occupations. A few women did farm in the past, and currently women who have their own farms still trade, process agricultural products, work the harvest on the men's farms and supply water and cooked food to their husbands and children. Some, like Esther, own a bar or a shop as well. On the other hand, the pattern of growth cannot be reduced to a rather banal process of simple addition of land and person-hours to an occupation already culturally and institutionally validated. There have been misgivings, failures, unforeseen vulnerabilities and a variety of experiments that deviate quite far from simple duplication by a new generation of the farming careers of long-time farmers. The growth in female farming comprises several different processes: the simple expansion of farm area achieved by women who have farmed for a long time; the shift in crops and techniques undertaken by farmers like Esther; the adoption of farming as part of the female occupational repertoire by a high percentage of the rest of the female population; the reshaping of the female occupational repertoire as whole; and the collective acknowledgment that – even if not yet entirely worked through – female farming has become a fixture of life to be faced in the institutional contexts of families and compounds. One institution that has not emerged so far is the classic conjugal peasant household.

One empirical method for capturing changing configurations rather than linear developments is to define and describe the threshold moments at which a new pressure or a new possibility made a marked *qualitative* difference. When the dates of women's entry into farming were plotted, there were two clear moments of change. Of those who were farming in 1988 an average of just over two per year said they had started between 1970 and 1976. In 1977 there was a sudden leap upward, and from then until 1984, over six per year started their own farms. Then from 1984 to 1987, the number went up to twenty-five per year. This stepwise pattern of women's entry into farming suggested taking a cohort approach to analysing change: that is, to define 1976 and 1984 as threshold moments to be looked at in particular detail, and to examine separately the configurations of life and work for the women who started farming in each of the three eras.

COHORTS OF FEMALE FARMERS

To review the pattern of change, Figure 9.1 shows the points of entry[2] into farming of the 153 women now claiming to have farms of their own.

Nineteen women (12 per cent of those farming, 9 per cent of all women) said they had been farming for twenty years or more, and from 1970 to about 1976 there was a fairly steady, small stream of women into farming. Ten per cent of current farmers began farming during that period of seven years. This pace of entry may reflect the same pattern of women's farming as I saw in the late 1960s, although the proportion is somewhat higher than I would have estimated then. About 1977 the annual entries take a leap upwards; thirty three per cent of today's women farmers initiated their farming careers during the eight-year stretch from 1977–84. A yet further and more dramatic leap from 3 or 4 per cent per year to 10 or 12 per cent per year took place from 1985 to 1988. Fully 42 per cent of the women farming in 1988 started during the three years 1985, 1986 and 1987.

These numbers are too dramatically different to be accounted for by demographic processes alone, even though in a growing population there is bound to be a birth-cohort effect in that each new generation is larger than the preceding one. While there certainly were women who fit a demographic or life cycle model – a twenty-five-year-old with three years of farming experience

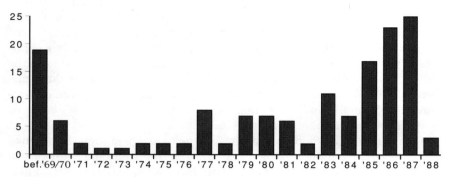

Figure 9.1 Women Entering Farming (before 1969 to 1988)
Note: N=153, from total sample of 222

and a seventy-six-year-old who started at least thirty-six years ago – for the women in the middle and older age ranges there is at present no correspondence between age and years spent as a farmer. An over-eighty-year-old had been farming seven years and a sixty-seven-year-old for six years. In 1987, women aged twenty-one, forty-two, fifty-three and sixty-two all started farming on their own account for the first time. The great variety of ages at the time of entry into farming, in all the cohorts, confirms the inference that the life cycle is an almost completely separate variable from historical innovation, at least over this period of rapid change.

This period from about 1977 to 1987 seems to be a discrete decade of experience, with two phases. Before 1976 there was a pattern of entry consonant with the steady maintenance of farming as simply one possible minor theme in women's occupational repertoire. After 1987 there may well be a slowing off in growth because the remaining 25 per cent or so of women who do not farm are mainly those who could not easily manage to do so, such as the old, the sick, some very young women, some pregnant, and some committed to artisanship or trade. There are, then, four meaningful groups of women for a historical analysis of the expansion of women's farming: those whose farming pre-dates the collective spurt; those from the earlier years of the growth spurt; those from the later years; and those not yet farming, not interested in farming or not able to farm.

There are two correspondences between these data and other which support an interpretation on the basis of women's independent responsiveness to economic circumstances. First, the dates at which their patterns of activity shift match significant dates in the regional economy. Before about 1975 the effects of the oil boom on the urban hinterlands had been very limited. The Department of Geography Study carried out in Ibarapa in 1976 mentions that transport services to the villages, especially in the western part of the division, were provided by 'old, slow and unreliable vehicles', making marketing 'uncertain at the best of times' (Daly et al. 1981: 36). About this time transport began to pick up dramatically (see Chapter 6). Under civilian rule between 1979 and 1983 the local government started fairly serious work on the rural road network, and the influx of labourers from Benin, Togo and Ghana accelerated because of the high value of the naira relative to the franc CFA. Tractors started to be available for hire. This cohort's farming therefore might plausibly be understood as a response to the growth of transport and the conditions of the oil boom.

The year 1985, by contrast, is the time of economic crash at the national level. The decline in oil revenues and the growing debt finally cut very deeply into federal government spending. Pressures built for devaluation of the naira, cutbacks were made in the civil service and the military, some migrants returned from the cities as prices rose and employment contracted. The national vehicle fleet began its slow decline into decrepitude. Migrants from Benin and Togo began to go home. The picture for the rural areas was not uniformly negative by any means,[3] but the deterioration of urban conditions lowered the cost of casual male labour and raised the demand for cheap staples such as cassava flour to feed a slowly impoverishing urban population. Unemployed men turned to trade and transport to make a living; transporters bought cassava fresh from the field, thus cutting out the local primary processing; specialised cassava-processing locations developed in the immediate urban hinterlands, using mechanised techniques;[4] and agribusiness started farming, most notably to serve the breweries. Whereas the era between 1977 and 1984 opened up possibilities for women farmers, the era after 1984 placed intense competitive pressures on women's processing and trade.

The single overarching continuity for these farmers from 1977 to the present, across the 1985 threshold, has been that the urban food market continued to grow, both from within Nigeria and beyond its borders. The decline in the value of the naira relative to the franc CFA of the neighbouring countries has made naira prices very attractive since 1985, resulting in an apparently huge demand for Nigerian goods all around its extremely porous borders. Since growth in demand has been continuous, women could retreat into farming when competition in trade and processing intensified.

The second striking consonance is between the women's response to the market and cultural bases for women's options in life. In Yoruba thinking, a person is a person first and gendered as a secondary characteristic (see also Chapter 3). During a woman's reproductive years, specifically female qualities are foregrounded but she never loses the basic personhood of compound membership and spiritual identity that can be refocused at the forefront after menopause. A woman may reach a level of great influence in her natal compound, even acting as its spokesperson by virtue of seniority and talent without officially being its bálé. Both men and women can be

praise singers for their compounds. It is even slightly vague whether women
are eligible for chieftaincy titles held within compounds; the fact that it has
never happened does not rule out the 'in principle' possibility.

In the ritual domain where these concepts of gender are enacted, even the
biological differences of reproductive age are rendered context-specific in
their relevance, rather than being affirmed as a fundamental axiom perme-
ating all of social life. According to Matory's (1994) analysis of ritual, a
woman is not in all contexts a wife, and a wife is not in all contexts a woman.[5]
Matory's inferences apply outside the ritual realm to daily activities. The
relevance of gender to life and work can be created by the actors, and therefore has to be discovered rather than assumed by the researcher. The
specificities of tasks by gender tend to have a certain situational rather than
categorical quality to them, and are always subject to the cross-cutting criterion of seniority. There is nothing shameful in a man cooking or pounding
yam, for example, and the tasks that women have apparently always carried
out in agricultural production can also be done by men. Women generally
work specific harvest tasks for the crops that need plucking (cowpeas, peppers,
tomatoes, maize, pigeon peas) or extracting (egusi, cocoa) in return for pay
in kind or in cash, and they do not generally uproot yams or climb palm trees
to pick the fruit. But there is no injunction about these matters. The expectation that women would headload crops from farm to village and from
village to market was one of the pillars of the newly expanding commercial
involvement during the 1960s when the transport system was so poor. It was
considered a wife's duty. But men also headloaded, even senior men, and
often extremely heavy loads. Women may peel and soak cassava for *láfún* for
their husband's sale as well as for home consumption, but often a man and
his wife worked together at basic processing tasks.

The one consistent concern men had about women's farming was the
advisability of bending down in the sun all day. Unlike the case in many
'traditional female farming systems' where the bending posture and circular
motions of hoeing are considered distinctively female, in Yoruba conceptions this is an inappropriate stance for women in the childbearing years. In
fact, hardly any of the kinesthetics of women's work involve bending from
the waist; they kneel, stand and sit on stools, but they never spend the whole
day, elbow on knee, in the habitual stance of the women farmers I knew in
Cameroon. The only tasks that women regularly perform that require this
bending stance are spreading crops out to dry in the sun and sweeping the
courtyard, whereas men spend hours every day bending over the ground.
One man told me that this was his greatest objection to his wife farming, that
it required bending over all day in the sun.

So tasks tend to be gender-weighted rather than fully gendered. The criteria for weighting vary with the task: opening up the land gives right of
disposal of the crop that corresponds to the male obligation to provide the

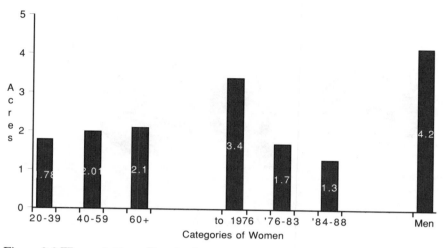

Figure 9.2 Women's Farm Sizes by Age and Cohort

staples of the diet; hoeing involves bending over all day and according to the farmers should therefore be discouraged for women in the reproductive years; weeding has to be done for long hours and many days at a time in the sun which tends to dry out and darken the skin in unpleasing ways; and serving the early afternoon meal makes farming for the whole morning impractical for whoever does the cooking. Wide flexibilities are opened up by the situational linking of person to possibility.

Occupations differ from tasks by virtue of being part of a person's social definition, and they may place particular spiritual demands on the practitioners. Many occupations are only *de facto* gender differentiated rather than *de jure* ascribed, so there is the occasional case of an eccentric or greatly talented person who crosses over, while most people will stay within the ordinary expected bounds. For example, one of Idere's compounds taught its daughters to be drummers in the past, and there was a female goldsmith in the later 1980s. Farming is such an occupation. There is a cult of the farm, *òrìṣà oko*, but no specifically male or female acts or qualities that it calls on to promote fertility. So the low involvement of women in farming in the past tends to be explained pragmatically. Women had the cultural 'permission' to claim the designation *àgbẹ̀*, farmer, long before many women took it up.

Even seniority seems to have little effect on farming style, at least between the ages of twenty and sixty, so little do the standard criteria of status generate differential patterns amongst women. The forty farms (forty-one farmers) in the female sample that was studied and interviewed in more detail were

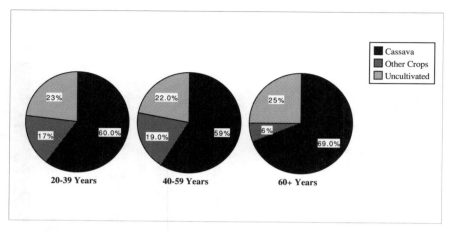

Figure 9.3 Proportion of Farm in Cassava by Age of Women Farmers, Idere, Nigeria, February 1988

divided into three twenty-year age categories; 20–40, 41–60, and over 60. Their mean farm size and mode of clearing the farm was tabulated in order to gain a preliminary sense of how age and farm activities might interact. Figure 9.2 shows how similar the three age categories are in farm size, differing significantly only in that the oldest women seem to hire tractors very little. The cropping patterns for the three age groups, also show limited differences amongst them. The mean proportion of land devoted to cassava, the women's main crop, varied only from 59 per cent to 69 per cent (Figure 9.3).

In brief, classic status categories such as gender and age correspond poorly to both the pattern of women's entry into farming and their style of farming practise, whereas Yoruba notions of situational and contingent gender and a continuity of basic personhood and career are plausibly consonant with the cohort-based shifts that we see. Women's moment of entry into farming has had lasting effects. The means calculated on the same variables as above – farm size and cropping pattern – by cohort rather than age shows much clearer differences.[6]

While the mean farm size for women is about half that for men, Figure 9.3 suggests that the longest-farming cohort has very considerably larger farms, up to 81 per cent the size of the male mean. Each successive cohort has a smaller mean farm size. Cropping follows the same pattern: the longest-farming cohort has the highest variety of crops and the lowest dominance by cassava, and the proportions of cassava increase with each successive wave of entry into farming.

These simple and graphic indicators of variation by cohort support the historical/personal agency approach to analysis that has been suggested by

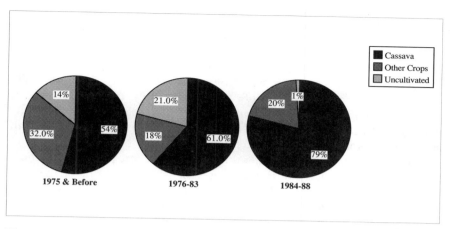

Figure 9.4 Properties of Farm in Cassava, Cohorts of Women Farmers, Idere, Nigeria, February 1988

the history of women's entry into farming, rather than an age/status approach.

COHORT 1: FEMALE FARMERS FROM 1975 AND BEFORE

At the end of the 1960s women farmers were benefiting like the men from the arrival of migrant workers. Before that, I doubt that any women farmed the open savanna unless they had access to subservient workers such as debt pawns or possibly sons-in-law. I have never come across a woman who cleared her own farm from open savanna and doubt very much that it ever happened, except possibly when the brush was very light. The number of women whose husbands cleared the fields for them was minuscule, possibly because it might compromise woman's free and clear claims on the crop. An older woman was astonished that I would even ask whether her sons helped her. She hired labour and paid for it herself. Because of this bottleneck in land clearing, the women's farming that I knew in 1968 was probably a recent phenomenon that depended on the early commercialisation of labour in the regional economy.

Each of the nine women interviewed in detail who fall into the pre-1975 category has particular idiosyncratic conditions around her entry into farming that I will indicate briefly for each one, since their histories differ so clearly from the following cohorts. Four are true 'countryfolk'; they are the now-elderly daughters of that generation of men who built up the abúlé system of farm hamlets in the early years after the imposition of Pax Britannica. One elderly woman, now surely close to eighty years old, is the son's wife of one of the village founders. These women grew up with pioneering professional *àgbè* men who were colonising new land and adjusting the cropping systems to local soil types, environmental particularities and growing market possibilities. Many of the generation of women growing up in the *abúlé* have always known how to farm and have farmed on and off throughout their lives. There was an explicit eccentricity about *abúlé* life when it was more isolated in 1968, that one can still recognise in some of these older people. In such a context, with few plausible occupational alternatives, and with access to land through descent, women learned to farm and actually practised farming when the need arose.

One fairly young woman, in her thirties, fits this same pattern of learning farming in childhood, although for other reasons. Her father had taught her to farm and she had originally farmed independently as a teenager on his land. It became clear as we talked that her striking beauty was combined with intellectual limits that neighbours later told me obviated almost any kind of sustained logical conversation. Trade or an apprenticeship was clearly out of the question, so it seemed in retrospect that perhaps her father had taught her to farm throughout her childhood, as an alternative way of making a living that he personally could ensure for her.

The case of Esther has been described briefly already. She had been a farm worker in commercial tobacco close to town, developed her own onion farm in the riverbed behind the town, and moved into her own farming venture when her husband's support for the children began to lapse. She resembles two other women in this cohort in that none of them could count on either enough food or enough money from their husbands. These last women, each having six children, are polygynously married to salaried workers whose cash incomes could not possibly cover the needs of a large family and whose time commitments to the job precluded working large farms themselves. One of these wives managed to go back to selling nearly all her crop as some of the children have left home and now insisted that her farming is strictly for sale. In the beginning however she indicated that there used to be provisioning considerations, as there were for the female farmers in the villages in 1968.

All these women started slowly and on a small scale, alongside other occupations, but kept up the farm and expanded it over the years, several of them gradually letting the other jobs fade out. Inter-urban trade in particular became difficult to manage once children had to be encouraged to school. A mother can only travel regularly if she can rely confidently on another adult to make sure the children observe the routines. One woman defined her old major occupation of trade in cassava flour to Lagos as *àfikún*, an addition, something she now does only from time to time. Another who did a trading apprenticeship in her youth now only trades in the dry season.

Asked to summarise their reasons for going into farming, five of the nine women said simply *owó*, 'for money', and a further one said she used farming to generate trading capital. The final three said 'for food'. So these are women who love farming and chose it as an occupation, or who took to farming when access to a man's farm for the children's food supply was unreliable or insufficient. The polygynously married wives of the new wage employees of the 1960s were particularly vulnerable. The advent of migrant wage labour allowed such women to take on agriculture, so even at this modest level, women's farming was part of a growing and diversifying regional commercial economy. This pattern might have stabilised at a low, replacement level, but a new configuration of circumstances induced a different set of women to begin farming in the latter half of the 1970s.

COHORT 2: THE COHORT OF THE OIL BOOM, 1976–83

The most important of the new circumstances, besides expansion of the transport system, was a heightened awareness of the speculative potential of cassava production. Four of the thirteen women who fell into this cohort had been inter-city food traders before going into farming, two had been in other branches of fairly substantial trade such as beer selling, two had been cassava processors, one was a teacher, one a soap-maker and only three had been in local and small scale activities such as preparation of cold corn pap for sale. They gave up their other activities only slowly and partially. On the whole they saw their entry into farming as a positive move, a shift of elements in their lives, rather than a radical step up or step down in welfare. The following three examples indicate some of the terms in which women described the addition of farming to their repertoire during this time. As already suggested, one sees elements of the configuration faced by the earlier cohort, but with some added considerations.

Ogunyoyin grew up in a farming village of which her brother is now the *bálé*. She had little plots from time to time throughout her life: two *adé*s (about one-eighth of an acre), she said. But she has only been a farmer for ten years. Presently in her late sixties, she lives in her natal village with her two sons, three daughters-in-law plus one of their sisters, and ten grandchildren.

She used to make black soap for a living. At a certain point the work was too hard and the earnings insufficient 'for food'. She said that a man's farm could not feed everyone. Rural people were sending sacks of cassava to adult children in Lagos because the urban price of food was high and rising. Also, as she spontaneously observed, their children were bearing children of their own at younger ages than in the past, so the number of dependants was rising. Her mildly-expressed criticism that the expansion of parties and celebrations, with pop music over loudspeakers and beer drinking lasting well into the night, was encouraging youth into earlier sex was tempered by a very positive outlook on having more children as a result. The older generations, however, have to pick up the extra work of food provision. Ogunyoyin had no trouble getting land to farm because she is a daughter of the landowning compound. Her farm is in a choice position, close to the village, and she benefited from contributions to the family economy on the part of her co-resident son who was a successful larger scale farmer and cocoa trader.

Moradeyo's circumstances at the time she started farming in 1976 were initially more pressured. With four children in school, two of them requiring fees, and without regular financial support from their fathers, she found her trade in egusi, cooked pap, cassava flour to Lagos and retail bottled beer insufficient. Her mother's death took away a major source of help at home and she decided to take advantage of the newly introduced service of tractor hire to clear about two-and-a-half acres of land. Why farming? 'Ebi npa mi': 'I was hungry'. But the size of her farm went far beyond the dimensions of the usual food farm by virtue of the cheap tractor hire. Since she was bringing up her first husband's children he was willing to give her an area of his compound's land. Her first sales were at N16 per bag of flour, but she had already seen the potential of price fluctuation and managed to realise N42 per bag from sales in 1979–80. With that money she was able to invest in building her own house in Malete and install her beer business in a concreted market stall. She is now a quite intermittent farmer, expanding and contracting as she sees the advantages and the costs relative to her other activities of beer sales and cold pap preparation. Only one child remains to be supported at home.

Bimpe is in her mid-thirties. She started farming at the end of the period, in 1983. Before this she bought cassava by the row in the men's farms to make into cassava flour for the market. She went into farming to source her own cassava because the men started to sell theirs to the traders straight from the field. As she said, 'They are now wise'. The advantage of the new arrangement to the farmers was persuasive enough that shrewd women processors knew that life would have to change. The gradual, row-by-row harvest, in amounts that were manageable for women using their own small-scale soaking pits, would become less and less viable for a woman who needed to raise a substantial income.

Bimpe is one of several who took to sourcing their own cassava for processing. Many of these women enjoyed a windfall when the price of cassava lurched upwards around 1980, and they used the profits to build their own concrete damù, soaking pits, and drying platforms for their láfun preparation. Concrete was very inexpensive and in plentiful supply during the construction boom and import bonanza of the period, which allowed many dam constructions on a scale that could not possibly be afforded after 1986.

Like Ogunyoyin and Moradeyo, and echoing conditions from the earliest cohort, Bimpe uses her farm for the family food supply as well as for sale. Unlike them however, she is currently married to a full-time farmer, who has a farm of over nine acres and is in his peak years of production. The reasons she feels the need to supply food do not relate to absolute shortage in her own case, but to subtle shifts in intra-familial relations that are far from generalised yet. Her husband has made a speciality of tomato production; almost his entire cash income over six months was from tomatoes. According to his budget, he spent 37 per cent of this income (46 per cent of his current expenditure) on food, medicine, household goods, school books and fees for the family of two wives and seven children. But he spent almost exactly the same amount of money on inputs to the farm enterprise – labour, tractor hire, fertiliser – and incurred another, almost equal, amount as a debt to be paid to the Agatu at the end of the season. The costs of production have become a major expense. The present is therefore a period of testing, when some men are moving towards a high degree of commercialisation and devote a higher proportion of their cash income to the diet than in the past, mainly in the form of already cooked food, fish, meat and oil. They then expect their wives to complement the strategy from their own farms, thereby shifting a little of the weight of staple food supply onto their wives. These women do not pick up the entire responsibility for the dietary ingredients but they do contribute if they have a farm.

There are other families where women have resisted this move, since they were not responsible for the staple diet in the past. There is a fierce emphasis to their declaration 'a ntà', we sell, and if they have to make up a shortfall in self-provisoning over a period of a husband's illness or misfortune they try to get back quickly to the old pattern.

Some of the women who went into farming during the oil boom made windfalls, while others have been edged into increasing their contributions to family provisioning. What had certainly been put in place by the time the crash and the structural adjustment period set in from about 1984 was a plausible variety of ways, from a variety of social positions and for a variety of reasons, in which a woman could be a farmer. Income-earning was now at the head of the list of motives. The much heavier emphasis placed on cassava, as shown in Figure 9.4, reflects the commercial orientation of this cohort by comparison with its predecessor for whom crop variety was still desirable.

The subsequent cohort only required a nudge to move into farming. That nudge in 1984 was the continued intermittent peaking in cassava prices and the increase in the costs of living, particularly for health and education.

COHORT 3: THE COHORT OF STRUCTURAL ADJUSTMENT

Nineteen women in the sample, with a mean age of 40, started farming between 1984 and the beginning of 1988, eight of them only the year before they were interviewed. By contrast with their predecessors, these women were markedly locally-based as small-scale operators before they went into farming. Only two of them had been in any occupation one would classify as inter-urban trade. One purchased kinds of peppers and onions not grown in Ibarapa and brought them from Ibadan for local sale, and the other had tried out the used clothing trade for two years. All but one of the others were in cold or hot pap preparation, all kinds of very small-scale retail sales (Omo laundry detergent, salt, beans, oil, dried fish), intermittent processing (gari, guinea-corn beer), or harvest labour and porterage. Two had salaried husbands who could no longer make ends meet in the city and had sent their wives and children home. The last had never had an occupation before; she had gone into farming as her first money-making proposition.

One older woman's occupational history bears repeating in more detail because it illustrates how farming was a defensive option in an otherwise downward career path. In her middle years Jemi traded successfully in second-hand clothes between Lagos and Ibarapa. About ten years previously, just at the time when trade began to be more competitive, she was forced to spend most of her trading fund to deal with family problems. She found it impossible to get back into the business and decided to stay in Idere to make *pitọ*, guinea-corn beer. During the next years she began a long-term relationship with an elderly but vigorous man farming in one of the villages. In 1985 or so she moved to the village with one of her grandchildren. She helps her husband with *láfún* preparation and decided to try farming, since she saw other women doing so and had nothing else to do. She is quite easy-going about whether this new experiment in life is for food supply or sale. Probably it is mainly for sale because there are only three of them regularly at home and both adults send money rather than food to their absent adult children. Her comment that she farmed because she saw other women doing it was repeated by others in this newest cohort, suggesting that when the number of women farmers reached a certain critical mass, those who were only marginally committed to their current occupations decided very quickly to join in.

Jemi's story illustrates the sudden conjuncture of personal problems and competitive market conditions in the late 1970s that resulted in a slow downward spiral that led finally to a small farm plot. Tutu and Titilayo's situation illustrates the position of weaker economic participants in the mid-to-late 1980s. These two women are middle-aged co-wives who have lived in the village all their married lives, with a rather impressive figure for a husband. Their regular cash incomes had come from cold pap sales on market days, which they augmented with a whole series of other activities such as working the egusi harvest and shelling the seeds. About 1986 they began to have a lot of trouble with credit customers who failed to pay up due to straightened circumstances. Although nothing could be cheaper relative to income than corn pap, customers everywhere were trying to cut corners as the price of many consumer goods, school fees, medicine, transport and so on began to climb. Those who failed to bargain powerfully were simply passed over when it came to meeting obligations. It was their husband who decided that they should start farming instead. Up to that point he had forbidden them because it was too strenuous, and involved too much exposure to the sun. Now, he found the labourers to clear the land, bargained for the price and stopped short only of paying for the work. He also advised on what and how to plant in a way that was very rarely the case for the other women. On the whole, the men have not 'taught' these women how to farm. This particular case illustrates the fact that a certain proportion of rural Yoruba women are not successful traders and marketwomen. They are still multi-occupational, seasonal workers, with low personal incomes and a daily routine of cooking and childcare. These women can quite easily farm on a small scale with a simple crop inventory, as soon as the possibilities have been opened up.

The other woman whose husband helped her establish a farm may represent a wave of the future, as women assimilate farming as a regular career. This young woman has started her income-earning career in farming, rather than taking it up in her thirties as appears to be the dominant pattern for the first cohort. Modina was twenty-two years old, newly married to the junior brother of the head of the household in which they lived. Her husband was himself a returned migrant to farming, trying to make money to pay off a debt. Because neither of them had any financial means, he cleared and heaped her land and gave her the plot, explicitly as a gift. After a baby was born she neglected the weeding and he paid labourers to do it for her, although the crop is still hers to do as she wishes with. Other very young wives were similarly indecisive. They started up a plot and then postponed the work. Four said that they farmed mainly because they saw others doing so.

This last cohort has clearly started on farming from a weaker economic position than their predecessors, even though all but one of them are, like the second cohort, currently married. For them, farming is an increasingly attractive way of adding to a low but probably quite steady personal income without needing start-up funds. This last wave of entry into farming is too recent for success or even viability to be assured, and it is still unclear whether they will follow the patterns of expansion of their seniors.

To see the characteristics of the space that farming by women occupies in the rural economy one needs a two-stage approach: first, a detour out of the temporal mode of analysis to take up a structural vantage point on the overall shape of women's farming in 1988 in comparison and contrast to men's farming; and second, a return to the social and historical dynamics.

WOMEN'S STYLES OF FARMING, 1988

There is a series of marked similarities and differences between the farming styles of male small-scale farmers and the women, taken as single categories undifferentiated by age, occupation or cohort. One should not dwell initially on the *differences*, however, because the fact that there are *similarities* at all is remarkable. The overall pattern is an exquisite commentary on the Yoruba cultural premise that a woman is a person 'first' and gendered 'after', ọmọ (a child) first and situationally qualified where relevant as ọkùnrin (male) or obìnrin (female). The meanings and shapes of that qualification obìnrin for the majority of local women who are now living the formerly male occupation of àgbẹ̀ are only just being created.

It is worth emphasising again that the Idere women are not taking up farming in a situation where the men have migrated away as in parts of Southern Africa, been lost in war, or otherwise become unavailable. The men's farming is also expanding and at least replacing itself demographically. Women's move into farming is not a culturally devalued measure, implemented as a stop-gap under duress and only assimilated through long term power struggles about gender ideology. The farming styles and work patterns of these women are not prescribed. If this were the case one would see far more differences between men's and women's farming: for example, women specialising in horticulture on small, labour intensive plots close to home, or in particular specialty crops such as soup ingredients (leaf vegetables, okra, groundnuts) or inputs for domestic industry such as indigo for dyeing or indigenous tobacco. In fact, women are growing major staples for consumption and the market. Furthermore, women do not encounter profound male antagonism, certainly not organised antagonism. Rather, within their own life circumstances they have had to work out ways of dealing with a whole series of ongoing implications: negotiation of land access in different locations, assimilation of the labour demands of different crops, mobilisation of cash to pay for tractor clearing, management of bargaining with labourers, and exploration of the consumption-versus-sale question. None of the outcomes is dictated. Insofar as they cluster into patterns they are an expression of the cultural and social reworking of specifically female qualifiers attached to attributes of personhood.

Women's Access to Land

Land access and farm size determine the broad outlines of farming practice for both men and women. As indicated earlier, women in this area do not in principle have different bases from men for claiming land for a farm. A female member of a land-owning compound can go to the *bálé* and ask to be shown where to farm. As is the case for men, her descent status will influence the location she is given, since all 'children of a house' exert their primary claims against the compound land worked by their closest kin, namely siblings. A woman claiming land has to coordinate with brothers, half-siblings and other ẹ̀gbọ́n and àbúrò (senior and junior siblings) who have claims on the area. Her access is not necessarily more difficult than that of a young man returning from the city.

There is, however, space for secondary differentiation: over the location of the land, over access to land for farm expansion, and over the gender of the applicant's membership link to the compound. As noted already with respect to men, a person can claim land in the compounds of their mother, father's mother and mother's mother as well as their paternal patrilineage. I know of no cases of a female compound member being refused land in her father's compound, but I also came across none who were farming on land of their maternal or other compounds, whereas for men this was very frequent. There is one woman who described her farm *expansion* on paternal land in terms that suggested a discretionary cession rather than the invocation of a right. In a situation where the absolute land constraint on farm expansion is not fully operative, the issue of women's expansion possibilities has yet to be faced squarely. In fact, most of the women farmers have not yet built up the standard field and fallow roster that they need to maintain the old rotation pattern, let alone faced the issue of expansion.

It may well be that both men and women will find it increasingly difficult to claim land in their maternal compounds if a land shortage emerges. The possibility of this being a criterion of secondary discrimination focused specifically on women – where a woman has a reduced chance of exerting rights through her mother than does a man – may well be lying dormant in the repertoire of exclusionary measures. However limited and idiosyncratic a single case of secondary discrimination may be, the possibility cannot be ruled out that such cases will operate as precedents as the dilemma is addressed on a wider scale in the future. Of course, if women recognise the danger and combat it they may ward it off, but there are already some practices that indicate other solutions. For example, in three cases women had loaned already-worked plots to each other for one or two seasons, a practice I have never seen amongst men. Borrowing allows a woman to expand production for a while, or to allow her own land to be fallow, without putting demands on the landowners where she is already farming. If this practice became more prominent it could mean that women are resolving some problems of land access and farm establishment amongst themselves, on the model of friendship or *ẹgbẹ́* membership rather than pressing their demands on descent.

A woman looking for land beyond the boundaries of her natal compound's territory acquires it primarily through affinity. Co-residence with her husband is the main reason a woman cannot farm on lineage land, so it is through her husband's rights that she negotiates her own land access. All the married women in my sample have been given land through their husbands. The contingent, derivative nature of their landholding is clearly indicated by the fact that no woman I know of pays *iṣákọ́lẹ̀* to the landowners for her farm. A woman's farm is implicitly covered by her husband's payment of *iṣákọ́lẹ̀*. *Iṣákọ́lẹ̀* was conceptualised in the past as a recognition of ownership, not an economic payment, so a father's payment covered his sons. More recently, when the payment was monetised it became individuated. But the tributary nature of *isákólè* is still implicitly recognised in the way that a man's payment covers his wives. From the women's point of view, I have never heard of a husband refusing to find a plot for his wife and have not yet heard complaints about possible restrictions on farm expansion on a husband's land. Her rights on that land, however, in the case that he pays *isákólè*, are twice removed: by her husband's tenancy and by her own marriage. Under conditions of greater stress on the land her rights could be vulnerable at each of the linkage points.

At the moment, land rights are not yet the main pressure point in the small-scale farming economy. Male farmers still gain by their wives maintaining co-residence, so one can see a strong rationale for a husband to grant land to his wife, in order to give her a localised source of income now that artisanal processing has come under market pressure. Apart from the desirable domestic aspects of co-residence for farmers, there is the peak period and other support work that wives still do for their husbands in the farming economy. A woman who divorces her husband and moves out forfeits the farm she has made on his land. Marital mobility is rendered somewhat less desirable for a woman when she has a field of maturing cassava on her husband's land, so one cannot rule out the possibility that men are encouraging an otherwise restive and occupationally-pressured population to invest in rural life. In the case of both wives and labourers, the granting of a plot of land after the manner of the *àbùṣe* of the junior male dependant of the past, is an effort to stabilise relationships. It may be a successful strategy because, as I will discuss later, most of the women in the larger sample who left their households between July 1988 and December 1990 did not have farms.

Although there are minor indications that land access may become a problem for women in the future, there is no evidence that it has yet emerged with any clarity, either with respect to initial access or with respect to the subsequent expansion necessary to implement customary rotations and fallow practices.[7] The quite striking alacrity with which physical and jural space has been made for women's farming reflects the lack of acute pressure on the land, the cultural construction of compound membership, the positive interests men may have in the enterprise of women's farming, and the fact that women are not growing tree crops that establish long-term rights.

Women's Farm Size

The size of women's farms cannot be interpreted as a direct result of the land access. They are, however, significantly smaller than men's farms. The mean woman's farm is only 44 per cent of the acreage of the mean man's farm. Table 9.1 summarises differences in farm size.

Table 9.1: Size of Farm in Acres, Male and Female Farmers, 1988

	Male Small-scale Farmers	Female Farmers
Number in Sample	50	41
Farm Size		
Mean Farm Size (acres)	4.3	1.9
Mean Number of Plots	5.4	2.9
Mean Acres per Plot	0.8	0.6

Women's farms are smaller than men's mainly because they have fewer plots, and to a much lesser degree because their plots are smaller (unlike the difference between the part- and full-time male farmers of the past). Two complementary lines of enquiry need to be pursued to explore the difference and similarity between male and female farm organisation. Given that land access is not the major issue, one needs to look at possible constraints on *other* inputs, and then, in the context of these constraints, at the values that women are expressing in their farming styles.

While labour is still the key input into farming, since the advent of tractors for hire in the mid-to-late-1970s access to cash funds is also a possible differentiating factor between men and women. Tractor-clearing has to be paid at the time of the work, so the farmer has to be able to tap lump sums. Table 9.2 tabulates the acreage and proportions of present total farm size, for men and for women, that were initially opened up by each of the various available methods, showing that tractor access does in fact differentiate by gender.

Neither sex receives significant family help in opening up land. Women and men prepared similar acreages by hired labour (1.3 and 1.2 acres respectively), but since women's farms are smaller, they are proportionately far more dependent on the conditions of hired labour supply than men; two thirds of their land had been opened up by hired labour in 1988.

The fact that the input of hired labour averages out to such similar acreages between men and women suggests that the labourers themselves do not discriminate, either positively because one sex pays or feeds obviously better than the other, or negatively because of other values beyond the bargain. The mean cost of opening an acre of new land entirely by hired labour between 1984 and 1987[8] for male farmers was N169 and for female farmers was N180. The difference is minimal and perhaps simply estimated with a slightly higher level of bargaining accuracy on both sides by the men, due to longer experience. From the labourers' point of view a job is a job, regardless of who employs them, and they devote similar work to women's farms as to men's.

Women clearly do less of the work on their farms themselves, and rely proportionately far more on hired labour. By comparison with the men, who

Table 9.2: Mean Acreage Initially Cleared and Prepared, Male and Female Farms, by Method, 1988

	Male Small-scale Farmers	Female Farmers
Tractor only	1.8 (42%)	0.5 (28%)
Hired Labour	1.3 (30%)	1.2 (65%)
Farmer(s)[a]	0.7 (16%)	neg. (1%)
Tractor and Hired Labour	0.2 (5%)	0.1 (5%)
Tractor and Farmer(s)	0.1 (2%)	–
Hired Labour and Farmer(s)	0.1 (2%)	–
Family Labour	–	neg. (1%)
No Data	0.2 (3%)	–
Total	4.3 (100%)	1.9 (100%)

[a] Includes use of àáró (exchange) labour, but as a very small proportion of the total. Àáró is mainly used for weeding and certain harvesting tasks.

cleared nearly one acre (20 per cent) of their land themselves or with exchange labour, and only hired labour for 30 per cent of the clearing and one in five weedings, on women's farms, virtually none of the clearing was done outside the labour market, and 65 per cent of total farm clearing and about half of the weeding (102 out of 208 plot weedings in 1987) was done by hired labour.[9]

Self-clearing is one factor that gives men's farms a size advantage. Tractor access adds to the differential. Again, the difference is one in degree rather than kind. Women do hire tractors; over a quarter of their land has been tractor-cleared. However both the mean acreage and the proportion of the farm opened up by tractor are considerably lower for women than for men. This has the single largest effect on the differences in mean farm size. All the logic outlined above would suggest that women would be amongst the tractor hirers' most enthusiastic customers. The cost is lower than clearing by hand, at an average of almost N50 per acre for the years 1984–87, by comparison with about N175 for hired labour. One needs to ask why, if women are in the hired labour market to the same extent as men, they are not in the hired tractor market to the same degree.

Two finer analyses suggest that the gap may be narrowing. First, the gross figures are affected by the fact that men started using tractors much earlier than women and therefore have more tractor land under current cultivation. For land cleared *after* 1984, the difference between male and female tractor hiring is considerably reduced: from 1.8 acres for men and 0.5 acres for women for the whole cultivated acreage, to a mean of 1.2 acres versus 0.5 acres, for the area opened up from 1984 onwards.

Second, the difference between female and male tractor *users* rather than the entire male and female samples, is again narrowed: the mean tractor acreage for female users was 1.8, or 72 per cent of their total farm size, while for male users it was 3.6 acres or 65 per cent of their total farm size.

There are probably, then, several convergent reasons why more women do not hire tractors more often. One that they mentioned is that tractors have always been something of a hassle to arrange, especially in the farming villages, so it may take activation of personal ties with a driver to get him to come. Women said that they 'didn't see' a driver, and therefore chose other methods. The main reason is that tractor hire demands instant payment in cash, unlike hired labour that can be contracted on credit. A certain proportion of the women go into farming because of lost trading funds or at other moments of crisis, so they cannot afford to start farming without some kind of extension of credit, either from the labourers or from a money-lender. Credit on the money market can be expensive if the free sources from credit associations, kin and remittances are not available. Those women who can get a son or daughter from the city to pay for the tractor will do so, while the others will take the credit option in the hired labour system. Men, by contrast, have been farming for years and can save some of the previous year's crop to finance the cash-on-the-barrel tractor payments. Finally, there may be a limit to the size of farm some women want to handle. Tractors only plough in one-acre plots, which may be more than a woman wants to add to her farm all at once, and this dissuades her from being a tractor-user at all.

In summary, the overall differences in farm size between women and men stem from a set of convergences and divergences and not from absolute differences in access to resources. For the women who farm seriously to make an annual living, there are surprising similarities between their farms and the men's farms. In fact they are overlapping categories. A few women's farm size and number of plots almost exactly corresponds to male farms. The mean total farm size for the fifteen female tractor users (out of forty-one farmers) was almost exactly the same as for the twenty-one male non-users (out of fifty farmers). The longest-farming cohort of women has a mean farm size much closer to the male than the following two cohorts. The farm size of five of the female farmers is above the male mean. Although gender accounts for some of the specific divergences, the overlap between the male and female farm sizes is considerable.

Women's Cropping Patterns

The final major set of issues on gendered styles of farming concerns characteristic cropping systems. If women's smaller farm size were a function of their different social structural position, one might expect them also to practise different cropping, techniques and work rhythms. Again, Idere women converge and diverge in nuanced ways in relation to the male pattern of activity. Table 9.3 summarises male and female crops for the two growing seasons of 1987.

Table 9:3 Percentage Acreage by Crop, Men's and Women's Farms, 1987

	Season A		Season B	
	Men	Women	Men	Women
Cassava	24	42	43	74
Egusi	23	30	3	2
Maize	4	3	13	2
Yam/Guinea corn	9	0	17	0
Tomatoes	11	7	1	3
Peppers	2	3	3	4
Other	15	3	16	4
Not planted/no info[a]	12	12	4	11
Total	100	100	100	100

[a] No information applies to one large, man's, farm, in season A.

Women's farms are clearly low on diversity and on the prestigious traditional staples. Women grew no yams worth measuring at all, while men had 17 per cent of their land in yams at the end of the year. Women also grew relatively little (5 per cent at most) of the other old staples, maize or guinea-corn, to which men devoted a total of 27 per cent in the second season of 1987. The final category on which women's farms were very low, at 6 per cent of total acreage, was a collection of minor crops including peppers, indigenous tobacco, pigeon peas, groundnuts, vegetables and okra, to which the men's farms devoted a year round average of about 20 per cent of the farm.

Two crops predominate on women's farms: cassava and egusi which account for almost exactly 75 per cent of their acreage. In the early season women devoted 44 per cent of their acreage to cassava, while men devoted 25 per cent; in the second season women devoted 76 per cent to cassava, while men devoted 46 per cent. The second most popular crop for women was egusi-melon. In the early season of 1987 women put 30 per cent of their acreage into egusi while men put 27 per cent. These two crops share the technical conditions that they demand relatively little weeding and the cultural condition that both are already associated with women's labour through the harvest. These are the crops they know best, which happen also to be highly marketable and to be grown with methods that least contradict the guidelines for female work.

But is this level of specialisation a plateau, or are there are seeds of diversification? Certainly there are women now growing, or having grown in the past, almost every crop on the list of cultigens, so the question is not one of the simple presence or absence of diversity but of a pattern of change over time. The main way of exploring this is through looking back at the cohorts.

THE DYNAMICS OF CHANGE

Women start their farming careers with cassava and gradually reduce the proportion of their farm in that crop to incorporate egusi and then other crops. They do not, however, reduce the absolute area under cassava. While 79 per cent of the most recent cohort's farms are in cassava, and only 61 per cent for the middle cohort, the absolute areas in cassava are identical (1.03 acres). The oldest cohort devoted a lower proportion (54 per cent) to cassava in the second season of 1987, even though they grew a higher absolute acreage (1.8 acres). Their 14 per cent of land uncultivated in the dry season, ready for planting egusi in March, was almost twice as large as the area saved by the middle cohort, and at the same time their 'other crops' are absolutely and proportionately much more important. It is the smallest farmers who are the most specialised, and the larger farmers who are the most diversified.

If the cohort patterns can be seen as a pattern of growth, that growth is characteristically achieved by the gradual addition of other crops as the total farm is expanded. Diversification, expansion of farm size and *total* volume of involvement in the market go hand in hand. The most fragile farms in the rural economy are those that are most highly specialist and almost completely commercialised, namely the smallest women's farms. The evidence for their greater commercialisation bears reiterating: these women are entirely dependent on hired labour or tractors to open up their farms; they employ more labour for cultivation tasks; they rarely organise àdrò cooperative labour for weeding; they focus on the crops that are the backbone of local farm sales; a significant number of them say that they went into farming 'for money'; for many it is still only one of a repertoire of income earning activities; and many have rather intermittent or fluctuating careers in farming.

Since this last point cannot easily be made quantitatively let me refer back to Moradeyo. Her farm had been quite large and very successful in the early 1980s when she hit the cassava price at the right moment. She used the money in part to build up her beer-selling business while continuing to prepare cold pap for daily income. An accident sidelined the farming for two years or so, but she did not return to it on the same scale as before until the rise in beer prices during structural adjustment cut into her income. In 1988 she was back at the farm, harvesting the small area of cassava planted on this now-neglected tractor-cleared land from the past, and she was preparing the plot anew. Several other women's plot histories included seasons when nothing was planted, not for the technical reason of fallow management but because – they said rather vaguely – they could not come up with the money. Women are highly responsive to the market because they have been more deeply dependent on its fluctuations, and thereby more vulnerable to ephemeral coincidences in the price of inputs relative to the price of the product in a volatile market. Diversification expresses a greater commitment to regular farming; specialisation reflects an attempt to capture windfalls.

Table 9.4: Changes in Women's Farming Activities, 1988–90.

	N	%
Still farming: larger farm	90	41
Started farming	11	5
Still farming: smaller farm	27	12
Left farming	10	5
Still not farming	31	14
Moved	45	20
Died	6	3
Other	2	1
Total	222	101

Diversification is also, however, ambiguous as a commercialisation strategy because is allows the self-provisioning wedge to be driven into women's sales. Although only about a fourth to a third of the women went into farming 'for food', diversification clearly makes it more possible for them to contribute in kind to the family staple food supply. If women's farming moved in this direction it would indicate a shift in the gender division of responsibilities, and a changing shape to family dynamics, consonant with the emergence of a form of organisation more approximating a 'household'model. One should note here, for comparative purposes, that if this model began to emerge it would certainly not be the result of the dynamics of production, as is predicted in evolutionary theory, but the result of the exigencies of consumption in an economy where prices fluctuate widely, leaving imperative expenditures such as school fees and health costs to surpass the capacities of any individual, male or female.

Finally, are there any ongoing directions in the way that women see their own participation in farming to be developing? The larger sample was reinterviewed in 1990, concentrating on any changes, particularly entry or exit from farming, a larger or smaller farm. Table 9.4 summarises the results.

This table suggests that the growth in *numbers* of farmers may have plateaued, while the growth in *farm size* continues.[10] Only 5 per cent started farming, exactly balancing out those who stopped. Of those who remained, far more increased farm size than reduced it. The main reasons women gave for expanding their farms are summarised in Table 9.5.

The domestic orientations of women's thinking seem clear. They lie on the complex confluence of a suddenly rising cost of living, a suddenly increasing urban demand for cheap staples, and an apparently increasing male farmer orientation to commercialised inputs and outputs, with the possible pressure this places on family provisioning.

Table 9.5: Women's Reasons for Expanding Farm Size, 1988–90.

	N	%
Support children	34	38
Food	27	30
Money	21	23
School fees	6	7
Other	2	2
Total	90	100

CONCLUSION

Women's farming is the single most difficult element to triangulate in the three contextual frameworks set out in the introduction: the development of new farming patterns in the humid savanna, the logic of urban supply, and the moving frontier of Yoruba social life. Women's farming is more exclusively commercial, less intensive and less diverse than any other pattern of production except large-scale farming. Although women's farms approximate *in size* the farms of the home-provisioning part-timers of 1968, they share no other characteristics: either number of plots or crop diversity. They and agribusiness constitute Ibarapa's first attempts at narrow, commercial specialisation. Both are governed by a 'vertical integration' model, albeit on very different scales, where the primary processing exigency drives the profile of the farming.

As women's farming has progressively institutionalised, however, it seems not necessarily to be maintaining this focused profile. For the moment, the longer they stay in farming, the more these women tend towards patterns of cultivation that approximate a diversified male model, again within certain particular limitations and facing particular challenges that will almost certainly prevent their farming from completely duplicating the male pattern. At the same time, however, the men's farming that I describe in Chapter 11 is also shifting the bases for diversification, and developing a cassava-plus balance of crops that – at some point – may converge with the women arriving at that point from a different direction.

NOTES

1. The sample included every resident woman, daughter or wife, of all ages past school age, in one compound from each of the four town quarters. They were interviewed at a time when most residents would be in town for the major Muslim festival of Id-el-Kabir, including women who would normally be trading, living in the farm villages or otherwise absent from town for occupational reasons.

2. Just as the four-day market week is referred to in Yoruba practice as five days long by counting the the two market days that frame the temporal duration, so when a person is asked how long ago they started doing something they give separate identities to the starting point and the present moment. In this way, a woman asked in 1988 how long ago she started farming will answer 'two years' if it was last year, 'five years' if it was 1984.

3 .Cereal imports were banned. President Babangida inaugurated several polices to stimulate rural economic growth: The Directorate of Food, Roads and Rural Infrastructure; Better Life for Rural Women; The National Board for Community Banks; and various means of bringing producers and small industry together.

4. A detailed study of this phenomenon has been undertaken by Mimi Wan.

5. The self and the community are seen as hollow vessels 'that potentially host a variety of beings, who may change places at ritually induced moments' (Matory 1994: 135). A 'wife' epitomises hollowness and receptivity to being 'mounted' by another being. Hence the term for wife can apply to male religious functionaries in relation to their god, and to ritual servants in relation to the king. See also Drewal and Drewal (1983).

6. It should be noted that the patterns of entry into farming and farm organisation in this sample broke down more clearly between 1975 and 1976, 1983 and 1984, than the one year later suggested by the larger study, and have therefore been adopted as the defining cohort boundaries.

7. On men's farms, the proportion of the total land area that had just ended its fourth or less year of cultivation at the beginning of 1988 – that is, clearly within the framework of the old rotation of four years cultivation and eight years fallow – was 74 per cent. Comparing this to the farms of the first two cohorts only – that is, the women who were farming in 1983 and before, and therefore could have some older land – what emerges is that 84 per cent of their land is within the four-year rotation pattern, showing no clear female disadvantage in access to new land.

8. That is, the land currently in cultivation in early 1988, mean cost per year averaged over the four years.

9. Only one woman cleared any land at all, and this was a member of the oldest cohort, deeply imbued with farming expertise and farming as a way of life. Not all farmers, male or female, are strong enough to clear on the scale that present-day farming requires. No older man clears his own land. The only man I knew who cleared his entire farm himself was in his forties and quietly, but explicitly, proud that he still had the *agbára*, the strength, to do so.

10. I am not sure what this high rate of physical mobility (20 per cent) reflects; possibly the peripatetics of life rather than major change in residence. Indeed, a person 'travelling' may not be clearly defined as moving, except in restrospect, and obviously these data were contributed by other compound members who answer all questions about someone else in as vague a way as possible, to preclude inappropriate inference.

10

THE YOUNGER GENERATION
OF MEN

Young men are new entrants into local agriculture, in the same way as are
mid-scale farmers or women. The current styles and life trajectories in farming are not necessarily much clearer for them than for the others. Social
conditions changed markedly over their youth, and differentiate their situation from their fathers and senior brothers. Many took apprenticeships and
migrated to cities for work, and then had to return home when markets
shrank after 1985. By 1988, the returned migrants were still unsure of their
options in life. The pattern of reproduction and slow growth for male farming that is described in the following chapter depends crucially on this next
generation's ability and willingness to pick up all the knowledge and social
commitments to make it work.

The full-time farmers I knew in 1968 were brought up in the 1930s to the
1960s, in an economy on the fringes of the urban system. Hardly any of
them have formal education in the national secular school system.[1] Some
learned to read the Bible in Yoruba through religious adult education, but
the oldest men with formal schooling were only in their mid-fifties in 1988.
The most enterprising farmers moved into cocoa-growing areas, but the
majority took up arable farming as soon as they became independent, growing the crops and living the lifestyle they had learned as juniors to their
fathers or senior brothers. Although struggling, they are probably doing
better now than they expected to do in life. Some men who were young in
the 1960s branched out beyond the local traditional occupations and cocoa
farming. With the expansion of local government, new salaried jobs opened
up for a few young men with enough education to do formal sector work:
sanitary labour, road repair and jobs demanding some literacy, as clerks and
teachers. A very few went into the army during the civil war. The new farming possibilities of the 1960s were commercial tobacco and serving the food
market.

I expected to see high mobility amongst the younger generation of 1968
when I returned in 1988 but found that the stability had been remarkable.
Very few of those who were already established in farming had gone to live
anywhere else or tried any other occupation over the twenty-year interim.
Even though the urban economy diversified and offered new jobs to many
migrants in transport and construction, the men who were in their twenties

and already farming in the late 1960s barely took part. A local career was still attractive by comparison with the other options for men with little education and no English; free primary education instituted in 1955 had only resulted in an attendance rate of one-third of children by 1964 (Barber 1966: 60). One of the most energetic farmers of 1968 had become frustrated at home and taken the risk of moving to the city, only to be stuck in a night-watch job. This is the present established generation of farmer who, like the previous generation in the cocoa belt, invested in their children's education while maintaining the farming economy.

The present younger generation of men in their twenties and thirties has a different life history altogether. They were teenagers during the early years of the oil boom and most received some education. Many have travelled, received training and been employed in the urban economy. Due to education and experimentation in the labour market, this new generation is entering farming at a later age, having already tried other possibilities. The established generation has to sponsor them, not necessarily by giving them cash to survive, but by feeding and housing them during the start-up period for a farm and maintaining the institutions of the farming economy: land control, pathways, markets, village organisation, àárò labour and so on.

If the conditions of the oil boom had continued, the present cohort of young adults might have been a switch generation, mediating a radical change from broad sprectrum farming to artisanship, from agriculture as a personal occupation to specialised cultivation as a sideline to a 'modern' trained skill, from working the land to managing farms worked by others. If the older generation's plans for the youth had worked out, the 'peasantry' might well have 'disappeared' (Berry 1985), leaving the farming economy dominated by a small-scale yeomanry of local land-owners and farm managers, or by large-scale outside interests.

Economic instability has prevented radical scenarios from unfolding. Most of the youth are artisans rather than professionals, and under current economic conditions their other jobs pay less and are more unreliable than farming. With solid urban demand, food farming more or less guarantees that a man can make a living and also establish the family and community identity without which he amounts to nothing in the social world. Unsure of exactly how to combine their occupations, or to take advantage of shifting conditions, this generation is zigzagging back and forth from farming to training over a stage of experimentation that did not exist in the late 1960s.

It does seem, however, that the farming population is at least replacing itself, if not growing, in spite of the occupational indecisions of the younger generation. Every adult in the farming sample of 1988 was asked about the occupations of their children.[2] Twenty-eight of the fifty male farmers interviewed in 1988 had children who were adult and out of training, a total of 145. Table 10.1 summarises their occupations.

Table 10.1: Occupations of Adult Children of Male Sample.

	Male		Female	
	N	%	N	%
Known farmers	28	40	5	7
Other occupations	25	36	40	53
Unemployed or unknown to father	17	24	30	40
Total	70	100	75	100

Perhaps due to slowly rising standards in the health infrastructure, the parental generation of men who had any adult children by 1988, had an average of five, in many cases with younger children as well, so the younger generation is considerably larger.

It is sheer coincidence that the number of 'next generation' male farmers – at twenty-eight – is exactly equal to the number of fathers of adult children, but it does dramatise the conclusion that when a population is growing there can be occupational diversification and out-migration without the farming population necessarily failing to replace itself. Even those who have received training grew up in a farm context, so they have some agricultural skills to come back to if a career as an artisan falters or if they decide to combine occupations.

The crafts that the non-farming children do for a living are very varied. Male occupations represented include printer, medicine-seller, goldsmith, driver, bank-worker, pastor, mechanic, typist, tractor-operator, tailor, battery-charger, teacher, security guard, taxi-driver, technical construction worker, carpenter, photographer and 'panabita' (panel-beater, that is, automobile body-worker).[3] Female occupations include trader, typist, seamstress, teacher, goldsmith and nurse. Parental investment in training had been very considerable. To give an example of a young woman apprenticed in the 1970s when training picked up momentum: her parents spent N400 on the apprenticeship, N400 on the sewing machine and another substantial amount on the freedom ceremony when the apprenticeship was over, for a total value over $1,000, at the current exchange rates of approximate parity between the naira and the dollar.

By 1988, when the urban economy was in severe constriction, there were four viable pathways that these young people could follow. Some children went straight into farming, even if somewhat fitfully after forays here and there to look at other possibilities. Those who had trained as apprentices in crafts that could be practised locally, such as tailoring, motor mechanics and motor cycle repair could stay at home and farm as a sideline. A third category had been trained in urban-based crafts that continued to be in demand because in a recessive economy no one can afford to replace items;

everything has to be repaired. These are the children who can afford to remit money to the rural areas. For example Esther's son, an electrician in Lagos, sent several hundred naira for the installment of electricity in her bar when the cables were finally extended that far. A final group has been forced to abandon their urban-based work, return home and pick up farming from scratch at a relatively late stage of life.

If current retrenchment in artisanship continues, probably well over half of the male children will eventually pick up farming as their major occupation. A further quarter or so may come back at some stage, spending time as marginally employed, here and there. The final quarter may be earning a meaningful income elsewhere in the economy for substantial parts of their careers. Remittances will go in both directions depending on the state of the larger economy. Under the conditions of structural adjustment, the flows of goods benefit the urban-dweller who can barely afford the retail food prices. Many families send sacks of cassava flour to kin, and certainly never go for an urban visit without taking substantial amounts of rural produce. Under some circumstances the flows go in the other direction: an accountant helped the family to define compensation in a land case; an electrician sent money for ploughing; a civil servant helped to pay lawyers' fees. The help flowing into the rural economy tends to be intermittent and ear-marked for particular expenditures. It probably takes many years before the value of the returns begins to approximate the parents' expenditure on the apprenticeship, especially given the present cost of urban living.

I review briefly the period of entry into farming in a man's life as it was in 1968, and then describe the experiences of the present cohort in the farming that they eventually take up.

ENTRY INTO FARMING AND THE FARMING STYLES OF YOUTH

In 1968 the age curve of farm size was relatively flat. Young men worked upwards from a gradual beginning, and once a man was launched into an adult career, the regular occurrence of both major and minor social demands throughout his adult life meant that the farm had to be kept up. Individuals geared up and down as their aspirations changed, but the aggregated pattern reveals an expected rise, maintenance and gradual fall in work effort over the life cycle. From age thirty to seventy-five, mean farm size for full-time farmers changed fairly little.

The age curve is sharper in 1988, favouring men in early adulthood, from thirty to forty-five. The age-pattern however masks a major difference in this age group between those who stayed at home and those who migrated and returned. While mean farm size for the entire group was just over five acres, those who had stayed at home averaged 7.1 acres while those who were returning were only at 2.4 acres. The returnees include the nightclub waiters, factory workers and urban unskilled who are coming back home later in life to try to put together a viable career as farmers. They are already quite disadvantaged in this endeavour before they start. Most of them lived in extremely crowded conditions in the city and earned very low incomes. One worker in a battery factory lived for a while in a single room with seven other people: three slept in the bed, one in the chair and three had mats on the floor. When they return home from a work experience of this sort it is often with debts rather than assets. Most of them have no money at all when they arrive. In fact, they have usually exhausted all resources trying to find more work in the town before they come home. They arrive almost destitute and even in debt, and they have to start again in a small way at the age of thirty exactly as if they had been eighteen or twenty: they depend on kin for food and for locating land; they clear as much land as they can afford to pay for at the end of the growing season; and they usually postpone marriage and housebuilding. Fully adult patterns of work and farm size did not become markedly evident until a man was in his twenties in 1968 but a whole ten years later, in his thirties, in 1988. The slow start-up is a cyclical generational effect; its lateness in the thirties instead of the twenties is a cohort effect, dominated by the employment crisis for youth.

Unlike the people who stayed at home and worked up their farming skills, the returnees are at a poor starting point for developing the full range of farming options. Without cash for tractor clearing, and within the credit restrictions for farm labour (end of year payment), it takes several years for someone who starts out indigent to build up a complete complement of fields, even if they have all the advantages of resource control by right of access through descent. People have to establish and prove themselves by performance.

Some examples illustrate the dilemmas. Tijani was a shopkeeper for a woman beer-seller in Abeokuta after leaving Islamic School. After two years he went to Lagos where a brother found him a job as a barman for N40 a month plus tips. As inflation cut into his wage gradually over eight years, he decided to come home and now lives with his wife and child in one room of his senior brother's house in a farming village. He will not travel again because he has reached the age, in his early thirties, when it is imperative to establish a family. In 1988 Tijani's farm consisted of only three plots, totalling 2.5 acres: almost exactly the mean farm size for a man between the ages of fifteen and thirty – that is, without family responsibilities – in 1968. He managed to pay for the clearing and heaping of just over two acres by hired labour, which he first planted in tomato, to make a quick nest-egg of cash, and then put into cassava while he started opening up other small fields for tomatoes as his main cash-crop. By early 1988, he was still dependent on his senior brother, and was still only growing two major crops.

Lamidi's is a similar story, with a stint as a primary school teacher following the period as a barman and a factory worker in Lagos. He decided to come home one full growing season before Tijani, so was doing better by early 1988. His farm was still only 2.6 acres, but he had seven plots and a somewhat more varied crop repertoire, including small areas of yams and maize. He, too, had specialised in tomatoes when he first came home, to the extent of half of his total farm, demonstrating quite clearly that subsistence, in the sense of food in kind, is not the primary need, but rather a solid place in the commercial side of the economy.

Hassan came home from Lagos yet earlier, primarily because of illness. He had started an apprenticeship in fan repair, even though his father had died young, leaving him with limited support for training. But by 1985 he had already decided to return to farm. Like the other two, he first opened up as large a field as he could manage, drawing on *àdrò* group labour, and put it into a cash crop, in his case cowpeas. Then he opened up two new plots to devote to tomatoes and peppers, and finally another large plot for cowpeas again, for a total farm of 3.3 acres and four plots, devoted to five crops: cassava, maize, tomtoes, peppers and cowpeas.

None of these men brought any money home when they returned. The first two are well into their thirties, while the third is still in his twenties and unmarried. In 1988 the farming of all of these men was gradually moving into a fully adult category, at a much later stage of life than their predecessors, and concentrating at the outset on commercial crops rather than self-provisioning.

The other pathway is slightly more encouraging, but agriculturally different. Men who have apprenticeships and skills that can be deployed locally can move back and forth from one occupation to the other and accelerate the establishment of their careers. For example, Sunday spent eight years in Lagos: three as an apprentice to a bricklayer and five more working. Since his father was dead his master did not ask for money, and his friends paid for the freedom ceremony. By 1984 he said that 'Lagos was no more Lagos', and he came home. A friend asked him to build a casssava-soaking pit, and gradually he has built up a small irregular business doing concrete work and repairing house walls, from which he earns about N15 each day that he works. This is not much more than a farm labourer earns to clear and heap a new plot, and in his own case all the money from his last job had to be spent on a school uniform for one of his two children, rather than on augmenting his farm. Both his wives have left him, so in 1988 at the age of nearly forty he was trying to develop a new marriage. He can afford, however, to be somewhat independent and to emphasise the commercial side of his farm.

Sunday's five plots totalled 4.3 acres: the average farm size for adult men, but well below the average for his age group. Again, he started out in tomatoes, but instead of gradually adding to his crop repertoire, he has kept the majority of his acreage in cassava, at various stages of development. At the end of a cassava cycle he grows a year of yams, or a season of maize followed by tomatoes, but there are no signs of him becoming either a more generally diversified farmer, or a cassava-plus-speciality farmer.

Mosudi spent eight years in Lagos between 1978 and 1986, training and then working as a housepainter. Jobs became very scarce when people stopped painting their houses so he returned home and is starting out anew at farm. Like Sunday he would apply his skills at home if he could, and then use the money to extend his farm. His small farm of 1.7 acres was entirely devoted to tomatoes, with cassava to fill in the rotation. The fully-established local artisans can use their own apprentices for occasional farm labour in a farming enterprise that has these same monocropping tendencies.

Career trajectories back and forth from old to new skills, and from artisanship to farming, are also idiosyncratic. Idowu's occupation put him into a level of debt that only farming can get him out of. In 1978 he took an apprenticeship in tractor-driving, and then took a job in a hotel in Lagos for six months to save up the N100 needed for his licence, which then took another two months to get. Driving was irregular work because of the weather. Finally the tractor broke down and the owner could not afford to repair it because of the rapid rise in the cost of spare parts. The solution was to persuade the farmers known well to Idowu to pay for ploughing in advance, at a slightly lower rate than the one prevailing on the market. Money was raised and the tractor fixed, but the entire area they had promised to the farmers could not be ploughed before the tractor broke down again. Idowu had borrowed in his own name, and now owed the farmers N480 for the repair of a tractor that did not belong to him and no longer worked.

It is a slow process to return to a style of life in which one's immediate peers from childhood, who did not go away, are already well established, with wives, children, and a full complement of fields and budding local social careers. Only if the division of labour is intensified within the rural area will the skills that these men once learned become viable bases for making a living at home. In the meantime they are an element of volatility within the farming economy, often pursuing some eccentric explorations in cropping patterns, hunting and minor paid work, and only gradually putting together a classic farming enterprise. They are not, on the whole, returning to the countryside with the deeply negative feelings described for other parts of Africa. After all, this is a viable life, linked into the urban dynamic and not so far away that visits to town are unaffordable. But these men do return with a sense that in order to move on in their social lives they have to cycle back in their occupational lives. Given the acute sense they have of the stages of an acceptable adult life, the need to catch up probably precludes these same people ever moving out again.

There is some grey area between this pattern and full-time farming: understandably, since the youth themselves are not sure of a viable sense of direction. Their emerging style of agricultural practice does however differ in that it is commercially oriented for both inputs and products, combines ideally – in their own view – with actual or potential other sources of cash income, and seems more narrowly focused on tomatoes and cassava than the drift towards a varied speciality farming that I describe for most adult male farmers in the following chapter. In these senses it shares more with the commercial experiments of the women and mid-scale farmers, than with the immediately older or more established men, which suggests that sheer knowledge and experience in a diversified agriculture may be a relevant variable. I refer to their style provisionally as side-lining. It is quite distinct in orientation and plot/crop plan from the self-provisioning part-timing of the past.

CONCLUSION

There is a core of men in their twenties and thirties who never really considered any occupation other than farming. There is also a large proportion, at least one third, who have other training and career trajectories and many of these have returned to farming in recent years. None is as skilful a farmer or as established a member of the community as men in their forties who have farmed all their lives. Their social careers have been slowed down by about ten years in comparison with the young men who were urging their fathers to pay bridewealth and release them from service in 1968. The difference is remarkable: the late teenage/early twenties youth I knew in 1968 now have almost adult children of their own, two wives, their own houses, and run quite lavish naming ceremonies for their children, whereas their junior siblings of only a few years may have very little.

Agriculturally, two sub-groups of youth coexist: farmers and commercial sideliners. Many of the farmers are starting late, and many of the sideliners are a volatile element, still searching for the windfall that will allow them to pick up their occupations again. Market growth is a historical process, where many of those who account for successful short-run response do so on the basis of technical and social experience forged in another age. Over the longer-term, the present middle-aged, ambitious farming generation that I describe in the following chapter will be replaced by a generation with very different experience and possibly also knowledge and aspiration. Some of the aggregate patterns of change are likely to reflect not choice *per se*, but different choosers.

NOTES

1. Free primary education was instituted in the Western Region in 1955.
2. Since the female sample is partly overlapping with the male sample with respect to children (being their wives), I use only the data from the men here.
3. Thanks to Paul Richards who remembered the meaning of *panabita*.

11

THE SMALL-SCALE MALE FARMERS
IN 1988

Throughout the twenty years from 1968 to 1988, the male small-scale farmers have been the single largest group of producers in the agricultural economy. These are the farmers who by their sheer numbers account for the largest part of the increase in commercialised crops and inputs in the rural economy, who will be its anchor if the logic of small-scale production prevails in a growth economy and its backbone if economic decline pushes the region back into the periphery. They, too, have responded to the market, but not by means as dramatic as the sudden entrances of others appears to be to the outside analyst who brings a concern with the emergence of differentiation, the development of the gender division of labour or new intergenerational relations. Their own changes have been less striking. Theirs is configurational change: they do use tractors, but only up to a limit; they have shifted their cropping patterns, but in rather specific and subtle ways; farm size has grown substantially, but proportionally much more amongst two subgroups – the old part-timers of 1968 and the full-timers aged thirty to fifty – than in other categories; and so on. Their moments of maximum change and growth have also differed from the others, by what appears to be a three or four year 'lag-time' (about 1981 and 1987–88) but on closer examination is a response to specific conjunctures when the conditions were there for consolidation as well as innovation. The points of triangulation do meet at key points. The maintenance and style of diversity is at the centre of that intersection, and the major innovation that locates it is the rapid change that took place in the cassava market around 1980.

MEN'S FARMS: AN OVERVIEW

Over the past twenty years, small-scale farmers over the age of thirty have substantially expanded their farms and changed their styles of farming. There has been a rise in mean farm size from 2.9 acres per man to 4.3 acres. Modest as it may seem, growth of 40 per cent in a small-scale system still entails a whole complex of subtle shifts. As I argue in more detail below, about 25 per cent of the growth met the food consumption demands of an increased population of dependants. All the rest of the growth is due to deeper engagement with the urban food market: another 25 per cent due to occupational change as the old part-timers took up full-time agriculture, and the final and largest single component of growth stems from two spurts, in 1981–82 and in 1987–88, both of which are best seen as responses to favour-able price conditions. The first spurt depended on prior use of a new cassava variety, experiments with tractor hiring and the expansion of perishable crops in response to changes in transport. The second spurt started in 1987 and continued through the study period, dependent on the growing stream-lining of the cassava trade as the urban population's purchasing power declined and cereal imports were banned under structural adjustment.

The four sections of the chapter explore this pattern of growth. The first summarises demographic and occupational changes that have altered the supply and demand conditions within the local economy, which account for about half of the growth. The second outlines a history of agricultural and commercial conditions, highlighting the centrality of cassava in the regional market economy, and accounting for the other half. The third section ex-plores the limits on growth, and the maintenance and transformation of patterns of diversity. Finally, a section on work, incomes and styles of life suggests the motivations and implications for the producers.

DEMOGRAPHIC AND OCCUPATIONAL CHANGE

The census figures suggest that it took thirty years (1934–63) to double the Idere population from about 3,000 to 6,000, and only eighteen years (1963–81) to add another 3,000: an annual growth rate of about 2.5 per cent. The base of the population pyramid is broadening, giving higher dependency ratios. The age of child dependancy has probably risen as well, due to edu-cation. At the same time, the proportion of men in the adult age ranges who expect to provide the family diet from the farm may be slowly declining due to occupational diversification, and even the full-time farmers are buying more food than they did in the 1960s. This more complex commercial engagement of the 1980s means that the demographic changes cannot be assumed to have a direct and immediate effect on farm size. The change in the age pyramid, however, is probably great enough to contribute its own pressures towards growth. Table 11.1 shows the age pyramid from a census carried out in 1981.

A rough idea of worker/dependant ratios might be about 1:0.8 in the late 1960s, by comparison with 1:1.1 by 1981.[1] The estimate for the 1960s is bound to be a little low because we cannot estimate the child mortality rate, but all qualifications considered, it seems reasonable to work with the notion that the full-time male farmers may be supporting the food needs of between 20 and 30 per cent more dependants in the 1980s than in 1960s.

Translated into the farm area needed to feed a dependent population in kind, this amounts to increasing the self-provisioning acreage from one to about 1.3 acres, which means that about 20 per cent of total farm growth could be attributed to the increase in dependants' food needs. Other needs

Table 11.1: Age Pyramid in five-year blocks (0–20), and ten-year blocks thereafter, Idere and Surrounding Villages, 1981, and Worker/Dependant Ratio

Age	% Population	Dependants[a] and Workers[b]
0–4	13	
5–9	15	
10–14	11	
15–19	9	48[a]
20–29	16	
30–39	14	
40–49	9	
50–59	5	
60–69	4	48[b]
70 and above	4	4[a]
Total	100	Worker/Dependant Ratio = 1:1.1

Source: Brieger and Ramakrishna (n.d.)

– for clothes, school fees, apprenticeship training, medicine, transport and so on – have to be financed by cash income, so their effect on farm size works through the commercial and socio-political nexus.

Occupational change in favour of farming accounts for another fraction of total growth. As I outlined in Chapter 4, in 1968 full-time farmers averaged a farm size of 3.7 acres and the part-timers averaged 1.4 acres, that is, only about a third of the farm size of the full-timers. The 'catch-up' among part-timers has been a major change in farming patterns. Twenty-three male full-timers from 1968 survived and stayed in farming (59 per cent of the original sample of full-timers), while ten part-timers did so (53 per cent). Table 11.2 compares their farms, showing that the mean farm size of the former part-timers is now over two-thirds of farm size for the full-timers, compared to one-third in 1968. They have closed the gap while at the same time the overall mean farm size has risen. Put another way, part-timers have increased their farms by 250 per cent while the full-timers have increased by 13 per cent.

The old part-time farmers contributed a mean of 1.8 acres to the growth of mean farm size overall, so if part-timers of one sort or another were up to 20 per cent of the total male farming populations this would average to about 0.3 acres per man over the entire farming population, or about the same as the contribution of demographic growth and changes in the dependency ratio.

Table 11.2: Surviving Part- and Full-time Farmers, Comparison of Mean Farm Sizes in Acres, 1968 and 1988.

	1968	1988
Full-timers of 1968	3.8	4.3
Part-timers of 1968	1.2	3.0

Adding demographic and occupational change to one another, one might conclude that 0.7 acre or exactly half the growth in men's farms could be accounted for by demographic pressure on the worker–dependency ratio and by part-time catch-up. This is a generous estimate, to give full space to the importance placed on demographic growth in the literature on agricultural change. These two factors still leave half the farm size increase to be explored.

I suggested in the last chapter that none of the changes in farm size were accounted for by the under-thirties and the over-eighties. This leaves about 0.8 acre or about a 20 per cent increase in the farm size for the large population of full-timers to be understood in terms of the push and pull factors that adult men between the ages of 30 and 70+ engage with in the urban food market.

THE HISTORICAL PACE AND PATTERN OF GROWTH IN MEN'S FARMING

Farm size, Constraints and Opportunities

The points of growth for men do not occur at the same moments as for the other farmers. Most growth has taken place over the last ten years only, with 1981 and 1987 particularly standing out. This is quite markedly a discontinuous process of growth, for which the new resources that seem to have had such an immediate effect on women and larger scale farmers constitute enabling but not determining conditions.

Farm data and farmers' narratives help to reconstruct the decisive moments. The plots still in use in 1988 contain a cultivation history. There are three salient categories of land, given the cultural framework of a four-year rotation cycle: all fields cleared from 1984 to 1986 inclusive, that would still be in cultivation up to January 1988 when the study was done; fields cleared in 1983 and before, representing an extension of the rotation cycle; and fields cleared in 1987 when rates of clearing were greatly increased.

An analysis of the land in each of the three categories by age of farmer – under and over 50 – eliminates the possibility that there were striking age-specific differences to farmers' timing of their response to market conditions. For the two age groups, the percentages of land from different years of initial clearing that were still in cultivation at the time of study in early 1988 are almost identical. Whatever affected the timing of change, it affected both age categories at once.

These data show that one means of farm expansion has been relevant across the board, namely the extension of the length of the rotation beyond the classic four years. The rate of farm clearing in the middle years, 1984–6, is entirely consonant – at about 0.6–0.7 acres per year – with the smaller farm size of yesteryear. A regular annual clearing in this range would result in a farm of 2.6 acres, almost exactly the mean size of farms in 1968. A

Table 11.3: Total Farm Areas Cleared, by Year and Age Category of Farmer

	Under Fifty (N = 21)		Fifty and Over (N = 27)		Total	
	Acres	%	Acres	%	Acres	%
1983 and before	23.7	22	25.0	25	48.7	23
1984–86	43.8	41	45.6	44	89.4	43
1987	39.0	37	31.2	31	70.2	34
Total	106.5	100	101.8	100	208.3[a]	100

[a]Two farmers' fields, a total farm area of 7.6 acres, were measured but could not be dated; added to the total here, this gives a total of land measured in 1988 of 215.9 acres, as reported elsewhere in the text.

simple extension of the rotation alone could therefore account for a good part of farm growth, up to 1987; a four-year cycle that becomes a five-year cycle has increased its acreage by 25 per cent. In fact, for this sample, it is the tractor-cleared land rather than the hand-cleared land that is being differentially carried over into five or more years, so rotation change and tractor innovation need to work together to produce this effect. Tractor-clearing alone does not produce a simple 'extensive' expansion.

Although the *timing* of change has been similar by age of farmer, the *magnitude* of change is greater for men under fifty. The possibility that the use of tractors and hired labour are the most critical differentiating factors can be examined by looking at these data by age category over the three time periods.

As a result of doing a little more recourse to the oldest and newest (and cheapest) methods of land preparation, namely 'own work' and tractors, younger men can economise on the most expensive method, namely hired labour. The younger generation had cleared 69 per cent of their land by methods that cost less in cash (own work and tractor) whereas the older generation had cleared only 60 per cent by cheap methods. The older generation's greater recourse to hired labour over the other methods could certainly constitute part of the explanation for their smaller farms. The differences, however, are again fairly small. The only large difference between the two age groups is in how soon the under-fifty cohort experimented with tractors; the greatest difference between the two is in the proportion of old land, still in cultivation, that had been cleared initially by tractor, in the first years of the 1980s. Only two factors therefore favour the younger men since the early 1980s: their alacrity at trying new methods, and their own greater physical strength and willingness to assume heavy tasks themselves. It is still however a small margin, leaving the greater farm size in the thirty-to-fifty age group to be understood more as a function of incentives and ambitions than differential resource access. All male small-scale farmers have expanded their enterprises. The men under fifty have simply expanded more, to a level

Table 11.4: Percentage of Area Still in Cultivation in 1988, by Method and Date of Clearing.

	1983 and before	1984–86	1987	Total
Farmers Under Fifty				
Farmer	1	32	19	20
Labour	3	37	40	31
Tractor	96	31	41	49
Total	100	100	100	100
Farmers Over Fifty				
Farmer	28	13	8	15
Labour	36	40	44	40
Tractor	36	47	48	45
Total	100	100	100	100

Note: A total of nineteen acres (9 per cent of the acreage measured) was prepared by a combination of methods such as cleared by tractor and heaped by hired labour; for these cases each acreage has been divided in half between the two methods used and assigned to an unambiguous category.

much higher than the equivalent age group in 1968, and by means that reflect both an early involvement with mechanisation of land clearing and at the same time greater willingness to do their own heavy labour.

The spurt of 1987–88 is large and created by all age groups, which tends to confirm an incentive understanding of their strategies. A full 34 per cent of all land in cultivation in 1988 was cleared in 1987. To give a slightly longer time line on this sudden surge we can tabulate the farm clearing for the budget sample of nineteen male farmers, for whom all new land cleared up to the end of August 1988 was measured. Table 11.5 presents the pattern of farm growth for these men from 1983 and before up to August 1988.

This sub-set of farmers had somewhat larger farms than the total mean, even up to January 1988, but the growth in their farms is exactly the same as for the larger sample up to that time. The phenomenal growth during 1988 continued and accelerated the increased momentum that picked up in 1987. More of the new land is cleared by tractor (52 per cent in contrast with 40 per cent in 1987), but it hardly seems likely that this reflects increased tractor availability. The vehicle revolution began before 1981, and in 1987–88 owners were having a very hard time keeping their tractors going.[2] The pattern of growth suggests, rather, response to new market possibilities. Rising prices gave farmers the possibility of anticipating substantial margins if they expanded acreage and shifted cropping patterns.

To offer circumstantial support to the idea that price incentives were particularly crucial to the male farmers, I recorded local wholesale prices,[3] not giving primary credence to nominal price levels so much as to what farmers and traders said about the overall successful years (for figures and further

Table 11.5: Mean Acreage Still in Cultivation in 1988, by Year of Clearing ($N = 19$).

1983 and before	1984–6	1987	1/88–8/88	Total Mean Area, Sept. 1988
1.1	2.6	1.5	2.1	7.3

details, see Appendix B). Several people mentioned 1981: one of the *pàràkòyí* (market sales mediators) built his house in that year, and farmers bought motor cycles, mainly from the sale of cassava and egusi. Tomato sales picked up, less in price than in volume. A specialist tomato trader said they started coming to Igbo-Ọra in 1980. Yam prices, in contrast with the other crops, remained stable over the early 1980s.

In reporting their stories, the farmers and traders tended to jump straight from 1981 or so to 1987, which saw the beginning of a general price rise. In 1979, for example, according to the market traders, egusi sold at N65 per bag in the plentiful season and N75 per bag in the low season. Prices rose in 1981 and again in 1987, and by 1989 were expected to be at N200 per bag. Cassava began to sell by the pick-up in the late 1970s, at N60–70, went up in 1981–2, but was still N80 in 1986. By 1988 the price had risen to N160, N240 by 1989, and from then on there has been an even more rapid rise that takes us beyond the period of study. The same sudden lurch upwards in food prices was noted in the urban newspapers as a national 'food crisis' in early 1989 (*Newswatch*, 13 March 1989).

The farmers' responses to the 1981–82 price rise are only now discernible through the large amount of land cleared by tractor around that time, and in their purchase of goods, primarily motor cycles, houses, furniture and roofing. The response to the 1987 rise is already visible in the increase in land cleared: 1.7 acres per farmer cleared in 1987 as compared to a mean of 0.6 acres per farmer for each of the preceding three years. The budget sample increased its farm size by a mean of 2.1 acres in 1988, which involved a major cash investment: the cash cost of farm inputs stood at 38 per cent of all expenditure in 1988, where it stood at 6 per cent in 1969 and probably only at around 25–30 per cent in 1987 (see Adediran's case, later this chapter).

That price incentives should have been translated into farm size increases is not quite as obvious as it seems because land-preparation was not the labour bottleneck in 1968. Both tractors and hired labour had existed in the rural economy for a long time before they were subject to such intense demand. Changed prices gave the incentive, but also there had to be innovations in the agro-ecological pragmatics that mitigated what I had argued was the most important determinant of farm size in the past, namely the need for weeding labour. The changing organisation of the cassava economy, especially in the most recent and largest surge of farm expansion, answered several of these problems in a remarkable fashion.

Opportunities and Pragmatics in the Cassava Economy

While in all of 1968–69 and the first season of 1987, almost exactly 25 per cent of men's farms were devoted to cassava, in the second season of 1987 fully 46 per cent of the land was under cassava. Even the newly cleared plots opened up by farmers in the budget sample in 1988 had been devoted to the extent of 16 per cent to cassava as the *first* crop – a practice completely unknown in the past (Table 11.6).

The rapid rise in cassava prices from 1986 actually completed a congruence of conditions, some of which had been put down earlier, and which drew into a powerful synergistic configuration in the mid-1980s. There were four basic conditions in place before the price rise of 1987: new cassava varieties of the 1970s and 1980s; harvest by the buyers and transporters; cultivation on flat fields cleared by tractor; and the old advantage of lower weeding demand of cassava by comparison with other crops. Each depends on the history of small but significant innovations.

The cassava economy is really a twentieth-century phenomenon in Ibarapa. In the early decades of the century, farmers grew only two major varieties of cassava (*páki*): *abakókò*, which can be eaten fresh, boiled and pounded into *iyan*, like pounded yam, which is the preferred staple food; and *olowude*, which was dried and cured in the sun, for making into flour (*àmàlà páki*). Working in the dry season of 1988, I found many of the older farmers' houses had a few tubers of *olowude* on the roof or on a piece of corrugated iron in the courtyard, alongside the drying yam skins that would be used in a fairly innocuous kind of market adulteration that made cassava flour look and taste more like yam flour (*èlùbọ́ iṣu*).

There are now very many cassava varieties, defined and distinguished by many criteria, and two main modes of preparation that can be carried out year-round. The most important criteria of judgement are: whether it can be cooked fresh like yam, pounded into *iyan*, rather than requiring the soaking and drying treatment for *láfún*; the timing of maturation; and the durability in the ground.[4] All farmers grow many varieties, and always have at least some of both bitter and sweet varieties. For example *abakókò* is one of the

Table 11.6: Crops Planted on Newly Opened Land, First Season 1988, Budget Sample (*N* = 19).

	Acres	%
Tomatoes	16.4	41
Egusi	15.3	38
Cassava	6.4	16
Other	2.0	5
Total	40.1	100

oldest varieties grown for pounding fresh, and it has been superceded since about 1980 by *wolódò*, coming in from Meko in Benin, which yields much better. Nevertheless many men still grow the old variety, usually as *ilákọ*, in rows planted at ten-row intervals in plots devoted primarily to other crops. The market has been built on processed rather than fresh cassava up until very recently, so cassava production for the regional market has focused on the varieties suitable for *láfún* (flour). Varietal experiment is very dynamic. For example, *amiyáyá* was a new and relatively untried variety in 1987, usable only for processing, but quick maturing and yielding large tubers.

The single most important varietal innovation in recent times has been *odóngbó*: a *láfún/gari* cassava introduced in the 1970s. The longest growers of *odóngbó* date it from 1973, and everyone was growing it by the end of the decade, that is, well before the price rises of the early 1980s. The unique quality of *odóngbó* is that it can be harvested with good size tubers inside one year, and also can be left in the ground successfully (i.e. without becoming woody or oversoft) for very much longer. It weathers the seasons and continues to grow. People already had mature and therefore high-yielding *odóngbó* when the prices rose in 1981, and hence made windfall profits of the kind they had never seen before. One man named the motor cycle he purchased in the early 1980s Odongbo Bayin, after the *odóngbó* whose sales gave him the cash.

The next innovation was the mastery of the complete harvest: *tán* (at once, complete) rather than *dièdiè* (little by little). The old style of harvesting *dièdiè* corresponded to the very high perishability of fresh cassava. It has to be processed within twenty-four hours of digging up, so the amounts harvested have to correspond to the processing infrastructure. When specialised and partially-mechanised cassava processing developed around the cities in the mid-1980s, the *jálukere* economy could be tapped by a processor to rent a small vehicle, hire three or four workers, bargain a lump sum price with the farmer and clean-harvest a whole field in time to get the tubers into the transformation stage within a day. Farmers said that this practice began about 1985 or 1986, in other words, long after the beginning of the *jálukere* economy and the development of *odóngbó*.

What clean harvesting means to the farmer is that he can much more easily put his cassava field onto a rotation where it would be *immediately followed* by another crop. In the past, this was awkward. The only hiatus between growing seasons that was long enough to completely clear out a plot by gradual harvesting was the dry season from November to March. The ground is however so hard in the dry season that the harvest is difficult and potentially damaging to the tubers. As a result, in 1968 almost all cassava was grown as the last crop in the four-year cycle: it was weeded in that fourth year and then more or less left without cultivation, and harvested gradually until the land was left altogether. *Ilákọ* – cultivation in one out of ten rows –

was another very convenient way of augmenting cassava production under gradual harvesting, because the shade it cast was sparse enough, and the space small enough, not to interfere with whatever other rotations were to be put in place. Now, with clean, complete *tán* harvesting and *odóngbó* cassava (maturing in less than a year), the farmer could move cassava up in the rotation cycle, and plan to follow it later with another crop at any convenient moment from one year to two or even more after it was planted.

The one problem that the farmers still had difficulty controlling was that when large acreages are harvested completely there results a huge amount of work to clear away the stalks before they start rooting (given that cassava grows from stem cuttings). The hired harvesters of the *jálukere* owners do not clear up the fields themselves; they harvest and leave as quickly as possible. Inability to deal effectively with the clearing up can undo the entire advantage of being able to harvest and replant with another crop almost immediately. So the mid-scale farmers have no great advantage in cassava cultivation over the small-scale farmer, unless they can draw on a committed labour force at exactly the right moment to get the stalks from several acres cleared away quickly.

The small-scale farmers said that one acre is a good size to devote to cassava for complete harvesting, and they emphasised that no farmer would ever keep all their cassava for this mode of harvest, not only because of self-provisioning needs – which are met by *dièdiè* harvesting – but because the price is volatile enough that any careful farmer needs to have some cassava at a harvestable stage at all times. *Odóngbó* lends itself to price 'speculation' because it does not deteriorate in the ground, but farmers still mix varieties and stagger the timing of their planting because of the added commercial flexibility this offers. One of the most skilful farmers can offer an example. He has a large farm, with half an acre of three-year *odóngbó*, that he is keeping for the right price, along with plots at other stages of growth.

The third component of the new cassava economy is tractor-cleared land. The 'one acre' suggestion the farmers made about cassava for complete harvesting corresponds to the minimum area than can be tractor-cleared. Cassava can be grown on the flat, without heaps, like maize and egusi, so it participates in the new crop sequences that tractor-clearing has opened up, and is gradually moving into these larger fields. Table 11.7 summarises the situation in 1987.

Table 11.7: Percentage Hand- and Tractor-cleared Land Planted in Cassava, 1987.

	Season 1	Season 2
Hand-cleared land	30	52
Tractor-cleared land	26	43

Finally, the limited labour requirement of cassava after the first year is the long-standing factor that favors its growth. Low weeding demands and a commercial harvest operation make cassava remarkably suitable to living with the labour constraint as farm sizes are expanded.

In summary, cassava has raised its profile very considerably, due to the gradual accruing of components to what was already a favourable configuration. The possibilities of *odóngbó* casssava, accompanied by complete harvesting, contribute to the lengthening and reordering of the crop rotation, which in turn makes a measurable contribution to the increase in farm size. The overall increased importance of cassava is reflected in men's incomes. Cassava and cassava products accounted for 33 per cent of their total income in the six months covered in 1988, compared with 18 per cent for the same period in 1969. Cassava has always had the great advantage in a seasonal economy of yielding a steady week-to-week income, because of *dièdiè* harvesting (see Guyer 1972: 127, for monthly income of cassava *vis-à-vis* other crops), but it now offers lump sum income as well, due largely to the *odóngbó* variety and complete harvesting.

For the moment, however, the farming economy has not become so focused on cassava as to constitute an entirely specialised system. Only the concomitant expansion and shifts for other crops must qualify what would otherwise seem *the* decisive contribution that *odóngbó* has made to agricultural growth.

LIMITATIONS, CONTINUITIES AND THE DYNAMICS OF DIVERSITY

Farming may go into these spurts of expansion around particular crops, but what sets the limits on them when they happen? I argued from the 1968 data that the answer was weeding labour, and I still think so. Initially I thought that the fact of farm growth by 1988 had demolished my old argument: if they could expand with such alacrity, what did the upper limits I had calculated and proposed about 1968 mean? A closer look at reported weeding practices in the larger sample, days spent weeding in the budget sample and reports on the use of hired labour in weeding all suggest that a concerted combination of measures has had to be launched to cope with the larger areas under cultivation.

Farms appear on the average to be weeded less often than in the past. Farmers weeded twice per growing season in 1968, but they spoke of weeding only three times a year in 1988, and they employed young people and labourers to do much of the work. The only changes in farmers' own labour patterns between the two years of study are precisely in the increased number of days spent weeding in 1988. These three pieces of evidence taken together, along with the knowledge that much of the expanded acreage is in a crop that demands less weeding, suggest that the technical demands of weeding guinea-savanna land are very pressing and that there is a strict limit to how large a farm can be relative to the labour input, regardless of the availability and costs of means for clearing new fields or the profitability of new crops. To expand farms as far as they have been able to do, the male farmers have to address the problem of weeding labour: to shift rotations, hire the weeding out, and to some degree just neglect it. If they hire it, they have to produce the crops to support the cost. Hence the tighter commercial nexus on the larger, male farms shown in the farmers' budgets.

In brief, until there are new technical possibilities to deal with weeding, new social possibilities to produce much more cheap labour, and new sources of income from higher-value crops to finances the input costs, there are probably no returns to scale in this savanna farming system. This condition places a great premium on making crop mix work as a means of managing the market opportunities.

The diversity of farms and crops is the most complex variable, but the one where market, ecological and social forces meet most tangibly. African farming practice has been both admired and criticised for its 'diversity', but the counterposing of intercropping and monocropping, or diversity and specialisation, oversimplifies the possibilities. The combinations and permutations are far more varied and less deterministic: fortunately for life but less conveniently for analysis.

Community, individual and farm-level diversity are produced by different processes. Intensification through population pressure alone should logically reproduce diversity at the farm level, with comparable pattens from farmer to farmer, at least uniess accompanied by other forces encouraging or enforcing specialisation. In the context of a market, if each farmer specialises in his own different crop, individuals can be specialised producers while aggregating into high levels of community diversity. Conversely, individual farms can remain quite diverse but if each farmer develops the same market speciality the community comes to be seen as specialised. The development of specialist fields or field types and rotations within the repertoire should correspond with different overall logics, and indeed – given the instability of prices – people themselves are likely to be looking for strategies that retain both buffers against the market and means of profiting from it.

The data suggest that all processes are at play. In a specific way cassava is becoming a dominant crop in the regional repertoire, but otherwise the total profile of crop diversity has not changed radically. Because cassava offers a certain self-provisioning security, and now market security, each farmer and each location can afford to use it as a multi-purpose anchor while adopting a narrower-spectrum cropping pattern than in the past. There is greater focus at the individual level, and also greater difference amongst farmers, which in turn maintains community-level diversity. Farmers are becoming cassava-plus-personal-speciality producers, through three means: different weighting of the hand- and tractor-cleared options, now that their crop rotations are beginning to precipitate; pursuit of localised options for crop combinations; and individual preference.

Specialisation by Type of Field

Farmers are tending to precipitate their rotations into two types: one on hand-cleared land that is heaped (as were all fields in the past), and another on tractor-cleared land that is on the flat. The old staples of the commercial economy, maize and egusi which together accounted for 56 per cent of agricultural income in 1969 but now account for considerably less, have been maintained by concentrating them in the tractor-cleared fields, at higher crop densities. The new crop of tomatoes, that accounted for fully 24 per cent of agricultural income in 1988, was almost entirely grown on hand-cleared plots. The differentiation is not complete but it is quite striking. Table 11.8 shows the proportions of land devoted to the major crops, by type of land.

Cassava and 'other crops' are distributed more or less indifferently to type of land. For most of the other crops however there is a definite preference. The egusi/maize sequence is definitely favoured for tractor land, by a factor of almost four. Tomatoes are virtually reserved for hand-cleared plots.[5] If we couple the data on these changed rotations with the finding that tractor-cleared plots tend to be kept in cultivation longer than hand-cleared plots, we can discern two developing variations in land use. One is land intensive: farmers are keeping large plots of land in cultivation longer, increasing the crop density, adding fertiliser (to maize only), and growing the old commercial staples: egusi, maize and cassava. This pattern is also labour extensive, in that these crops require less weeding and tending. The other pattern is land extensive (shorter cultivation period, longer fallow) and very labour intensive as in the old system. It maintains old crops such as the yam cycle, peppers and vegetables, while also being devoted to the new substantial money-earner, tomatoes. Farmers have used the new possibility that tractors offer to preserve old staples of the commercial market while new

Table 11.8: Crop Complexes by Type of Land, Two Seasons 1987, $N = 49$, Percentage Total Area.

	First Season		Second Season	
	Tractor	Hand	Tractor	Hand
Cassava	26	30	43	52
Maize, egusi	46	18	30	3
Tomato	4	25	0	0
Yam/guinea-corn	10	13	13	26
Other crops	14	14	14	19
Total	100	100	100	100

money-earners in the perishable category of crops are maintained through the old style of cultivation.

Village Specialisation, by Micro-ecology

Chapter 5 described how villages had their own patterns of cultivation according to soil type, even in 1968. Table 11.9 summarises changes in village-level cropping patterns since then.[6]

Most of the changes are in the same direction, across the locations, suggesting that there are indeed general processes of homogenisation in relation to the market: egusi/maize has declined everywhere, as has millet/yam to a lesser degree, but particularly markedly in Afunije; tomato, pepper/cassava has risen everywhere, again particularly markedly in Afunije. 'All-year cassava' and 'other' seem consistently to play off against one another: where cassava has risen in importance, other crops have not held their own in the total diversity of the cropping system.

It is worth noting, however, that each location has had a characteristic *weighting* to its cropping system in both years, and for its own reasons. At the local level, this process is better termed 'weighting' than specialisation because it has no necessary progressive dynamic. It is not clearly going towards a particular end state and could, in principle, shift back again over a couple of seasons. Onileka has the highest yam acreage in both years, largely due to the suitability of the soils and its reputation as a yam-producer. Jagun has

Table 11.9: Percentage of Total Farm Acreage, by Annual Crop Sequence, Four Locations, 1968–69 and 1987.

Location	Year	Egusi/ maize	Tomato, peper cassava	Millet/ yam	Cassava all year[a]	Other	Total
Idere	1968	38	3	26	24	9	100
	1987	29	16	20	24	11	100
	Difference	−9	+13	−6	0	+2	
Jagun	1968	38	0	23	22	17	100
	1987	33	16	9	37	5	100
	Difference	−5	+16	−14	+15	−12	
Onileka	1968	29	0	36	24	12	100
	1987	20	13	26	15	26	100
	Difference	−9	+13	−10	−9	+14	
Afunije	1968	52	1	11	27	9	100
	1987	12	48	8	28	4	100
	Difference	−40	+47	−3	+1	−5	

[a] The acreage of cassava for the lower of the two seasons, the difference between the two being assimilated to the tomato/pepper rotation (on the assumption that the increment is newly planted that year).

brought egusi/maize and cassava into greater prominence than any other place, largely because the higher incomes these farmers get from cocoa in October to January allow them to put a lot of their arable acreage into tractor-farming, a mode of land preparation that on the economic side requires cash on the barrel, and on the agro-ecological side is more suited to crops such as egusi, maize and cassava that do as well on the flat as on heaps. Afunije, with poor tractor access due to the rocky nature of the site as well as seasonal income factors, has more or less switched out of these same crops and into highly labour intensive tomato production using wage labour for land preparation.

General changes have not, then, homogenised the micro-ecological variations. Sub-groups do differ. One very important factor here is the asset of having a reputation that will attract the *jálukere*-buyers to their villages. As the transport network is opened up and buyers and transporters increasingly purchase in the villages rather than the wholesale markets, a reputation for bulk and quality in a particular crop may be a critical asset for a village to develop. The names of places are used all the time by buyers and sellers alike in a mental map of the urban hinterland that reflects niches of organisation and concentration, laid over the baseline conditions of accessibility that define the classic rings of market orientation. As the change in cropping patterns in the villages shows, the historical process of local concentration on a narrow spectrum of crops is not only shaped by ecological suitability; it reflects a collective investment in reputation.

Individual Preferences

How great is purely individual variation in cropping pattern and with respect to which crops does it show up? The simplest way to measure diversity as a personal strategy is to tabulate the proportion of male farmers who grew each major crop in the two study years. Table 11.10 represents this.

The most striking conclusion to be drawn from this table is that in 1968 each farmer was growing most of the major staples of the provisioning and market economies: egusi, cassava, maize and yams, plus the heterogeneous category of 'other crops'. For five crops, more than 60 per cent of the farmers had fields devoted to them in 1968. By 1987 this was quite dramatically not the case. More farmers were growing tomatoes – a crop destined entirely for the market – than were growing egusi, maize or yams. Cassava was the lone crop grown by more than 60 per cent of farmers. In 1968–69, 56 per cent of farmers grew *all* the staples. In 1987 only 20 per cent of farmers grew all of the major staples, and these were all considered consummate full-time farmers, with large farms. We might call this change a shift from broad-spectrum to narrow-spectrum farming, a process of concentration where the certainty of cassava is allowing farmers the leeway to develop quite idiosyncratic preferences with respect to their other crops.

Table 11.10: Percentage of Male Small-scale Farmers Growing Each Major Crop, 1968–69 ($N = 66$) and 1987 ($N = 50$).

Year	Egusi[a]	Cassava[b]	Maize	Guinea-corn /yam	Tomato	Pepper	Other
1968–69	100	81	87	75	21	21	62
1987	40	100	52	54	58	34	52

[a] For 1968–69 this proportion has to be based on the budget sub-sample. It is probably somewhat high, but not excessively since many of these same farmers have been the ones to give up egusi since then.
[b] This refers to fields devoted primarily to cassava. Everyone had cassava planted at intervals in other fields, as ilàkọ. This proportion is also probably slightly under-stated for the reason that farmers were still practising cassava cultivation as the last crop in the cycle in 1968, so some very bushy, partly harvested fields of cassava were not measured.

This kind of shift in individual farm plans must surely reflect consumption as well as production: a varied diet is now no longer planned for and guaranteed through self-provisioning, at least by individual male farmers. In fact, their budgets show that more food is now purchased: 27 per cent of expenditures devoted by men to food and minor household needs in 1988, as against 13 per cent in 1969.

'Diversity' in Aggregate Cropping Patterns for the Entire Community

Aggregated cropping patterns have been looked at briefly earlier, but the question here is whether they show less diversity in 1988 than in 1968–69. In fact, the overal pattern of crop diversity by acreage has changed considerably less than individual farmers' strategies, as Table 11.11 shows.

As shown already, cassava took a leap forward in the second season of 1987 but has otherwise remained a fairly stable component of the cropping system. The other changes are all probably accurately estimated at under 10 per cent: the millet/yam sequence down a little, peppers up a little, 'other crops' up a little. There is movement in this cropping system but the pattern of variety has changed very little over the twenty years of growth. We can look at the aggregate pattern of diversity in another way by looking at the sources of farmers' income (see Table 11.12).[7]

Egusi was sold later in the year in 1988, so the income from that crop is under-represented, but taking into account that the income from egusi sales would eventually be very substantial in 1988, there is probably a real emphasis towards cassava in farmers' incomes, as we see also in their fields. Otherwise, in 1969 three other crops (including 'other' as one category) and in 1988 four (including egusi, and again 'other') contribute between 10 and 25 per cent of total income. This pattern of income diversity seems very little different from 1969, even though the crops that constitute it differ in some

Table 11.11: Changes in Cropping Patterns, 1968–69 and 1987, as Percentage of Total Cropped Acreage, Men's Farms.

Crop[a]	Season A		Season B	
	1969	1987	1968	1987
Cassava	28	24	23	43
Maize	8	4	34	13
Egusi	41	23	1	3
Millet/yam	19	9	24	17
Tomatoes	0	11	1	1
Peppers	1	2	0	3
Other	4	15	14	16
Not planted[b]	0	12	3	4
Total	100	100	100	100
Total acreage	56.0	215.8	167.6	215.8

[a] Intercropping for two crops has been accounted for by dividing the acreage and assigning half to each crop. Further nuances – three crops in one plot, small corners with variations – have been dropped out for present purposes.

[b] This category contains areas already newly cleared but awaiting planting, and a very few fields just left for the season. It reflects the organic scheduling of a long growing season, not mistakes or failures.

respects. The two inferences are, I believe, related in that cassava – as a commercial crop – now constitutes a bedrock to other market experiments for individual farmers with their own specialities within the continuing diversity of the collective crop repertoire.

This crop diversity is not primarily a defensive coping strategy. The need to pace cash income over the weeks and months is often given as one economic reason for crop diversity, but here the seasonal income peak is more marked in 1988 than in 1969. Incomes in 1969 were kept quite smoothed from month to month by the sales of several crops on different harvesting and storage schedules. The lowest two months, March and April, yielded fully two-thirds the level of the income gained in the highest two months, July and August. In 1988 the trough of April was lower and the peak of

Table 11.12: Crops as Percentage of Total Income: 14 Male Farmers 1969, 19 Male Farmers 1988, Six Months, March–August.

	1969	1988
Cassava	18	35
Maize	31	1
Egusi	25	3
Yams	4	4
Guinea-corn	5	2
Tomatoes	1	27
Other arable crops	15	16
Tree crops	1	12
Total arable crops	100	100

August higher. People must be far enough from the subsistence minimum to opt for more fluctuating incomes, even though the ecology would allow more even income distribution if they wished.

Diversity in marketable crops is possible where the market demands a variety of crops whose relative prices are always fluctuating. As we see, however, the picture of diversity here is more convincing for the community than for the individual farmer, whereas it is the individual who is thought of as the risk-taking agent in theories of risk-management (for an exception, see Udry 1990). Unless, therefore, there is a community policy to preserve diversity, Idere's persisting aggregate pattern of crop diversity cannot be explained in terms solely of individuals' rational adaption to risk. There must be some other process that explains the coexistence of personal innovation and collective conservatism about crop diversity.

The importance of preference was clearly present in farmers' own descriptions. The Cherubim and Seraphim pastor was the only man still growing an old variety of cassava that he liked; there were several farmers specialising in indigenous tobacco; an older man produced large quantities of vegetable seed to sell to urban gardners; a returnee from Lagos was the only one producing a large crop of cowpeas; there was one major producer of tangerines (see below); one farmer gave part of his *okógbó* (forest farm) over to *ewura* (water yam), which is not a kind that can be pounded and is not very highly regarded even though the tubers can grow very large; and farmers seemed divided simply by temperament and preference over whether they found the management of the women's egusi-harvesting teams to be unnecessary trouble and therefore a reason to give up egusi production altogether, or simply a customary peak of activity.

It is people's *interest* that maintains the search for possibilities, sources of change and experimentation. Farmers do not necessarily follow similar market-based calculations to each other, but rather apply the collective repertoire to their own situations. The critical importance of personal interest is that it more or less guarantees to keep the crop repertoire large and a variety of planting stock available. Without a pervasive market in planting material, the flexibility of the whole system depends very critically on this process. The social complementarity that underlies the Yoruba division of occupational labour, and which I turn to in the final chapter, seems reflected in the growing practice, within farming itself, of collective diversity.

SOME EXAMPLES OF FARM ORGANISATION

As a final illustration of changes in farm size and farm practice I describe the farming of particular successful men. The first is an elderly expert from 1968, the second, a diversified farmer of the next younger generation, the third has more clearly 'weighted' his farm practice to leading crops, and the last has moved into a more fully specialised style of production.

Adediran

In 1968 Adediran was fifty-five years old working 5.8 acres together with his twenty-year-old son. Now seventy-five, he is a chief in the town hierarchy and working 6.6 acres with hired labour. He has been in public life on and off for thirty years, having been a local government councillor in the first elections of 1956. Experience in government gave him connections beyond the town and encouraged an outward-looking set of interests. Although his complex farm was in almost exactly the same location in 1988 as it used to be, he had been through a series of experiments since then, including NTC tobacco farming and the ownership and lease of a tractor.

In 1988 he had basically three parts to his farm: the tractor plots for egusi and maize (three acres), some old plots for long-growing crops such as second-year cassava and pigeon peas (about two acres), and a set of plots totalling about one-and-a-half acres for yams, tomatoes, new cassava and a variety of other crops. Just under four acres were originally cleared by tractor and the rest by hired labour. None of his farm is cleared by himself, but he does still do weeding and other tasks, mostly with the help of a young grandson whose father – his own son – died. The child finished Primary 6 but did not seem destined by temperament to further education.

On their eleven plots, there were twenty-six weedings during 1987 (not including tasks such as re-heaping and harvesting which sometimes incorporate weeding). He did five of them alone, and twelve with his grandson, or occasionally with other children or grandchildren. The other nine weedings were done by labourers at a total cost of N419. The total number of weedings is well under the three per plot per year that was the absolute minimum in 1968, suggesting a savings by changed rotations and possibly by reduction of standards of at least 20 per cent. Self-employed labour accounted for 4.3 acres-equivalent of weeding: close to the mean farm size of full-time farmers in 1968. Much of the hired labour in weeding was devoted to the large tractor-cleared plots. The one-acre minimum for tractor clearing makes for a huge area to weed all at once, and thereby enforces a discouragingly routine work style for men who are accustomed to the varied work rhythms of the past, and who must be available at any time for administrative duties in local social life.

The clearing and weeding labour means that the costs of production are high relative to Adediran's income and obligations, and he expresses concern about the constant need for money. He is gradually buying blocks to add to his house which is too crowded. Every man should have a room alone with his wife but family growth has outstripped the space they have. Being a chief, he says that people are constantly asking him for money, food, drinks and so on. His income, however, is not particularly low. He planted egusi-melon and tomatoes throughout his largest, tractor-cleared field and harvested enough to clear about N1,200 from these two crops alone, even though the weather was bad and even though certain amounts were given to the harvesters and kept for eating. After the egusi he planted maize, fertilised it for N200 and harvested enough to clear about N500 at the prevailing market price. The rest of his farm did much more poorly because of the erratic rainfall, but they had plenty of yam, cassava and vegetables to eat, and by no means everything had been sold by January of the following year. The cash income he mentioned added up to well over N2,000, which is certainly considerably lower than he would ultimately realise from that year's work. Cash costs of production, however, cut deeply into this income: N420 for weeding, N200 for fertiliser, N60 for opening up an acre of new land by tractor and N160 for hired labour to clear and heap another, for a total new acreage of 1.7. Running costs were then about onethird of his cash income.

Adediran's farm illustrates all the major points about the growth in farm size amongst the established farmers. All ages of farmer responded to the possibility and needs for growth, although for the older men the proportional farm size increase was less than for those in the mid-years. The pattern of growth over time was not incremental, but rather involved spurts when fairly large areas were added. Size increase brought new costs of production that had to be financed in cash, because farmers were already close to the limits of an acceptable labour regime. Crop rotations were shifted, aimed at making more money out of the land. The ambitions and needs of a public career are the rationale for growth and change.

Başiru

Başiru is a practitioner of his compound's traditional occupation of facial scarification and circumcision, and has no other marketable skill. Although he says that farming is a burden, his own farm is over ten acres and he has always been a committed and successful farmer. After a few years of trying life in several farming villages he started a cocoa farm in 1968 and moved to live near it in 1976. Since then, he and his junior brother built their own house in town fifteen years ago when he was about thirty years old. He purchased a motor cycle several years ago when prices were accessible, and uses it to travel to and from the three sets of food plots, plus a cocoa farm, in different places, that make up his farm. In the early 1980s he started to hire a tractor to clear land, ambitiously opening up five acres all at once to grow maize and egusi. The other two areas were cleared by hired labour, and far more of his weeding is done by labourers than most other farmers. His use of labourers allows him to maintain a full variety of crops, even those that are labour intensive, by contrast to several of the other farmers with large areas who essentially started to farm less labour intensively on certain plots of their land in order to support the acreage. Even with hired labour, Başiru's own work was devoted largely to weeding, since he had crops such as yams and tomatoes that demanded care. Otherwise, he regularly prepared cassava flour (*láfún*) for market, earning a very substantial income – about 80 per cent of his six months of agricultural income in 1988 – from this source.

Başiru supported his eight children with this income, including two in secondary school, at the total cost of N240 in fees per year, plus the various development funds and contributions. He said that his entire income was taken up with life cycle ceremonies, including two naming ceremonies costing a total of N900 for children born to him in 1987, school fees, medical expenses and the cost of hired labour. In fact, according to his budget, maintenance for his motor cycle and expenses on food were also high.

Başiru's case gives a sense of the kind of incentives that have drawn out the peak of response from men in their forties. This is the cohort whose children have arrived at secondary school age at a moment when school fees have been reintroduced and medical costs have gone up. For the first time, raising and educating children drives production, and it affects primarily this age group: a group already committed to farming as their prime occupation by virtue of limited formal education levels in their own early youth and no training in artisanship.

Sunday

Sunday's farm is 7.7 acres, of which five were cleared by tractor in a single season in 1984. The size was a challenge to maintain, so he eventually planted about four acres in pigeon peas, a crop which can support some weeding neglect, lasts two years and is a nitrogen fixer. Unlike many others, he has only just over an acre in cassava and considers himself more oriented towards the labour intensive production of peppers, okra, tomatoes and leaf vegetables. He was one of the very few who had a significant plot of okra for the market, as distinct from having small patches for food and petty local sales. He has a motor cycle, so can envisage the farm-to-trader rapid transport that this demands. His children are too young to require school fees, and his ambitions of the moment include enjoying himself on a flexible time schedule, hence the combination of large plots in low-labour crops plus a small area under a labour-demanding regime, being worked in intensive spurts.

Adedigba

Adedigba had taken specialisation to a different level, after the pattern of cocoa production. He turned nine acres of old cocoa into a tangerine farm. It happened by chance rather than design. He liked tangerines, so he planted a few trees to provide fruit for himself, during farm work. In about 1980 he took a few to market, and people rushed to buy, so he extended his acreage until most of the farm is now an orchard.

The trees are quite wide apart, so he used to be able to plant maize between the rows and now plants some cassava to provide the basic staple of the family diet. Other crops are planted here and there, and he has a plot of yams that are used primarily for feeding the workers who pick the fruit. He has a regular relationship with a buyer. At certain moments in the year, the two of them inspect the yield of each tree in turn, and fix a price for its near-ripe fruit per *igba* (200) which is symbolised by a piece of a leaf, and the leaves are then grouped into categories and the total computed. The advantage of citrus over cocoa is that it fruits for longer.

Adedigba is still fairly young, but with a long interruption in his family career. He has had several personal tragedies – widowerhood, divorce, a health problem with a child – so the whole enterprise is part of personal re-establishment rather than ambition. He can support his youngest child, with a new wife and the children she brought with her to the marriage, while also sending money to an adult daughter learning nursing in Lagos.

INTEREST AND INCENTIVE IN GROWTH AND COMMERCIALISATION: SOME EXPLORATIONS

Congruences of possibilities and forces do not explain people's actions; there also have to be reasons. Only occasionally, when new crops, new techniques or new protectionist measures are introduced, is it possible to make higher incomes in small-scale agriculture without one category of the population or another having to work considerably harder than they are accustomed to do. Classic theories assume a human nature that balks at increasing the work load and will do so usually only under pressure: the pressure of declining living standards due to rising population densities in Boserup's formulation; the pressure of political forces (including rent and taxes) in the Marxist formulation; the pressures of rising costs for near-necessities in an extrapolation of Chayanov's theory of peasant economy. By contrast, many of the theories of West African economic change rest on the assumption of rising aspirations to be met through money income and organised by reallocation of underused resources: the vent-for-surplus theory, Polly Hill's 'rural capitalism' (1970), A. G. Hopkins's 'open economy' (1973), Belasco's 'entrepreneur as culture hero' (1980).

The inference of motivations for the kind of modest growth we are dealing with here is a particularly fraught problem in the literature. Against the yardsticks from theory, these changes are all very ambiguous: some lengthening of the crop cycle but no signs of elimination of fallow, certain kinds of specialisation and not others, commercialisation of inputs but without a debt trap or reproduction squeeze, and with rising costs of consumption as both carrot and stick to increased effort. At one point people are trying to build houses, at another to compete for titles and at yet another to educate their children. Their farms will reflect who is willing, and with how much effort, to foot these particular bills, and the technical and economic resources of the time that they can mobilise. Nevertheless, aspirations seem to me central to explaining change.

Table 11.13: Male Farmers' Six-month Mean Income, March–August, 1969 and 1988

Income	Agricultural Products	Other	Total
1969 (Pennies)	5,808	1,815	7,623
1988 (Kobo)	121,681	9,310	130,991
1988 in real 'pennies'	7,605	582	8,187
Percentage change	+31	−68	+7

That aspirations rather than pressures shape production patterns, even in a poor population such as this, is circumstantially supported by their income and expenditure patterns over time. The official price indices for the urban markets offer the possibility of establishing the ratio of purchasing power between the penny of 1969 and the kobo of late 1986 (the latest available figures at the time of study). For food products it is 1:16, for manufactured products it was slightly lower (1:11), but given the structural adjustment conditions the 1:16 ratio seems adequate for gaining a general sense of real incomes (see Appendix B for detailed sources). Table 11.13 expresses the farmers' incomes by major categories in the two years.

By these criteria agricultural incomes in 1988 were 31 per cent higher in real terms than in 1968.[8] Total incomes – in which I place a little less confidence – come out only 7 per cent higher in 1988, reflecting the change in people's incomes from the part-time practice of other occupations such as hunting, drumming, house repair and trade. Remittances are clearly more important in 1988 than 1968, but came in on a very irregular basis, for such expenses as hooking up to the new electricity system. Urban kin did not send regular cash contributions; rather the farmers were sending bags of food to kin in the cities.

The conclusion that these farmers are one-third better off in real terms from their agricultural work needs to be qualified by the increased costs of production. In 1988, farmers spent a great deal more in inputs than in 1968.[9] Table 11.14 shows that the cost of inputs reduces the margin of real income increase to 20 per cent, or perhaps – with egusi – 25 per cent.

There has been, then, some growth in real income from farming. Male farmers have not been working entirely under price pressures that may encourage growth in output but leave the producers in exactly the same situa-

Table 11.14: Mean Agricultural Income, Input Costs and Net Income, Male Farmers 1969 and 1988, expressed in 1968 pennies

	Mean Agricultural Income	Input Costs	Net Income
1969	5,808	443	5,365
1988	7,605	1,125	6,480
Net margin		+1,115, or 21 per cent	

tion. Living standards and aspirations have also risen a small notch, to the tune of somewhere around 20 per cent. This is not very much, especially in the context of a rise in the dependency rate, due to population growth and later schooling. But it does distinguish the experience of these farmers from the downward ratchet of the 'simple reproduction squeeze' where assets have to be surrrendered in return for subsistence goods. Total incomes exceeded expenditures over the budget period in both years: they 'saved' 4 per cent in 1969 and a net margin, after costs, of 15 per cent of agricultural income in 1988.[10]

Some of these calculations of margins and savings become fraught with error. Their only purpose here is to show that in both years farmers were not generally in debt beyond their incomes nor limited in their expenditures to the simple basic necessities of food, clothing and shelter. On the other hand, and in spite of a higher level of managerial input and commercial engagement, they are certainly no more than 15–20 per cent better off in 1988 than in 1969. Given the magnitude of the changes in the larger national and regional economy, this is a positive but extremely modest share.

To what has increased income been devoted? What might constitute the incentives and benefits of increased production? In Table 11.15 I have grouped expenditures into large categories as well as into their constituent parts.

These budgets show some striking changes: an increase in cash income devoted to living expenses and farm inputs, and a very marked decline in the proportion devoted to ceremonial obligations and participation. If we are searching for incentives to income-earning they lie more plausibly in social ambitions in 1968, as I argued then, and in family welfare and investment in children in 1988.

We can note here how neatly consonant these findings are with the increased prominence of the thirty-to-fifty age group. These are the men with the largest family costs to take care of, whereas in the past it was the next older group of men who were seeking and enjoying social prominence. That is, it is changes in society that underlie the changes in farmers' cash economies, and not a simple individual price responsiveness across the board nor a cohort-specific innovation by youth.

One final analysis buttresses the inference that socially and culturally embedded values drive the level of expansion that has taken place. When we look at the labour data it is surprising how few extra days these men are putting into farming than they did twenty years ago. Of course, they are hiring more labour, but it is very striking how similar farmers' work diaries have remained across twenty years (see Guyer 1992). These men are working larger farms, investing much more cash in farming, altering the emphasis on the crops, shifting the rotations, earning slightly higher real incomes, and still not changing their own work-times nor the time devoted to social and political life.

Table 11.15: Male Farmers' Expenditures by Category, Percent of Total, 1969 and 1988, Six Months.

	1969	1988
Living		
Food, household	13	27
Clothes	9	2
Building	10	1
Medical	1	7
School	8	12
Travel	2	7
Other	3	1
Total	46	57
Producing		
Farm inputs	2	1
Hired labour[a]	4	4
Tractor	0	14
Total	6	19
Social Being		
Ceremonies and gifts	35	15
Associations	5	4
Credit associations	8	5
Total	48	24
Total	100	100

[a] Note that labour debts incurred but not paid over the period of study are not included for either year, although the data are discussed elswhere.

At this point we reach the limits of all arguments based exclusively on the structure of opportunities and constraints for individual producers. The social and cultural life that people are creating is in part the legacy and infrastructure to the present situation in production, and in part the incentive to the productive process, as I take up in Chapter 13.

CONCLUSION

The small-scale male farmers have not been edged out by the more dramatic activities of the other participants in the rural economy, bursting in with new agendas. They have followed their own pattern of growth and change, with its own moments of expansion. The logic of change corresponds to expectations of urban market dynamics: increasing commercialisation of both production and consumption, larger farms, more of the population farming, more production of perishable crops and sale of storable crops in perishable forms. The particular shape of change is less predictable. The lifting of specific production bottlenecks elicited the rapid emergence of new participants in the farming population, whereas the established male farmers responded to favourable movements in market prices.

The most striking finding is the development of personal and village-level narrow spectrum farming at the same time as the overall pattern of crop diversity has changed little. This variability is not an expression of social structure in the conventional sense of constraints on access to resources. Neither is it clearly a form of coping with risk. People were not poorer over-all, nor very much more pressured, in 1988 than they were in 1968, and in any case subsistence needs did not dominate farm plans. My original posi-tion was that farm practice lies on the intersection of personal careers and market conditions. Rephrased now to mitigate the structural understanding I had then of personal careers, I argue that farming style reflects a more emergent social organisation of identity and prominence. Preference and reputation are marking people's productive practice in a way that corre-sponds to the occupational diversity of the past, builds from the old strengths of the savanna agro-ecology in varietal management, and meshes with the naming and niche-making that we have seen on the part of new participants in the rural economy. It is, however, an incipient change, not fully developed. Just as there are categories of newcomers who have not yet established a space in the moral and organisational economy, there are pat-terns of cultivation amongst the established farmers that show only marked tendencies without yet developing the clarity that identifying and naming would confer. At the outer edge of this development are a few real specialists – tobacco farmers, a tangerine producer, a vegetable-seed grower – whose reputations bring the benefit of links to specific market networks.

If the commercial side of the Ibarapa farm economy – as distinct from the individual farmer – does specialise further, it seems unlikely that it will occur through the small farmer. This is not primarily because these are generic peasants who aim to cover subsistence requirements or hedge against risk, but because their patterns of commercialisation take the form of concentra-tion and niche development rather than an increasingly exclusive regional specialisation. It is a deeply commercial framework, predicated on the as-sumption of a market, responsive to comparative prices, competitive in the formal sense and contentious in the socio-cultural sense. The performance of the farmers, however, is at the centre of the culture and practice of pro-duction, rather than the performance of resources such as land or capital.

This chapter has explored the market response of the central operators in a farm economy that is commercial without being capitalist, even while its dynamics link into and confront the capitalist market. After a fuller discus-sion of the local ecological and collective institutional nexus that underpins its rationalities in the following two chapters, the final chapter recapitulates what I see as its basic principles.

NOTES

1. Accurate comparison with 1968 is vitiated by the lack of age data for that year, but one can take the population that was aged fifteen to thirty-five in 1981 to

indicate the dependant children of 1968, and assume a similar survival rate at sixty and above in both years, to estimate a dependency ratio.

2. It is possible that in 1987–88 tractor use was a kind of 'advance purchase' against predicted future scarcity under the ever-deepening problems of imported goods under structural adjustment, a kind of 'hoarding'; but this is speculation.

3. Official prices are of very limited utility for figuring out the advantageous years for local farmers because they report urban prices, and do so in a manner that is not very reliable over short time periods. Local market prices are affected by the weather and the season as well as by changes in the terms of trade for farmers.

4. Peter Ay, working around Oyo, found eleven old varieties and seven new ones. Their names reflect origin and conditions of adoption: Gold Coast, idileruwa (from Eruwa), rogo (a 'Hausa' variety), and IITA (International Institute of Tropical Agriculture), which is a variety known in Ibarapa as texaco because it came from the Texaco plantation. Varieties have come from the Agatu and from Benin with the workers.

5. The pattern becomes even clearer from the plot histories. Egusi grows best in the first season of the year; it is often planted on tractor plots, followed by maize in the second season which is sometimes fertilised and interplanted with cassava. In the second year cassava takes over entirely. With complete harvesting of the cassava about eighteen months from planting, the whole cycle can start again, making an alternating two-year pattern over four, six or even eight years. The hand-cleared and heaped fields are then largely devoted to crops that do very much better on heaps and at the old standard crop densities.

6. The crop data are simplified to reduce their complexity; rather than report each season separately, I assimilate the two seasons of the annual cycle into five typical single year sequences: egusi and maize, tomato/pepper and cassava; millet and yam; all year cassava; and 'other'. The percentage of land devoted to each set of crops in each season has then been calculated and a simple mean taken. For example, in one village 18 per cent of land was under egusi and 4 per cent under maize in the first season of 1987 (total of 22 per cent) and none under egusi and 19 per cent under maize in the second season (19 per cent); a simple mean for that 'crop sequence' for the entire year is reported as 20.5 per cent (rounded to 20 per cent). This annual figure offers a basis for very simple inferences about shifts in the cropping system.

7. I have one fairly serious problem with the comparison of these income figures, namely that the planting date of egusi was very late in 1988 so the harvest was not sold during the study period. We can however at least get some sense of different crops as sources of agricultural income, at a community/aggregated level, in 1969 and 1988.

8. As I mentioned above, I believe this margin is lowered by the omission of egusi sales for 1988, due to the change in planting times. Given that egusi is still an important commercial crop the margin is more realistically about 35 per cent, and may be more.

9. N180 in cash on farm inputs, tractors and farm labour, and they also incurred labour debts to be paid at the end of the season. (These are not included in the calculations for either 1969 or 1988.) This is 180,000 kobo or the equivalent of 1,125 real pennies, whereas in 1968 farmers only spent 443 pennies on labour and inputs (see Guyer 1972: 132).

10. The gross margin was 45 per cent in 1988. The amount saved over this first season in both years has to finance labour costs paid in October. If we subtract this very substantial amount (N267 per farmer in 1988) we still end up with a positive margin for for that season of N137 or 15 per cent.

PART III
SYNERGIES

12

'EVERYBODY'S FARMING NOW': AGRO-ECOLOGY IN THE LATE 1980s

By the mid-1980s a crescendo of activity was building up in Ibarapa farming. The full-time, male, small-scale farmers who were just beginning a phase of expansion in the 1960s had been joined by contract farming, migrant labourers, mid-scale farmers, agribusiness, a new generation of youth, the old part-timers and women. Their own farms had expanded and there were a few people moving out against the frontier, activating ancient claims in old towns in the distant savanna to the north, or acquiring cocoa plots in newly accessible forest patches. Some enterprises, however, were quite vulnerable: by 1988 the Texagri cassava plantation had closed, the Temperance poultry farm was no longer at full capacity, the Nigerian Tobacco Company still only had a handful of dedicated members after the decline of the late 1970s, and some of the women's farms were small and only intermittently planted or tended. The decline of the naira kept the Beninois and Togolese labourers at home, and the fleet of tractors and market vehicles was being held together by sheer ingenuity. Yet the period from mid-1987 to the time I left in mid-1988 was an era of farm expansion. The men opened up unprecedented areas, there were constant rumours about this or that outside concern trying to acquire land, and I ran into a former local government official who had been appointed to Ibarapa under military rule as he toured his new farm site in an area north of Aiyeṭe. There was a sense of turbulence: land law being created with little sense of how any measure would be actionable in court; cropping experiments being launched with vague plans for marketing; unprecedented prices paid for labour without a sense of what the produce prices would be later in the year to pay for it; and an advancing horizon to the costs of bringing children into the world and bringing them up adequately, entailing a rapid decline in deliveries at the maternity and perhaps – the midwife said – in births in general. Men in their thirties were not yet married, and many youth shuttled back and forth between Lagos and the home town. Local school-boys and girls looked for weeding jobs to earn enough money to stay in school, and buy uniforms and shoes. House-building and repair, and investment in concrete pits for cassava-soaking, had slowed down to a very low level. The entire society and economy was reconfiguring around the conditions of structural adjustment. '*Kò s'ówó!*': 'There's no money', was the ubiquitous explanation.

One argument implicit so far has been that there is very substantial elasticity in Ibarapa farming. Some innovations and shifts of emphasis have occurred quickly and could disappear just as quickly, without trace, like cotton in the early 1960s. At the same time there is a certain coherence to the frontiers as they have developed over the past twenty years. They rest on locational, social structural and ecological dynamics that are recognisable and interrelated. Each category of farmer is following its own social and ecological logic within an available repertoire, and developing the repertoire further, in relation to the social, economic and material activities of the others. The ecological synergies are explored in the present chapter because they set certain parameters around interpretation of the social syngergies that are addressed in the following one.

The population to farmland ratio reveals whether there is room for all these different people to continue their style of growth into the foreseeable future. Can all these participants be accommodated on the land available, or are they headed by sheer land shortage alone into one of the intensification scenarios: technical innovation in agriculture, the development of complementary occupations, dispossession by the powerful or multiple and enervating conflicts? Whether any of these is on the horizon depends ultimately on the space that is physically and socially available.

THE FARMING POPULATION AND AVAILABLE LAND

Idere's population doubled from 3,000 to 6,000 between the 1930s and the 1960s, and then doubled again by the end of the 1980s. In his official report in 1934 , Childs enumerated the population at 2,929 (1934: 23). A census carried out in 1963 put the town population at 5,300 and the village population – almost certainly under-enumerated – at 395 (Ogunlesi and Barber 1965: 176). By 1981 the total population was 10,758, of which exactly three-quarters lived in town and one-quarter in the villages (Brieger and Ramakrishna n.d.).

A study done in the late 1970s concluded from complex calculations of population, techniques, topography and soil types that Ibarapa was approaching a threshold of land scarcity: 'land shortage will begin to assert itself as a serious constraint on traditional hoe cultivation during the late 1970s and early 1980s' (Daly et al. 1981: 24). Since then, farms have expanded and more people are farming, but the deluge of land disputes that one might have expected has not yet struck and there are no obvious signs of the neo-Malthusian situation of declining yields. There certainly are oppositions, disagreements and some antagonism towards the largest corporate farms, but many requests for plots are still met with acceptance and even strangers can hope eventually to get a small piece of land somewhere. Farm labourers are getting some as well, partly as a concession to keep them coming back. Judging this situation is tricky. The ecology could be slowly and imperceptibly deteriorating, or alternatively, all the small innovations could be expanding carrying capacity. Possibly the original projection was based on over-pessimistic assumptions. With this kind of complexity of 'small change', it can be beyond feasibility to make a general and regional interpretation from partial information gained on the ground.

Remote sensing techniques vastly simplify establishing some basic estimations of carrying capacity because few assumptions are needed and the data are comprehensive across an entire area. Rather than starting from the parameters of the micro-level and projecting them onto a larger terrrain, remote sensing allows land use in the larger terrain itself to be described independently of estimates of production and population that have been built up from the ground. This means that inference of a 10 per cent (for example) margin for expansion or a 10 per cent over-extension beyond the threshold of long-term viability is much less likely to fall within the range of estimation error than would be the case if the inferences were drawn from ground-level measures. Remote sensing data can also help to verify the representativeness of the inevitably small and non-random ethnographic sample, since some variables can be matched across the two studies. These two advantages together greatly strengthen confidence in a larger interpretation of the ecological synergies.

The remote sensing data were collected in December 1987, just before my fieldwork began in January 1988.[1]

Land Use Dynamics

Six classes of land were discriminated: cultivated land, cleared land, granite outcrops, bottoms of valleys, savanna and dense vegetation. The class 'cleared land' includes fields but also some recent fallows and bare soils around towns or in eroded zones. The class 'bottoms of valleys' is characterised by a high soil moisture. The class 'savanna' includes fallow land with natural vegetation cover as well as never-cultivated land. Finally, dense vegetation includes forest, heavily wooded savanna, and cocoa plantations.

The relative proportions for the area of the image (surroundings of Idere) are shown in Table 12.1.

Table 12.1: Proportions of Total Land Area, by Type, Idere, December 1987, SPOT Data

Type of Land	Percentage
Cultivated land	11.6
Cleared land	7.6
Granite outcrops	6.9
Bottoms of valleys	23.9
Savanna	40.2
Dense vegetation	9.8
Total	100.0

Table 12.2: Aggregation of Land Use Categories

Land occupied by human activities	
(currently cultivated or cleared for other purposes)	19.2%
Land which offers a potential for the expansion of agriculture	
(savanna and forest, includes fallow)	50.0%
Land marginal for cultivation	
(rocky outcrops and bottoms of valleys)	30.8%

Land unsuitable for arable farming by present methods accounted for 31 per cent of the land surface (granite outcrops and valley bottoms). Dense vegetation, that might well be cocoa farms or forested land, accounted for 10 per cent. A total of 19 per cent was cleared or cultivated, and a final 40 per cent was open savanna.

The interpretation of the structure of the landscape is facilitated by the aggregation of these land use classes into broader categories (see Table 12.2).

With a 1:2 ratio of cultivated land to fallow, the total cycle requires 58 per cent of the land to be in the first two categories (19.2 plus a fallow of 38.4). This leaves 11.6 per cent available for the expansion of farming. The valley bottoms were assimilated to the category of 'marginal' land, which included rocky outcrops as well. Since we know that some valley bottoms are cultivated, as are some rocky outcrops (such as Okeyale's farm), and that some of the category 'dense vegetation' is already cultivated as cocoa farms, the judgement about available land cannot be exact. But even at the most conservative estimate of 19 per cent already in use and 40 per cent savanna, there is still a little room for growth. Whether we look at the ratio of cultivated land to savanna, or all cleared land to savanna plus forest, there is still a margin for expansion under the old land use system of four years cultivation and eight years fallow.

The indeterminacy about an exact threshold is due in part to some lack of clarity in the ethnography about possible differential land use and farming practices for land that appeared markedly in the remote sensing data as 'valley bottoms'. Apart from the single main 'valley bottom' (àkùrọ̀) behind the town, which was intensively cultivated in vegetables and okra during the dry season, the other areas very close to rivers were rarely used for dry season farming. In the rainy season there is no locational advantage because the river-banks are too insect-ridden, tree-lined and possibly also flood-prone to be regularly cultivated. In the dry season the water table goes too low to make hand irrigation in patches on the banks practicable. Some run completely dry by mid-season. Technical innovations such as pumps would certainly make this land more cultivable for dry season fields. So for the moment the riverine areas have been classified as 'marginal' whereas past experience with the town àkùrọ̀ may represent a plan for the future for at least some of the valleys further out in the countryside, if – of course – the trans-

Table 12.3: Proportion of Cultivated Land, by Type, by Proximity to the Town, SPOT data.

	Tractor-cleared	Hand-cleared
Around Idere	53.6	46.4
Outside Idere	33.9	66.1
Total Idere area	48.2	51.8

port system is reliable enough for the fresh vegetables to be quickly evacuated to the market.

The *àkùrò* is a very old technique. Initially a way of ensuring fresh vegetables for food during the dry season, the *àkùrò* immediately behind the town is now used for sales. The area is flat and marshy in the rainy season, broad and close to the water table in the dry season. Water still has to be lifted from the holes dug in the river-bed, but it is a question of wells and buckets, not climbing up steep banks. Both men and women hold small plots in the *àkùrò*. In fact, working an onion plot in the *àkùrò* was the way in which Esther started farming in the 1960s. The area under dry season cultivation at this site has been greatly extended over the past twenty years. It now runs several hundred yards and is completely cultivated in okra, *ewédú* leaf and various other vegetables. A plot can yield, as in 1988, several hundred naira of income during the season. But for the moment the water control techniques for larger scale dry season farming in more challenging topographies have not been developed.

If the upper limit of four years cultivation and eight years fallow has not yet been reached, and if differential land access is not yet a decisive determinant of technique, land use is still within permissive limits. To explore the patterns more closely demands matching the comprehensive data acquired by remote sensing data to the ethnographic sample. The index variable, that could be measured by both methods, was the proportion of land under cultivation that had been cleared by tractor by comparison with the proportion hand-cleared. Using the remotely sensed data we estimated the overall proportion of land presently under cultivation that had been cleared by tractor is 48.2 per cent, and by hand 51.8 per cent, and then introduced the additional check of assessing its spatial distribution around the town: within or beyond five kilometres. Table 12.3 shows the results.

Mechanisation is much more widespread around the town than at a distance: nearly 54 per cent of cultivated area near Idere has been cleared by tractor, whereas outside the Idere hinterland only 34 per cent has been cleared by tractor. Matching the comparable data according to the ethnographic sample with the remote sensing data,[2] Table 12.4 summarises the acreage cleared by tractor for men's and women's farms, for the ethnographic sample.

Table 12.4: Proportion of Cultivated Land, by Type, Ethnographic Sample (No. of farmers = 50 men, 41 women).

	Tractor[a]		Hand		No data		Total	
	Acres	%	Acres	%	Acres	%	Acres	%
Men	105.2	49	103.0	48	7.7	3	215.9	100
Women	25.2	33	51.7	67	–	–	76.8	100
Total	130.4	45	154.7	53	7.7	2	292.7	100

[a] A total of nineteen acres of men's farms and 3.9 acres of women's farms (8 per cent of the total) were prepared by various *combinations* of tractor, hired labour and farmer's own work. Since the present table refers to surface identification rather than labour analysis, *all* fields worked by tractor are included in the 'tractor' acreage (the 90.6 acres totally prepared by tractor and the 14.6 acres partially prepared by tractor).

We can conclude that 45 per cent of the small-scale farms in the sample were tractor-cleared, and 53 per cent hand-cleared, with 2 per cent no data, by comparison with 48 per cent and 52 per cent respectively according to the remote sensing calculations. Both the sources also show a higher use of tractors around the town itself and within a five kilometre radius: 59 per cent and 54 per cent for Idere; 38 per cent and 34 per cent for the villages beyond five kilometres. The two sets of data therefore correspond very closely in all major respects.

For the ethnographer, the closeness of the two measurements, undertaken independently, gives some measure of confidence that this sample does not depart dramatically from a picture gained from data on the entire population. One still proceeds with caution when using the ethnographic samples to draw general inferences about other characteristics, but the case is strengthened by comparing the two sets of results.

Fallows and Rotations

In 1968–69, farmers described the system as roughly four years of cultivation followed by eight years of fallow, that is, exactly the proportions that Ruthenberg (1980) suggested as a stable, threshold situation for savannas of the humid tropics. To recapitulate some points from Chapter 11: on men's farms, some land is now being held in cultivation longer than four years. Of the total documented acreage under cultivation on men's farms[3] in January and February 1988, 77 per cent had been cleared within the past four years (1984–87), 23 per cent being held over from earlier years (1983 and before). Seven per cent of total cultivated land had been in continuous cultivation for eight years.[4] The land held over, however, is disproportionately tractor-cleared land: 66 per cent of all land held over from 1983 and before is tractor cleared, with 18 per cent and 16 per cent for land cleared by hired labour and farmer's own labour, respectively. Of the land in continuous cultivation for seven or more years, 69 per cent was cleared by tractor (see Table 11.4) and this land is being cultivated in a different rotation from hand-cleared land, with lower crop diversity, more fertiliser and less labour input (Table 11.8). It is clear, then, that intensification of land use – in the sense of longer cultivation – is not a function primarily of population pressure, but of the economic accommodation of commercial inputs.

No one yet knows the longer term agro-ecological implications of tractor farming in this manner on these soils, but it has become a fixture of commercial farming over the past ten years. Some scattered experiments were already quite advanced in 1988. A few women were practising an intermittent short-term abandonment/return style of farming and a couple were using the nitrogen-fixing, long cycle (up to four years) pigeon-pea as a fallow crop, after the four years of a routine rotation. The ọba of Eruwa had been working a field said to be seventy-five acres, using fertiliser, continuously for six years. One corporate farm was experimenting with rows of leucena, a nitrogen-fixing shrub at regular intervals, to allow continuous cultivation.

The greatest ecological danger of land shortage is likely to be a function of this kind of expansion: very extended rotations by the larger-scale farms and the least committed of the sideliners. This is not only for the classic reason that they take a disproportionate amount of land out of a farming system that is already growing and will be needing its land frontier. More dangerous in the long run is the untried nature of their techniques, which they use far less conservatively than the small farmers. One hears of cases elsewhere in Southern Nigeria where the irreversible effects of soil-mining – loss of the topsoil and lateritic changes in the soil structure – under conditions of mechanisation and artificial fertilisation, have not set in definitively until about fifteen years after the land was opened up. For what has been essentially only a ten-year spurt of growth, the full tally is not yet in. For the moment the economic limitations of large farms indirectly protect the land from untried methods; they go out of business before ecological decline sets in.

Inferences on Intensification

The particularly interesting finding with respect to the small-scale farmers is that some of the methods they are currently using are obviously suited to adaptation to land shortage should the need arise in the future. The local small-scale farmers are also extending cultivation periods and using tractors, but on land areas that are intrinsically limited by the labour constraint and by methods that combine and mix field types and cropping patterns. Other possibilities that depend on much older ways of exploiting micro-ecologies include the development of orchard crops such as citrus, or palm in the gallery forests; the further development of the àkùrọ̀-style of dry season cultivation in riverine plots; and gardening amongst the rocky outcrops, which farmers themselves say is more fertile land. The existence of all these methods at once suggests that populations are probably developing some suitable techniques well in advance of the carrying capacity threshold: not necessarily for the purpose of dealing with absolute land shortage but in response to an active consumer market for varied products.

Without the synoptic and complete information given by the remote sensing analysis, one would have been inclined to extrapolate from the 1970s data for the whole district, and assumed that the pressures of Ruthenberg's threshold had already set in and accounted for the extension of the cultivation period. Other evidence might have been marshalled on each side of the argument, but it would all have been speculative, fraught with assumptions and based on the same very small sample. The alternative is at least rendered plausible by remote sensing analysis, namely that commercial prospects and some technical innovations have fostered intensification and diversification, ahead of land shortage. The remote sensing/ethnographic study therefore confirms the hypothesis put forward by Burnham (1980), Richards (1983) and Dommen (1988), that agricultural repertoires in the West African savanna are wider and more adaptable at the thresholds than a simple 'population pressure' model implies. Consonant with a tradition of crop-led change, this capacity owes a great deal to the external orientation of the farmers: to new crops, new inputs, new divisions of labour and growing markets. The pattern we see here in Ibarapa is a twentieth century extension of the crop/labour leading edge that has characterised African agriculture in the humid savanna for centuries. Production has been increased, but with what are – in the great scale of comparative studies – only subtle effects on permanent agricultural infrastructure and land use techniques. Changes in crops and crop combinations, in part facilitated by tractor clearing, have enabled small farmers' growth and intensification, and we see already an advancing recourse to a yet wider variety: *odóńgbó* cassava, citrus orchards, pigeon pea fields, fresh leaf vegetables and cocoa.

Seeing the crop repertoire rather than land use techniques (tools, agricultural infrastructure) as the leading edge of growth and intensification puts a great premium on the understanding of crop diversity. I have already addressed diversity in particular categories of farming in previous chapters. It remains here to summarise emerging regional patterns.

REGIONAL SPECIALISATION AND DIVERSITY

Beyond the gross distinctions between peripheral, accessible and immediate hinterlands, the rings of specialisation around the Southern Nigerian cities seem to be far from discrete. It is still possible in Ibarapa to sell the same products as are produced elsewhere. More distant, and perhaps more ecologically suited, supply zones have not completely undermined all possibility of the local farmers finding buyers. Varied prices for the same goods seem to exist in the larger hinterland.[5] The volatility of conditions in both transport and production may sustain such conditions that seem to defy the law of comparative advantage, except as applied to broad categories of crops, such as 'perishable' and 'non-perishable', savanna and forest.

Going back to von Thünen and the classics on the growth of European agriculture, one clear precondition of this relatively great local diversity is the lack of competitive pricing in land as an element in calculations of the costs of production. Land in Europe had been differentially 'priced' for taxation and defined as a potential financial asset long before it entered a market. It was a cost of production before it was bought and sold. Under nineteenth-century conditions, the land market made the cost of land increasingly important in economic calculations, and made credit 'a normal act not a desperate measure' (Kautsky 1988: 212). Competition with areas of low land prices forced specialisation on the high value areas, of which urban hinterlands were assumed, as early as von Thünen's writings in the first half of the nineteenth century, to be an obvious component.

These conditions do not yet prevail in Nigeria. Cocoa land and urban or peri-urban land have come under market valuation processes, although perhaps of a kind different from historic Europe. The valuation of land in the food supply hinterland has only just begun over the past fifteen years or so, although the Land Use Act passed in 1978 may gradually, and for the moment haphazardly, be giving birth to land value differentials. Neither is land taxed by value, again obviating the kind of calculus that entered into crop specialisation in other areas of the world. Hence, even amongst large scale farmers, one would not expect great pressures towards a specialisation that was based on the differential costs of land by location, as distinct from location in trade and transport networks. Decisive influences are the costs and availability of transport and confidence in the efficiency of market institutions, conditions that are shared by a wide range of crops. Hence the latitude that farmers in the Ibadan hinterland still have to farm in accordance with their knowledge and preferences.

The one factor encouraging the 'weighting' of cropping patterns by individual is the apparently increasing specialisation of traders, who now can access the villages directly. In the past, crops were sorted for sale by the pàràkòyí in the market-place and even then, many of the traders bought more than one kind of crop. In 1988 one heard far more about specialist traders, and far more about direct buying. If there is a single most important institution in fostering the narrower spectrum style of farming then, it is the reorganised intermediary sector rather than those determining the costs of production.

CONCLUSION

As Ibarapa approaches the limits of the old field and fallow system, it faces two feasible land-use frontiers: lengthening the period of cultivation, or increasing the labour input into fields of the old type, largely now devoted to perishable crops. While the male farmers practise both types, the new-comers and larger farmers concentrate on the former. Both are technically feasible for the moment. Both respond to a market demand. Neither – as far as we know – is completely inapposite to the environment, although longer cultivation on large areas that have been denuded of the stubby savanna trees is taking much larger risks than the smaller areas and combinations of field pursued by the small-scale farmers. Which particular frontier will be extended will then depend on the conditions for each set of *crops on the market,* and also on the fate of *each set of practitioners* in the larger social arena: the mid-scale and sideliners who have the incentives and the capacity to mine the soil, or the small farmers who move conservatively up through a series of land/crop/labour combinations that preserves the fallow, not only because they may have conservationist convictions and practices, but also because they lack the labour and capital resources to do otherwise and are already deeply accustomed to occupational careers that can be weighted towards certain crops without being fully specialised.

The low real cost of land is an underlying condition of both a small-scale economy that allows a variety of careers to enter the competitive arena and land accumulation in a speculative mode. The ecological dynamics of the urban hinterland are an outcome of both logics: one fostering the lateral variety of enterprises and the other fostering hierarchical differentiation. The main alternatives are already fairly clear. It is unlikely that the technical capacities for smallholder expansion will be exhausted before large opera-tors attempt to consolidate and expand their farms. The agro-ecology of the future thereby rests on the social organisations that each can mobilise to further their own style of production. The next chapter explores the social dynamics.

NOTES

1. Analysis was carried out by Dr Eric Lambin; the methods are summarised in Appendix A. We concentrated on the area immediately around Idere, and due to technical problems with the data received we were unable to compare them with other areas of Ibarapa or to do a general analysis of the entire region. The conclu-sions are therefore limited to the same area as is covered by the ethnographic data.
2. One needs some estimate of the ratio of male to female farmers since women use tractors rather less than men, and on smaller farms (as Table 12.4 summarises) whereas all the nine mid-scale farms – which were not measured accurately and are therefore not included in the table – were predominantly tractor-cleared. We worked with the ratio of female to male farms of 1:1.2.
3. Women's farming is too recent a phenomenon for clear patterns of multi-year land use to have emerged.
4. Of course this says nothing about fallow length, and nor can it accurately be related to what farmers were actually doing in 1968–69, as distinct from what they tended to say they were doing.
5. Intra-hinterland price variation at the rural wholesale markets seems to be very high, for reasons that remain obscure. For example, the prices for the two major

cassava products, gari and cassava flour, do not vary together. The 1979 Oyo State Rural Agricultural Sample Survey reported that amongst the twenty-two local government areas composing the state, the yearly average price of cassava flour varied from a low of 18 kobo per kg in Ibarapa to a high of 129 kobo per kg in Ila, while at the same time the price of gari was 42k in Ibarapa and 29k in Ila (Table 5.4). Possibly the conditions of processing vary, but there is also a high probability of reporting error.

13

COLLECTIVE DYNAMICS

A similar series of issues can be posed with respect to community and institutional frameworks as with respect to occupation of the land: are the people whose multifarious activities have been described in Part II at the limits of current social organisation, elaborating established templates in new ways or in the institutional maelstrom of a socio-political 'frontier'? By virtue of the relative lack of a formal sector presence, most of the forms – if not all the incentives – for institutional innovation grow out of local initiatives. As with the reconfiguration of farming itself, there are multiple challenges to social organisation.

At the arbitrary moment of study each category of actor may be at a different point of development in relation to the market. In 1988 the institutions of farm labour, transport, tractor use and trade were becoming more varied and complex. Others, such as artisanal processing, were under heavy pressure from competition. Speciality production may be in the process of sharper definition, with some crops leading the way, encouraged by specialist trading but modified by price instability in the regional produce markets. Women's farming is unlikely ever to become a discrete sector on gender grounds alone, although some women might well become organised speciality producers. There have been a few odd and failed experiments – in marijuana growing and in fresh egusi sale for the medicine market[1] – that will not develop simply because of the risk of major legal sanctions.

External presences have persisted only to the degree that they have developed ways of living within this context. Contract farming has gradually worked out a solid place within the rural economy, whereas the corporate farms remain to some degree enclaves. The NTC has a local constituency, an organisation, which faces the constant discipline of competition with the food economy to which it has also deliberately contributed by tractor hire, fertiliser provision and now technical advice about rotations combining tobacco phases with food-crop phases. The corporate farms only connect to the local economy through the harvest labour. Women harvesters have embarked on the path towards 'domesticating' them to a version of local labour practice, but with restricted success. Honorary chieftaincies represent the main other, and rather unsuccessful, effort to subject their owners to local disciplines.

There have been other problematic developments and outright failures. Collective capital investment has proved far more difficult to organise around than individual innovation, in part due to the chronic weakness of local government. Road repair, water supply, electricity, school funding and extension services have all been very vulnerable to official neglect and community efforts to compensate are simply too limited (Guyer 1992). A group attempt to build a new bridge over the Ofiki has been a long-term failure, in spite of several differently organised efforts to raise the money, employ the expertise and accomplish the work. Roads have been paved, fallen apart, and repaved. Electrification was short-lived due to thefts of cable between Eruwa and Ilugun, and the demise of all representative institutions eliminates the channels through which people could campaign for reinstatement. The water supply has deteriorated from piped water – newly supplied in the late 1960s, no longer adequate to demand by the 1980s – to the wells dug in the 1980s and the natural sources used throughout history.

The failures of the public sector place a premium on the local institutions that underly the capacity for constant competitive reorganisation. Most important are chieftaincy, the conceptual basis for the personal career, and association. The social arenas in which these premises are negotiated are contentious, but the style of contentiousness seems procedural rather than transformational. Disputes are intermittently resolvable and constitute an expected aspect of the process of change and expansion. Dispute is particularly time-consuming and inconclusive, not in moments of expansion but at periods of retrenchment and erosion of connection to outside markets and power centres, as may be happening again in the 1990s as the economic and political crises in the country drag on. With reduced possibility for outside linkage and forward-looking growth, the arenas through which the specialisation of personal career is developed, legitimated and organised become involuted. By contrast, the disputes that arise with respect to enclave development by corporate farms are more profound because they engage the operative principles of a different economic structure. The following sections examine each of these dynamics in relation to the local market.

THE ỌBA, CHIEFTAINCY AND COLLECTIVE FRONTIERS

Chiefs are not necessarily highly effective administrators; they are not chosen for those qualities. The chieftaincy is an institution with few constitutional powers in the national polity. The chiefs cannot, by law, impose taxes to carry out their own agendas and indeed they are not supposed to *have* political or economic agendas of their own. To the observer, the life of a chief is a constant round of paying formal visits, hearing about problems, receiving food from celebrations and mediating factional disputes. 'Being there' is one of the most critical and time-consuming duties. Presence, however, achieves a great deal in economic life. In increasingly important ways that people recognise, the very presence and daily routine of chieftaincy represents the capacity for contracts and organisations to be considered legitimate in communities that are still largely outside the realm of written records and that cannot depend on local or central government. One imagines that a comparative 'managerial' study might reveal that these functions could be fulfilled well or badly, and certainly the vision behind them can be forward- or backward-looking. But to a great degree – just as Barber argues that 'man makes god in West Africa' (1981) – the people make the conditions that they want endorsed by their authorities.

All associations – whether for occupational, credit, social or religious functions – link themselves to the ọba and the chiefs on an initial and ongoing basis. When a new ẹgbẹ́ is formed it has to be declared to the ọba, and when any special meeting is held subsequently, for which food is prepared, a portion has to be taken to the palace for consumption by the chiefs, or to the house of the quarter chief in the case of smaller groups. Even the smallest association prepares food for its meeting, and meets about once a month. In principle, then, the chiefs know of every ẹgbẹ́, every major rotating credit association, every occupational grouping and every religious congregation in the town. The main outlines of group activities can hardly be a secret, and in principle the chiefs can intervene somewhat knowledgeably should the need arise. There is a long history, for example, of the Onidere's consultation in the highly charged issue of succession to the position of Imam in the Muslim congregation, even though there has never been a Muslim ọba.

The behaviour of ẹgbẹ́ members, and particularly with respect to debt, can be backed by the threat of royal or chiefly sanction. The police and the courts do not deal in the myriad of agreements for which there is no tangible evidence, so all relations depend on long inter-personal histories and all terms of agreement reflect local standards. In a small town like Idere the ọba and chiefs carry out this function with some diligence. They may discipline the delinquent themselves, or bring in a relative to pay the money owed, as a means of humiliating the entire family. Clearly, the task is huge and the success rate at enforcement may not be very impressive. But the chieftaincy is the only social institution that will back verbal contracts of the kind that mediate every phase of economic life. The knowledge that backing and a source of recourse do exist, beyond social ostracism by the particular person or group that finds itself cheated, allows agreements to be made about very substantial sums of money without a sense of intolerable risk.

There is reason to think that there are many more social organisations that fall under the authority hierarchy now than in the past. Twenty years have seen the growth of new occupational ẹgbẹ́ that support farming: the tractor-owners, tractor-drivers, transporters, motor mechanics and motor cycle mechanics, as well as the greater formalisation of some groups of elégúsí women harvesters. The expansion of the markets entailed supervision by the *bàbá òja*, fathers of the market, and organisations of traders, *pàràkòyí* (mediators) and *onílódó*, measurers, for each of the main crops. All of these organised groups set prices and/or the terms of commercial engagement. The social and occupational *ẹgbẹ́* all have complex financial dealings involving the costs of operation in their productive niche, consumption costs such as matching cloth for ceremonies, and production loans. Without them, response to the fluctuating conditions of a competitive market would be a roller-coaster of daily adjustment that obviated all planning and all recourse to credit.

The risk for certain kinds of loan may in fact be quite low in a community like Idere with a political hierarchy that can stand behind verbal agreements made in the context of *ẹgbẹ́* organisations or long-standing types of transaction. Like the occupational *ẹgbẹ́*, credit organisations have become more varied. In 1968 farmers saved and mobilised credit in two main ways: through the rotating credit group they termed *àású* (*esusu*, in other literature), and through personal loans from money-lenders who were either men who would have had recourse to the institution of *ìwòfà* labour in the past, or successful women traders. Cash interest rates on individual loans seem to have been rolled over from the guidelines for *ìwòfà* (debt service through labour). I was told that under the *ìwòfà* system a £5 debt brought in either four days' work or five shillings per month, an equivalent of 5 per cent in cash or about 20 per cent of total workdays. Certain interest rates – for loans for a funeral, as distinct from loans for medical care or production costs – gravitate to the levels established in a pre-existing moral economy of labour rather than necessarily directly reflecting the calculated risk of loss of the principal. As I note below, one kind of loan carried the exact interest rate that was reported for *ìwòfà*.

In 1969 all substantial *àású* had to be verbally 'registered' at the outset with the ọba, and all the members and organisers named. There also existed in 1968 a system known as *àjọ*, for smaller amounts given at more frequent intervals, and paying a regular income to the organiser (because it was more work. *Àású* paid one extra payment per member for the organiser (Falola 1995). The farmers were not involved in the *àjọ* system at that time. It was mainly for the women traders. If a large *àású* had thirty members divided into three *igún* (sides) of ten each, and many farmers belonged to at least two at a time (see Guyer 1972, Chapter 8), one can get a rough idea of the supervision involved in keeping some kind of track of this entire activity in a town of at least 2,000 economically active adults.

In 1988 the types of credit system had proliferated although not necessarily the amounts of money that farmers regularly devoted to them. According to the budgets of the diary sample, only 3 per cent of expenditure (by comparison with 8 per cent in 1969) went to credit associations, and the amounts of each contribution seemed very modest relative to incomes. Two shifts had taken place: the farmers were more likely to belong to *àjọ* than to *àású*, possibly reflecting the tendency towards occupational specialities; and there was another kind of organisation altogether, called *mítìn* or *mítìnì*, from the English/pidgin 'meeting', that one farmer suggested was established around 1979. Members of the same family paid in a regular amount and then were allowed to borrow *on interest*, at a lower rate than the individual moneylenders were offering. One farmer quoted N10 per month on N200 (which is exactly equivalent to the 5 per cent of the *iwọ̀fà* system of the past). Not all compound members belonged to their *mítìn*, and one would need to explore much further than I was able to do their numbers, organisation and distribution within the community.

In 1991, on a re-visit, I saw the invention of another new credit system: that of repayment in kind for agricultural loans that resembles the crop-pawning that developed throughout the cocoa belt in an earlier era. When ploughing jumped in price to N100 per acre, and the tractor-owners' *ẹgbẹ́* maintained the pre-existing condition that ploughing had to be paid in cash at the time the work was done, women produce traders gave loans for repayment in bags of egusi at the rate of one per N100 loaned. Since the women traders are organised, their organisation would pick up the task of monitoring and sanctioning the arrangement. Solidity of organisation thus has important effects on cropping patterns: those farmers who wanted ploughing done on credit had to live with the demands of the traders that they produce egusi in the first season, which in turn rested on the traders' organisation and chiefly sanction. Again in 1988 as in 1968, people related cases of failure to repay *ẹgbẹ́* for loans being sanctioned by the ọba, and in 1991 they spontaneously mentioned that the ọba or balẹ would stand behind these new agreements for repayment in kind.

The economically most important verbal contract backed by the chiefs is the agreement between farmers and foreign labourers, because if a region earned a reputation for cheating the migrant labourers there is no doubt that they could be left high and dry the following season. Only a small proportion of work is paid for at the time the job is done, so crew bosses and farmers have to remember the amounts owed for several months. Needless to say, there is plenty of room for disagreement or outright failure to pay. Labourers talked about the difficulty of working in the Ijebu area because of the farmers' reputation for cheating, and explicitly noted that in Ibarapa the farmers paid well, promptly and accurately. Ibarapa is now deeply dependent on migrant hired labour. Without it, the mid- and large-scale farming would disappear, women would probably go out of farming again, and men's farms would reduce in size. No one can afford a bad reputation in this regard, but each payment is an individual agreement, subject to the usual vicissitudes of personal fortune and temperament. In the late 1980s, the ọba stood behind these labour contracts. If a farmer failed or refused to pay in October the ọba undertook to use his authority to raise the money by the time the labourers would return in March of the following year. And indeed he did take money and impound it. The continuation of the entire institution of labour-on-credit depends, then, not just on the willingness of individual farmers to follow the customary practice, nor just to recognise their own long term self-interest by paying up, but also on the labour policies of the chieftaincy.

The Ibarapa towns, and including Idere, are continuing to elaborate the chieftaincy institutions, like many other towns in Western Nigeria. The first annual community celebration, inaugurated in 1992, was the occasion for the installation of several new incumbents to chieftaincy positions, the re-hearsal of Idere's links to Yoruba traditions and a plan to build a new palace. Clearly there is an agenda in relation to regional profile and access to sources of power, as Berry (1985) suggested. But very significant local work is also still done by the chiefs. One can easily imagine the daily headache all these credit and debt cases must be to hear out, but it is hardly necessary to emphasise the importance, for a commercialising economy, of a set of guide-lines and sanctions for the collective management of money, particularly credit. Endorsing and symbolising a moral and administrative framework is probably one of the most important economic policy positions and adminis-trative tasks that ọbas and chiefs undertake. Even if it is done poorly or fitfully or with favouritism in practice, at least the ideal and the model are embodied institutionally. People can express this explicitly. When one wonders out loud about the worthiness of this or that incumbent of a chieftaincy position people say: 'we're used to it', meaning the institution. Do commercial rela-tions inspire more confidence with this kind of armature to guarantee them? It remains a question and a suggestion rather than a conclusion. But even agreements that are open for constant renegotiation must invoke a moral and jural authority of some sort. As I argue later, the conceptual stabilisation inherent in the niche economy is part of this armature, and it is both set up in the first instance and if necessary actively sanctioned by royal and chiefly authority.

Many of the more diffuse collective dynamics ultimately revert back to the concept of society as tied together, with a moral sanction that is em-bodied in, or passes at some point through the influence of, positions of authority in the town political hierarchy. That morality rests on the assump-tion of qualitative distinctions amongst different kinds of 'things' in the world – occupations, credit associations, cropping patterns, ceremonies, compounds – which act in characteristic ways, and have interacted with each other through cash for a very long time. Money and morality are not con-trasted because the framework of equivalences, expectations and sanctions that mediate highly competitive and individualistic careers are expressed in cash terms. There is an expectation that personal difference is constitutive, and will be managed collectively on a labour-intensive, contentious, case-by-case, daily basis. Chieftaincy stands for this. As Matory has eloquently expressed it: 'The kingship remains, though tattered, a central and redolent piece amid the various cultural and historical crosscurrents making up modern Nigeria. If any site in Yorubaland is credited with moral and social ordiliness, the kingship is understood to be its hub' (1994: 218).

FAMILIES AND THE INDIVIDUATED CAREER

Household control of assets and the organisation of production have long been associated with agricultural intensification (see Netting 1993). With this in mind, the single most striking social process to note in Ibarapa is the continued individuation of enterprise, and small mutations in familial economic relationships, within a complex nexus of larger kin and compound units. As Clarke suggested for the longer run, 'Small-scale farming enterprises and the households on which they depend have changed much more gradually' (1981: 821) than the large houses of the Yoruba past.

The 'household' of man, wife (or wives) and dependent children is even less a unit of production in 1988 than it was in 1968. Young people work for wages, even from their senior kin. Wives farm on their own account, and hardly any husbands intervene in any way with their wives' farms. If a man falls ill nobody works his farm for him even though close kin will certainly support him in other ways such as food provision and contributions to his medical costs. Hence the personal damage that endemic disease can do (Brieger and Guyer 1990). The work that kinsmen used to carry out for each other under the rubric of long term cash reciprocity, such as porterage by wives in return for ceremonial contributions and labour by juniors in return for bridewealth, have been obviated by changes in social life and translated into much more short-run forms. The result is a radical individuation of daily control of one's own activities. As I will explore later (and see Guyer 1992) this does not mean that resource control is entirely individual, nor that people's activities are uncoordinated, nor that families have no economic organisation at all. What it does mean is that there are no social groups that constitute units for the performance of production. Each production unit is based on a single person who adds others in explicitly short-term contractual relationships for carrying out specific tasks. The individual career rather than the household developmental cycle still determines economic decisions.

There are three sets of evidence that support this claim. The gender-*weighted* but not gender-*specialised* nature of personal budgets, that mirrors the patterns of men's and women's farming, supports the inference that intra-familial careers are individuated rather than functionally complementary. Second, there is much evidence of recourse to money as a mediator of daily familial relations. Finally, while compounds continue to command the time and attention of their members, they are less able than in the past to

Table 13.1: Percentage Days' Work by Task, Men and Women Farmers, March to August 1988 (182 Days).

Task	Men	Women
Clearing	1	2
Heaping	2	0
Planting	6	1
Weeding	37	58
Tending	6	1
Harvesting	5	7
Marketing	4	4
Other Agricultural	6	5
Sick	6	3
Non-Agricultural	26	19
Hunting	1	0
Total	100	100

command monetary contributions. These three processes – the affirmation of non-gendered personhood, the routinisation of money and the command on collective participation – underly all the family changes I can illustrate from the farm data.

In the chapters on farming I pointed out that the differences between men's and women's farms were differences of degree but not kind. Women's farms average 44 per cent the size of men's farms. They have a lot more cassava, a lot less crop diversity and are considerably more commercialised in both inputs and products. They are not however in a different class of organisation altogether. Insofar as some are specialist producers they are similar to sideliners amongst the male population. We see similar correspondences when we look at patterns of activity. I only collected labour and cash flow diaries from four women because of the sheer difficulties of accuracy, working with people with multiple income sources and high mobility rates. This particular four earned as high a proportion of their entire incomes from farming as I could find. I would make very little of such a small group were it not for the similarities between their diaries and those of the men. Table 13.1 summarises the percentage of men's and women's time spent in various activities.

Men's activities are more varied, and they spend less time weeding and more off the farm. Otherwise the balance is quite similar. There is a more marked difference when it comes to income sources, but again these are differences of total amount and of emphasis, not a completely different pattern (see Table 13.2).

If we look at expenditure we find a similar phenomenon: weighted differences rather than absolute differences. Here we need absolute amounts of expenditure to see the patterns most clearly (see Table 13.3).

The women were keeping up quite similar expenditure patterns to men,

Table 13.2: Male and Female Farmers' Sources of Agricultural Income (Percentage by Crop).

Crop	Men	Women
Cassava and cassava products	35	71
Maize	1	9
Yams	4	0
Egusi	3	2
Guinea-corn	2	0
Pepper	1	3
Tomatoes	27	11
Vegetables	1	2
Fruit	3	0
Cocoa	9	0
Other	14	2
Total Agricultural Income	100	100
In Naira	1217	505

although in 1988 they were driving themselves into six-month deficit to do so. They were paying school fees, keeping up ceremonial expenses, investing in their farms, buying food and financing building etc., just as were the men. All inputs into the farm are paid for strictly individually, and these expenses were second only to food and household necessities (kerosene, soap, matches) in the proportion of expenses that they accounted for. In general, women farmers are not doing something entirely different from men, either in their work life or in their budgets, and they are not dependent on others for any of the main components of an acceptable living.

This pattern of production and expenditure implies that the work of men and women is not coordinated or jointly managed, at least in the most obvious ways that are embedded in household theory. Men's and women's cash contributions to family and support of children are probably additive or substitutive according to discretion, rather enacted according to a prescribed division of complementary responsibilities and resource allocations. Often when I asked about who paid for this or that, or supplied food from the farm for the diet, people answered in pragmatic terms; it depended who had the money or the crops. The male farmers devoted considerable resources to family food supply and children's welfare, including payment for medicine and diligent attendance at hospital or the clinic when a child was ill. They spent a good deal more on food and minor household needs in 1988 than in 1968: 27 per cent of expenses as against 13 per cent. There were therefore no signs that men were pulling out of domestic responsibilities as women's occupations changed.

I reach the limits of confident intepretation at the threshold of marriages. It would take another research design to infer how this budgeting was done:

Table 13.3: Male and Female Farmers' Expenditures in Naira, March to August 1988

Category of expenditure	Men		Women	
	Amount	Percent	Amount	Percent
Ceremonial	133	15	92	13
Food and household necessities	244	27	261	36
Associations and credit associations	70	8	8	2
Clothes	18	2	4	0
School	111	12	40	5
Farm inputs (labour, tractor)	182	20	153	21
Medical, building, travel, other	148	16	171	23
Total	906	100	729	100
Balance over six-month income	+404		-182	

in what sense and by what means it had any 'joint' processes of decision making. Most middle-aged men had two wives and at least two sets of children and therefore as many units to concede independence to and provide support for as there were sibling groups among the children. If he had a set of children with no resident mother, for example through widowerhood, it could be difficult to get another wife to provide for them at a level comparable to their own mother. There must be very considerable subtlety in consumer decisions in the cases where co-budgeting does work, and almost total economic separation where it does not. In neither case is this the classic peasant household, with a head who organises the differentiated labour resources and unitary budget of the whole group. With the virtual disappearance of women's free head-porterage, the introduction of wage payment for youth, the apparent decline in self-provisioning, and rise in individuated costs of production, a family is a configuration of individuated careers to a greater degree than in the past. If there is a frontier of economic cooperation it is in the planning of consumption and the costs of children, rather than in production.

This pattern offers a comparative case alongside the Kofyar division of labour described by Stone et al. (1995). They show, as I have for this case, that gender is a qualifier and not a fundamental determinant of productive life. Kofyar production plans have a household basis however, whereas if conjugality affects Yoruba personal economies it is through the division of responsibility for consumption rather than through a division of labour.

INDIVIDUAL CAREERS AND ASSOCIATIONAL TEMPLATES

Personal achievement is at least as marked, if not more so, than in the past. Chapter 10 shows how men seem to be developing concentrations within farming. More could be done to define the terms in which farmers themselves see their identifications here but it is clear that people grow certain crops because it suits them, because they are interested. Precipitation of interest amongst farmers into their own formalised organisations around specific crops has not yet developed except for NTC tobacco, but the possibilities are there.

The collective life most closely relevant to farming is the town context for the establishment of profile and reputation. People still live an active social and ceremonial life, and to some considerable degree it still motivates economic activity. The acquisition of a title or position of responsibility in a religious congregation, and the capacity to finance a child's naming ceremony or a parent's funeral, are powerfully meaningful. The farmers I knew in 1968 who had achieved some kind of social prominence by 1988 were visibly animated and gratified when they talked about it, even while complaining about the amount of time or money that it consumed. If they held responsible positions, the activities and duties were mentioned often in their work diaries and clearly oriented their schedules of life. In the daily round of life they were addressed by title rather than name or teknonym.

In 1968 I argued that it was ceremonial life and social prominence, and not subsistence needs, that drove the farming system. Men spent an average of 35 per cent of their total cash expenditure on gifts and ceremonies (Guyer 1972: 132), devoted eleven days (6 per cent of total days) over six months to formal ceremonial and meetings, and an additional forty-four days to travel, community work such as road maintenance and housebuilding, 'rest' at home, associational meetings and religion including, for Christians, Sunday observance. The more money they spent on social life, the more time was involved. In 1968–69 it was the elders and oldest men of sibling groups who disproportionately devoted themselves to public life. In the years following the final demise of debt pawning, the only means of affording both the time and money that was needed to meet social and political commitments involved the activation of seniority. Older men kept their sons on the farm to help with the work, and ceremonial contributions were collected up from sibling group and descent group members by stepwise payments of juniors to seniors of their own generation and then on upwards in the generational hierarchy.

In 1988 social and ceremonial life was still very active but had been reconfigured. It accounted for only three percentage points less days than in 1968 (27 per cent as against 30 per cent), but the weighting had altered. Religious commitments such as Sunday observance had increased; formal ceremonials and meetings had slightly decreased from eleven to eight days. Much more striking was a decline in the proportion of expenditure devoted to ceremonies: from 35 per cent to 11 per cent. The quasi-totality of this fall could be attributed to the decline in the step-wise contributions that minor contributors had regularly syphoned in to their seniors under the old system. People gave less often and in lesser amounts, even though they continued to offer their presence. This meant that central celebrants – the parents of the new child, the children of the deceased parent, the immediate kin of the graduated apprentice – were putting up a higher proportion of the total cost of the ceremony than they had in the past. These expenditure patterns suggest that personal careers are more socially discrete from the sibling group and the compound than they were in the past.

Again, however, I would argue that there are new lines of collaboration rather than a simple attenuation of collective social life. People have not abandoned social commitment, but rather reorganised it so that even under the pressures of farm expansion, increased *ẹgbẹ́* participation and greater religiosity, one's presence at the key moments of social affirmation, can be managed. The most direct evidence that this is a collective process, rather than an ephemeral stage in a progressive social and economic individuation, lies in the reorganisation of the work week over the twenty years of growth and change in such as way that people's ceremonial and social life can be predictably synchronised.[2]

In 1968–69 the most important ceremonies of personal life – birth and death – took place immediately the event happened. Men's work schedules showed a remarkable irregularity as a result. Over the six months that they kept work diaries, the men spent an average of less than six episodes doing the same thing for three straight days (the Yoruba work-week, the fourth day being market-day), and less than one episode of six days or more (the Christian/Muslim work-week), for a total of 23 per cent of work days and seven work episodes per farmer. The days spent in ceremonial were completely randomly distributed throughout the week, with an average of six on Monday to Thursday, and five on Friday through Sunday. In 1988, work was more concentrated: 33 per cent of time and eleven episodes per farmer were in concentrated work on a single type of task, and ceremonial life was disproportionately on the weekend.

This shift is an accommodation of the local rhythms of life to the routines of Church and State. People tend to work all week, then spend the weekend fulfilling a whole variety of social obligations: Sunday or Friday observance, *ẹgbẹ́* meetings, visits to funerals and naming ceremonies, family credit *mitinis*, travelling and visiting. The minor participants in major ceremonies now limit their visits to the weekend, and their monetary contribution to very small amounts or nothing, leaving only the immediate kin to observe the entire week or ten days that may be demanded by a funeral or the functions surrounding a title ceremony. Without such streamlining the life of senior men would be impossible. The demands of work, the demands of religion and the demands of status would run into recurrent clashes and bottlenecks. Men who should not rush would be constantly rushing. Either farming or society would be neglected.

The reorganisation of work and ceremonial/social life can only be a *collective* process. Every *ẹgbẹ́* has numerous members, every religious congregation

encompasses numerous devotees, every ceremony calls in numerous participants, and every title-taking involves numerous town citizens. Farmers
would not be able to expand their farms unless social life was streamlined,
and they would not respond to the market and ecological change if the
demands of work so invaded social life that the incentives to produce at all
were greatly diminished. Incorporation into the urban hinterland is a social
as well as political, economic and ecological process. People are trying to re-
create a meaningful and effective social life as well as manage their farms.

The explanatory importance I gave originally to personal career in the
understanding of economic life therefore needs historical modification
rather than complete revision. Career paths that were conditioned by
ascribed seniority within sibling groups and compounds in the past are now
more enhanced by occupation, religion and association without, however, the
centrality of career-creation itself declining in relevance. Collective life is simply
more oriented around association and congregation than around kinship.

All sources confirm that personal success is not a new cultural criterion,
nor a direct function of recent commercialisation in Yoruba history and
society. Belasco writes of the 'entrepreneur as culture hero' (1980) in the
nineteenth century and refers to 'existential reversal' as the terms under
which market uncertainty is understood. Lloyd writes that 'the individual
sees his own attainment of an enhanced status as lying in his own efforts
rather than collective action' (1974: 219). Peil et al. note 'the almost univer-
sal urge of Nigerians for self-employment' (1988: 574). Culturally-based
studies add depth to the economic evidence: 'The image of self and
community as vessels potentiates certain forms of action ... [one becomes]
expert in the reification, externalisation and redesign of the subject' (Matory
1994: 169). In a sustained exposition of the relationship between career and
the money economy in the nineteenth century, Barber concludes that 'if
participation in the circulation of money was regarded as a necessary
condition of humanity, then participating successfully was the means to full
self-realisation' (1995: 211). The means to self-realisation can shift over
time, such that different qualities of the personal and the collective that
already claim spaces in the 'vessel' of the person are differentially combined,
while the indviduated career itself remains the unswerving goal.

THE DILEMMAS OF COMPOUNDS: THE LANDOWNERS
AND LAND LAW

Compounds and formalised kinship structures are decreasingly determi-
native of personal careers, but the interface with formal sector dynamics
makes them more important with respect to resource control than they have
ever been. The development of a market in land is uniquely indeterminate
and disputatious: because legal principles run counter to the performative
criteria of the local economy, and because compounds have been identified

by the formal sector as the means to mediating the transition at a time when their importance is otherwise changing.

There is no aspect of the rural economy more complex than land law and practice because demands are being put on the old system for which it has few useful rubrics, and the new Land Use Act of 1978 is itself fundamentally ambiguous. The principles of the local market and the national market – as represented in Land Use Act of 1978 – are at odds. In the first, access is based on 'ownership'/occupation in accordance with the performance of economic activities, in relation to others in the same economy. In the other, it is based on exclusionary legal principles. Farms acquired as exclusive property neither have to perform competitively nor in a manner that relates to the rest of the local economy, in part because they are financial assets as well as productive resources. Both sides reach out across this chasm of difference: the land law to define customary tenure so that land can be legally acquired from the customary sector, and the local society to create an infrastructure that makes new landowners accountable. As a result, land transactions are potential grist for more fundamental contention than contestation over the addition of some other practitioner to the competitive system. Since people are operating in all kinds of legal grey areas, maintaining contention on a wide variety of issues about land access, even in the absence of urgent land pressure, is one way for participants to make sure that almost anything can be done but also redressed, for whatever reason.

The rise of large-scale farming in Ibarapa post-dates the Land Use Decree (later Act) of 1978 and the transport innovations. For the first time there started to be numerous outside interests in Ibarapa, looking for farm land: the Boy Scouts of Nigeria, the former head of the national government General Obasanjo, the United Africa Company, civil servants, various churches and the shadowy figure thought to be in the background of many major schemes: òyinbó, the Whites. But in purely technical terms, the text of the Act was difficult to implement since it seemed to be contradictory on the status of land held in what was termed 'customary occupancy'. More or less all of the farm land of Ibarapa fell under this type of ownership. Shifts in customary practice were already underway by then, and they merged with confusions in the law to create a situation full of surprises and rumours for farmers, dilemmas for the compounds that controlled the land, insecurity for some of those acquiring land rights, and a determined belief – whether founded or not – on the part of the indigenous population that they could get rid of anyone to whom they eventually took a dislike.

The Land Use Act had one main purpose in the rural areas, namely the release of land to outsiders, including migrants moving into low-population density areas as well as middle-class agricultural investors. The stipulations of the law are that the state ultimately owns the land; dispensation over it is vested in the state governments; 'persons' only hold rights of occupancy granted by the state; and therefore the customary law under which people had lived over the entire colonial and post-colonial period no longer figures as a systematic set of principles. This simplicity masks the fact that the act contradicts itself in its specific provisions: on who counted as a 'person' (individual or kin group/collectivity), and on how the state acquired the rights to distribution from the customary occupants in the first place, since the category of 'customary occupancy' was explicitly named without being defined in legal and procedural terms.

There was 'no provision in the act for revoking an existing right' (Omotola 1982: 38). This extreme ambiguity with respect to pre-existing customary rights, their transfer and devolution meant that land transactions in the rural areas had to be idiosyncratic and inventive. No other kind of transaction was possible.

The direct influence of the act was spotty in the 1980s. Francis (1984) has shown how little it affected tenure in another rural area in Oyo State. A local government official told me that people went on trying to transfer rights by outright sale for several years, even though it was illegal. They did this by paying a premium on old runs of the stamp issue that had to be affixed to the licence, effectively backdating the bill of sale, and filing the documents as if they had existed before the Act became law. Several of those 'persons' who were interested in acquiring land rights in Ibarapa were not necessarily in the position to do this or to want to do it. Some were altogether too prominent or too directly associated with the policy to deviate from it in their own cases. Although response to the act was sluggish therefore there were distinct effects, both of the law itself and of the local whirlpools that emanated from the confluence of an ambiguous legal statute and a moving customary practice.

There are obvious difficulties in writing about land cases in a highly iden-tifiable area. I did not try to find out the exact details of the land transactions on which agribusiness in Ibarapa rested because it seemed impossible to do so accurately under the circumstances. The original provision of the Act was that it would be administered by a Land Board in the Local Government Authority, which by 1979, under the Second Republic, was an elected body. The potential for this body to block the transactions of very large and powerful parties was quickly realised, and as a result the Land Board was centralised in Ibadan in the state government. It is well known that the transfers of land were contentious, that 'compensation' to the landowners is nowhere close to an economic rent, and that subsequent devolution in the Texaco demise has been confused, just as Omotola predicted. I can, how-ever, outline how some of this looks from the customary-law perspective of the landowning compounds and the tenant farmers.

The customary landowners have started to alter practises with respect to customary tenancy. First of all, iṣákɔ́lɛ̀ is clearly not being transformed into a rent under the more highly commercialised conditions in the 1980s. Omotola suggests that tenants stopped paying the customary landowners when they heard about the stipulations of the Act that vested ultimate land-ownership in the state. I did not hear this, even though it is clearly plausible. In Idere some landowners themselves seem to have been complicit in the decreasing seriousness with which payment of *iṣákọ́lẹ̀* is treated. Many farmers said that they were asked for *iṣákọ́lẹ̀* rather irregularly. One of the very large landowers who was bemoaning the scarcity of tractors, was asked why he did not buy one for himself with the *iṣákọ́lẹ̀* money from the many villages of quite successful farmers that were established on his land. He answered spontaneously and dismissively that it would never be enough. He claimed that only a few cocoa farmers paid as much as N10 each. The total sum was too little to plan any enterprise with, including paying for tractor hire let alone for purchasing the tractor itself.

In 1985 one land-owning compound initiated record-keeping in an account book to keep track of *iṣákọ́lẹ̀* payment. The contents reveal a low, standard N10 p.a. collected from what seemed to be not very many indi-vidual farmers, considering the acreage of land at issue. But then, of course, the vast majority of Idere's own farmers can claim free land access through descent from one or other of their ancestral compounds. Ten naira is a much lower percentage of a farmer's total cash income in 1988 than three or five shillings was in 1968. Both taxes and rent – the feudal-based modes of ex-traction that were carried over in Europe to fulfil critical roles in capitalist development – have simply eroded away over twenty years, from a total of at least 10 per cent of annual cash income to about 1 per cent at most, the amount one might spend as a minor participant in a single ceremonial (see Guyer 1992).

The second entry in the same account book referred to a much larger amount, and it may be that the record-keeping was started with this new kind of transaction in mind: the payments from holders of certificates of occupancy under the Land Use Act. Agreements that grant a person the right to request a certificate of occupancy have to be mediated by a lawyer in order to have legal standing. Some of the agreements either are not legally mediated at all, or the terms highlight all the ambiguities to which Omotola pointed. For example, one significant land transaction was made, in part to try to gain political access. It ended up being based on a verbal agreement from only three of the six compound elders who 'should' have been party to it. At least, this was the opinion of the person who related the story. There are however no clear principles in either law or society about who should be consulted and what might constitute a veto. Compounds are a key institu-tion at the intersection between customary and enacted law but they are not entirely suited to this role. They may be corporate groups in certain respects, in relation to chieftaincy titles or house sites, but they have no undisputed mandate in custom or in law to act as legal individuals, nor to join together like individuals, in associations around common interests. In the end, this particular transaction was based neither on *iṣákólè* nor on an agreement under the law with respect to occupancy. While it may seem negative for the local community in the short run, situations like this in fact leave the local people with undisputed rights in the land. It is the outsider whose rights are insecure. The terms of these varied agreements are too sensitive to discuss, given that I only know any one of them from a limited number of angles, from limited data, and from the general 'knowledge' of local hearsay. Suffice it to say that the amounts of money involved in the initial transaction are large by local standards of income, but the annual payments bear no relationship to the financial strength or commercial viability of the enterprise for which the land has been ceded. In fact, there is no solid framework at all for estimating what an economic rent might be.

Disputes caused by the confluence of a changing local system and an invasive outside presence need to be separated into two different categories, even though any particular case may hold elements of both. The first stems from the link between land and status in Yoruba society and culture, where to be a founder or to be senior (coming first) confers status advantages. Contests over status can be enacted through the medium of contests over land, and contests over land inevitably imply status competition. The second stems from the negative institutional space around land as a component of the commercial economy within the expanding political economy of the hinterland.

The status concern to maintain ultimate reversionary rights is fought out with much greater expertise and experience than is applied to the muddle produced by negative institutional space in the commercialising hinterland. The largest land-owning compounds have lawyers on more or less permanent retainer because status-related disputes are regular and chronic. There have been at least two recurrent disputes in this area, arising in one case over a period of fifty-five years and the other over about thirty-five years. In both cases, the grounds for dispute keep shifting although the participants are the same, and the key issue at stake all along has been the position of a boundary. No one will let up, and new claims keep being concocted. For example, after thirty-five years of ongoing pressures on the boundary, one land-owning compound was accused in court of transgression of the fishing rights of the other by killing off the fish in a river abutting their land by throwing in old cans of Gamalin, a chemical used on cocoa trees. No one seems to expect the current decision on this case to be the last word.

Land can always be used to make points about status in a validating ideology where foundership figures prominently. To claim that a particular party does not own the land is tantamount to delegitimising their entire history. This makes land a tempting target in contests that have nothing to do with its material use. Some struggles are explicitly about the critical symbolic importance of particular sites or boundaries. During the intense struggle over the relative status of the beaded-crown ọbas that was attendant on the creation of Oyo State in 1976, an outsider made an unsuccessful land claim against the site at Ibona to which the Onideres are carried to be buried, and from which they are said to have moved to the present site of Idere to found the town. Burial at Ibona validated the entire history and political structure of the town, so it was impossible to cede. Then during 1988 there was an extremely sensitive legal case in process that involved a whole complex of issues: a title claim on a chieftaincy, town boundaries and an area of farm land. There were ramifications into the chieftaincy hierarchy of Idere, the free or servile status of the ancestry of at least one important compound, and the whole history of a formerly independent town. The case had been heard before in about 1930. Although it was ostensibly about a land boundary, the formal enquiry was held under the Office of Chieftaincy Affairs in the Oyo state government, and their report was marked 'confidential' because of the sensitive nature of the testimonies.

Most of the land disputes that I know of so far have involved status far more than they have focused on land as a commercial resource, so the commercial intentions of the outsiders who started requesting land in the 1980s brought in a new field of strategies, participants and legal rubrics. By virtue of a long interface with land cases fought out in the courts however, the new situation does not find the local population totally naive about legal institutions, nor unprepared to anticipate at least some of the implications of formalising agreements. They are, above all, quite quick to get the scent of formal agreements in the wind, and to mobilise strategies around their expectations. Rumours crop up about visiting strangers asking land-owning compounds for land, and these motivate other citizens and *iṣákọ̀lẹ̀* farmers to try to intervene. In January 1988 people were saying that an area had been ceded to outsiders by one of the landowning compounds. We do not know whether there was any truth in this at all, but non-compound members in the town at large were certainly shaping preventive and pre-emptive strategies. The only way for the rest of the community to influence the terms of an agreement, such as the area or the location of the land ceded, was to foment and finance discord *within* the land-owning compound, in the hope that a faction opposed to the transaction could be created who would then veto it within the family. Since any application for a certificate of occupancy had to be advertised in the *Sketch* (a national newspaper) and the *Tribune* (a newspaper for Oyo state), formal proceedings could not be held secret, unlike the founder–follower agreements of the past. Members of the community who did not belong to the landowning compound were thus keeping track of their sources to make sure they were ready with a workable strategy for derailing proceedings quickly if and when the need arose.

One striking fact in 1988 was that the parties to the agreements between compounds and outsiders to the community may end up with very different assumptions, not necessarily about the monetary terms but about the longevity of the contract and the conditions under which it could lapse or be abrogated. A true certificate of occupancy is for ninety-nine years, a founder-follower agreement is indefinite (subject to acceptable continuing recognition of the primary rights), and a private agreement on terms with the customary occupants lasts for as long as the parties care to specify. Over the longer term the ramifications of land commercialisation to outsiders begin to emerge. In one case, the land-owning compound made an agreement which they understood as a ten-year commitment covered by a lump sum payment that would have to be renegotiated. The law with respect to occupancy, however, does not technically give the opportunity for recurrent renegotiation, because it does not formally recognise the ongoing rights and the basic lease-period from the state is ninety-nine years.

A lawyer who handles this kind of case pointed out that the certificate of occupancy is technically an agreement with the state, which is the ultimate owner of all the land. The customary occupants do not, in fact, figure at all. The mediation with them is a private contract that specifies conditions that will allow the certificate-holder actually to occupy the land, as distinct from using the certificate as a financial asset. On the other hand, he did suggest that the customary occupants can successfully contest the transfer of the certificate of occupancy to a third party of whom they do not approve. If so, of course this defeats the purpose of the law. He confirmed others' observations about the back-dating of sales, but implied that this was technically legal since the law recognises verbal agreements, which could have been made at any time. In summary, he was inclined to think that in fact the customary occupants have a great deal of power to prevent final dispossession by private entrepreneurs (although not by the state), and that the only utility of the law was for 'people in government' to acquire land for private purposes, that is, implying that confident occupancy would be limited to those who had official backing.

Some cessions are never acted on, even if granted. Some are on ten-year agreements about the financial indemnity, and in several cases the term threatened to run out before anyone made any moves to use the land. Other cessions had been activated and then gradually abandoned in the face of the difficulty of making a success of mid-scale agriculture. Yet others had been agreed for acreages far in excess of what could be turned into a farm. A few incumbents are still there, facing a local population that accommodates and in some cases encourages them, but is convinced that the land can be repossessed because these occupants are fundamentally àléjò, strangers.

The land law represents a potentially dangerous situation for the ordinary farmer operating in the urban hinterland, in that official intervention for dispossession is always possible and this strategy has the force of an economic logic behind it, namely middle class investment in land and a soil-mining style of farming. It is very unclear for the moment, however, whether the dynamics of alienation that were set so suddenly in motion by the combined conditions of the end of the 1970s is really a progressive one, or a one-time historical experiment ultimately slowed down by a combination of local safeguards and legal vagueness, and perhaps also by the maintenance of the pastoral corridors and cattle-holding grasslands by the powerful interests that control the meat market. The selective cession of land rights has been tolerated, but only within limits whose very indeterminacy is – for the moment – in the interests of the customary occupants.

Compounds are in the eye of this particular storm, and at a time when their mediation of social life seems to be attenuating, for other reasons. Disputes at the compound level differ quite profoundly in their implications from negotiation and contention in other arenas, where incommensurability of principle is not involved. The local economy faces one market – the urban food market – to which it responds with alacrity under its own rubrics, and another – the land market – to which it relates on an uncharted institutional interface between two different sets of principles. The final chapter develops the principles of the former, in order to distinguish its dynamics clearly from the latter, at a moment in theoretical history when the two tend to be merged under a global concept of the 'market'.

CONCLUSION

Yoruba society is one in which social judgement rests on personal performance. Its institutions safeguard the space for performative initiative and originality by a combination of legal constraints, social incentives and cultural meanings for people to develop their own careers in a changing world. The social frameworks and contentions described in this chapter all promote a competitive process based on skill, acumen, character, personal networks, hard work and good fortune. The struggles over land do not show a pervasive refusal to alienate rights through monetary transactions or to accommodate the rich and the corporations. They show, rather, an effort to incorporate others *on performative terms,* in relation to the rest of the local economy and society. Collective ownership is less a legal tenet or religious injunction than a means of enforcing incumbents to meet performative criteria as skilled workers and diligent citizens. The old theoretical contrast between status and contract does not apply. People's status (as compound members, town citizens, recognised strangers) enables them to engage in a career of contract-making, every step of which is contingent on the quality of their occupational and social effort.

The institutions that are most relevant to career-building shift over time. At present, the kin-based forms of organisation are struggling with forces that both decrease and increase their relevance. Familial co-operation in production is attenuated by women entering farming on their own account, instead of following a variety of seasonal work and domestic tasks, and by the commercialisation of processing. But it could be strengthened eventually in budgeting and consumption by the rising costs of raising children. Compounds are less relevant to religious and occupational identity than in the past, but they are called upon by the legal system to mediate land transactions. Altogether less ambiguous is the chieftaincy system. Achievement of a title is one of the incentives to a career, at least for some people. But beyond the individual life lies an entire history of continual recreation of differentiation by occupation and status. The ǫba deliberately composed it in the nineteenth century. He and the chiefs still represent the terms of engagement amongst the elements, through their ratification and monitoring of associations and their recording and endorsement of verbal contracts. However well they may actually carry out the day-to-day duties, they are invested with guardianship of the principles on which diversity rests.

Accommodation to a multitude of small novelties, the continual creation of new elements, and the formation of working configurations describe the routine functioning of these institutions. Flexibility is less a basic attribute that they have 'in principle' than a result of people's pursuit of their own pathways and of the judgements that others make of their performance. The farming styles described in Part II and the previous chapter, as production is expanded and more profoundly oriented to urban consumers, reflect the same diversifying dynamic as career-creation more broadly. The remote sensing analysis in the previous chapter strongly supports the inference that people have not been pressured by ecological forces or population growth to make the changes they have made. They have moved into and through the possibilities that are offered by an institution that has long existed, and which – as I discuss in the next chapter – is one image of the world itself, namely the market.

NOTES

1. Several farmers were imprisoned for marijuana production in the mid-1960s. They were linked into a regional network by a trader who had married into the community. In the late 1980s fresh egusi was sold by a few farmers into the indigenous and foreign medicine market. The juice is used for a variety of purposes, one of which seems to be the production of fake malaria medication; the very sour taste of egusi juice closely resembles the taste of nivaquine.
2. For a more detailed analysis of work schedules, see Guyer 1992.

14

THE NICHE ECONOMY AND HINTERLAND CHANGE

The feeding of Ibadan over this period of rapid growth is an extraordinary achievement by any standards. General theories of 'the market', whether in terms of short-run price responsiveness or long-run processes of commoditisation through differentiation, offer only partial guides to understanding how overall growth has been managed, through periods of price instability, policy fluctuations and vicissitudes of climate. They help to block out certain parameters, such as the relevance of price, transportation and the presence of corporate enterprise, but they leave whole ranges of phenomena unaddressed. An adequate explanation has to aim to cover the entire configuration, including the terms under which economic life is generated over time within the producing communities.

Over this century, Ibarapa has moved in through discernible circles that surround the urban market. At the turn of the century and until the era of the Bedford lorry and the Ofiki River Bridge, it was remote, tapped only for very specific products that were either economically plausible or politically amenable to transport by headload. From the late 1950s until the mid-1970s, it was in the peripheral hinterland: reachable on a day-trip but poorly serviced enough that every product had to be amenable to sale in storable form. The transport revolution of the 1970s lasted until the late 1980s and brought the whole farming area into the accessible hinterland: a locus for experimentation, sale of perishable goods, incursion and expansion by different kinds of productive enterprise, and the syphoning off of educated and trained labour into the city itself. As long as urban populations continue to grow and transport continues to be available, there is clearly a progressive, cumulative dynamic to the overall picture of incorporation into and response to regional markets. If transport became yet faster, cheaper or more pervasive, Ibarapa could move towards a zone better characterised as the immediate hinterland, amenable to regular production of the most perishable goods such as leaf vegetables and the self-provisioning ambitions of weekend farmers from the urban population. If it collapses, as transport has done in the past, for example in Ilesha during the Great Depression (Peel 1983: 135), preservation will again become a criterion of production and an occupational niche, and the whole economy is likely to shift structurally further away from the urban consumer market. This pattern is entirely consonant with central place theory and the rationality of price responsiveness, applied to the crops and storage technologies of the humid tropics.

The specific form that commercialisation has taken in the Ibadan hinterland also follows from the historical logic of adaptation to the humid savanna ecology, namely the development of certain crops as leading edges of market engagement according to regional ecology, without the overall sacrifice of crop diversity. Ibarapa was the primary source of egusi, and then moved into cassava as the conditions in production, transport and processing improved. This weighting of regional systems as seen from the centre, however, does not involve complete specialisation, either of fields, farms or producing communities. Shifts in crop combinations have allowed a range of identifiable farming styles to emerge with greater clarity than in the past, in a manner that has so far conserved an overall profile of local diversity. This pattern has less to do with subsistence maintenance or even risk coverage on the part of farmers – since its components change over time, and the pattern itself persists even in the context of increasing food purchase – than with the nature of savanna rotational systems and styles of crop-led change that have been characteristic of these regions for a very long time and are probably eminently adapted to climatic and agronomic conditions. Crop combination cannot be abandoned for technical reasons, but differing styles of crop mix, weighting of crops, labour input and length of rotation can emerge. This too follows logics that are understandable in general rational and adaptational terms. They closely follow the inferences of Burnham (1980), Richards (1983) and Dommen (1988) about African savanna styles of intensification.

Progressivist models of commercialisation and differentiation also find confirmation, but within limits. People are indeed buying and selling more than they did in the past, but it is not helpful to see this as part of an evolutionary trajectory. Yoruba communities have been commercial and differentiated for as long as we have records. Neither is this a movement from autonomy to domination. The Nigerian state authorities and class interests have been less successfully integrated into the entire process of urban food supply, above all for the southern cities, than in many other African contexts.

Beyond certain basic correspondences between the predictions of rational/adaptational theory and the findings of the research, the patterns of change are a creation of social dynamics and cultural history, in a system that differs from both the self-provisioning logic that underlies peasant theory and the capitalist logic that is implicit in theories of the market. A set of propositions and templates lies behind the patterns and fluctuations, one that is consistent with assumptions of competition, a price mechanism and individual calculation of advantage, but not on the basis of returns to the classic resources of capitalism: land, labour and capital. The fact that the community has extended the variety of styles of farming within the population in ways that cannot be reduced simply to differential resource endowment suggests that the discipline of returns to factors of production in a competitive market is not exerting the decisive determining influence. The imprecisions of land costs and the virtual absence of capital in all but the corporate enterprises mean that neither land nor capital define efficient resource allocation. The central importance of 'labour', however, is masked if we reduce it to time worked or labour relations, in the differentiated sense. Labour is a complex variable comprising time, skill, personal predilections and use of the full breadth of organisational and institutional resources that mediates economic relations. The one major driving logic beyond response to market demand that emerges is the logic of career enhancement in the rationality of actors. Careers depend on the social organisation of competition, and on the culturally defined avenues for individuals to navigate their own ways.

NICHES: THE SOCIAL ORGANISATION OF COMPETITION

As I worked over the evidence, it seemed that I was seeing in a small place, over a limited social range and a brief phase of its history, some of the generative dynamics of a much larger phenomenon, of considerable historical depth and great cultural complexity. As places like Idere become more clearly 'agricultural communities' than they have ever been, the occupational repertoire seems to change range and composition rather than, in the local conception of things, necessarily narrowing. As new activities are added and old ones – such as palm-cutting, weaving, cloth dying and pottery-making – move out to their own areas of specialisation in the urban hinterland, the social organisation of work retains its multiplicity. The generic processes which von Thünen would see as specialisation are refracted through, and reshaped by, a profound capacity and propensity of the local society and economy to create *a multiplicity of niches*, each with its own terms of operation, each developing through a characteristic series of cultural and social manoeuvres towards the most institutionalised form of the association, with its ceremonial life and public recognition. Successes, failures and ephemeral or partial initiatives of niche creation reshape the repertoire of organisational and technical possibility. Only with an understanding of what those repertoires have become can one address careers adequately: how and why particular categories of people shifted activities at the historical moment they did, and concomitantly, how and why certain components of economic life – such as the male farmers' labour profiles – have remained so breathtakingly persistent in one attribute (total days of work) while shifting in another (phasing over the week).

The social definition and management of the difference and novelty that must be part of any process of growth lies at the core of this process. The following summary must be a descriptive rather than a theoretical model of the characteristics of the niche economy. The generative principles of temporal definition (the precedence of earlier over later) and nominalisation (of 'product' lines, and other defining attributes) that initiate niche creation are impossible to specify adequately in theoretical terms using the methods of study I employed, namely behavioural and social analysis. We would need to bring philosophy and practical life together through a concerted focus on the meaning and social practice of nominalisation, such as the operation of the ubiquitous prefix *oní-*,(*elé-*, *alá*) which announces the process of niche creation. This would constitute a technical cultural and linguistic study all its own, but ultimately a necessary one because the behavioural data testify to their power and because the categories of phenomena – crops, skills, social definitions of persons – that became eligible for niches are not predictable from our social science categories. Nominalisation applies to some phenomena – for example, to kinds of farm labour, modes of transport, market measures, certain kinds of farm and farmer, and occupations – but not so neatly to others, such as the gender division of labour. But neither do names necessarily proliferate indefinitely, as simple descriptors. The name for particular niches can be borrowed to include others or to apply analogously beyond its original designation: *oníkòkò* (owner of cocoa) can be used to apply to owners of all tree crops; *alabáṣẹ́kẹ́rẹ́* (owners of a small razor, i.e. a petty trader) can be applied to a farmer who is only marginally in the market. Sometimes one could clearly see brought forward, to apply to new phenomena, the templates from defunct niches of the past (such as interest rates and measures of a day's work coming forward from the debt–pawn system), or from other niches in the present (such as association structures applied to new occupations, like tractor owner and tractor driver). So there is a parsimonious economy of terms and organisational rubrics here, as well as profusion and invention, that demands its own terms of study.

Within the limits of inference that I can make without such a study, the outlines of a general processual logic can be discerned. Qualitatively different components of the economy are identified, named and thereby fixed in a temporal sequence not unlike the naming and seniority designation of people at birth. Naming can apply to activities (such as egusi harvesting as distinct from tobacco-plucking), categories of worker (Ṣaabẹ as distinct from Agatu), types of newcomers (Bororo as distinct from Fulani in general), varieties of crop (*odóngbó* as distinct from *texaco* cassava), kinds of vehicle (the *jálukere* pick-up as distinct from *bolakaja* lorry), measures (the enamel bowl *olódó* as distinct from the plastic bowl called *iki*; a new type of sack 'with three lines', as distinct from the familiar *alátika*), types of credit institution (*àásù*, *ajọ́* and *mítìn*) and so on indefinitely. None of the generic types is a closed category but rather an open list to be added to and subtracted from.

When it becomes socially established, a name defines a domain of actors, their distinctive activities and the value of their goods and services in a price system. At its most formalised, a named category is realised as a constituted *ẹgbẹ́* under ratification from the chiefs. At that point, certain key aspects of its functioning take on very noticeable stability and predictability over time, at least at the conceptual level and more often than I expected at the real level as well. For example, the cash wage rates for Agatu and the *elégúsí* women harvesters show remarkable stability over a decade or more, while new categories of workers and tasks have entered the economy, under different names, activity-profiles and thereby prices. Even interest rates on certain types of credit seem to be carried forward from precedents in the past.

This is not an automatic process, pursued without contestation. People move against the guidelines, but they move in characteristic ways. The competitive process takes several forms. The first is classic and very old in West African marketing, involving a deviation between nominalised standard and actual content, where the standard is performatively adhered to without dictating the value in 'real' terms of the transaction. It is not clear how far such deviations could go in the past, although the present study suggests that at a certain point they can themselves become explicitly nominalised. For example, the standardly-priced *olódó* market measure of a commodity is variably 'full' in the context of daily bargaining, but has three distinct levels of 'full', each with its own name, in the context of wage payment in kind.

Second, there is the augmentation or diminution of one of the lesser component elements in a package deal. For example the real wages of Agatu have been considerably raised by increasing the number of meals from two per day to three per day, and then allowing meal payment to be commuted to cash, even though it is still negotiated separately under the name of 'food'. A new element can also be granted, such as temporary access to farm land.

There are limits to internal elaboration of this kind. One senses implicit thresholds here. The economy is complex enough to offer major options for similar functions, and there are phases when these options are more competitive for the same clientele, and phases when they are less competitive. A growing economy offers more possibilities for these functions to find differentiated spaces, but even then, new elements are fighting for a place. The Ṣaabẹ are not just ethnically different from the Agatu; their labour organisation offers completely new possibilities to the farmers, and it is really this that the name refers to, not the workers' exact culture of origin. The new forms of credit have their own modes of operation, each under its own name, that may well compete for the clientele of savers. The female cassava processors are being undercut by the novel element of harvest in the field by *jálukere* labourers. If components of the relative prices in competing productive niches cannot be tinkered with satisfactorily any more to preserve their relative spaces in the market, the competitive process can result in the elimination of one or another altogether: by customers covering a domain in a qualitatively different way, or cutting it out completely. Fatigue with negotiations over the egusi harvest, for example, has led many farmers to abandon egusi cultivation altogether, rather than – for example – downsizing.

We see a similar process of potential elimination with respect to the vicissitudes of *iṣákọ́lẹ̀* tribute for land. It does not fit the conditions of land access by the mid- and large-scale farmers, but cannot be bent so far out of shape as to become 'rent', rising and taking on a calculated relationship to the commercial prospects of the enterprise or the size of the land allocation. Since it cannot become that, it is tending to become intermittently paid (or even requested by the landowners) and idiosyncratic in amount. Some landowners exact *iṣákọ́lẹ̀* under the old rules, and others only bother from time to time. Only with a completely new crop, cocoa, were landowners able to change the conditions of access and the price to be paid for land use. With food crops their response has not been to raise the price in accordance with a supply and demand model, but rather, at a certain threshold, to start instituting qualitatively different components to the agreements, including social criteria of access and restriction.

It is as if the price mechanism alone, for established occupational or product niches, were operated over a fairly narrow range of variance, with additions and subtractions of qualitative components taking over the weight of the competitive process as that range is exceeded. If components cannot be added or subtracted for whatever reason, the entire niche is likely to go into demise, with some of the 'functions' taken over, as competitors embark on their own struggle to become established. Old niches on their downfall and new niches struggling for a place in the local economy are repositories and arenas of experience in the social and technical engineering that goes into the entire process. Thus do the operations of price work through novelty and elimination, plus and minus, rather than continuous sliding scales of price, volume and quantity.

The founding moment is of critical cultural importance in defining the limits of variation. Waterman notes for popular music a very similar process of stabilisation around a 'naming moment' that I also found. While there is a profuse and continual process of musical invention, '(d)iversities which result from individual styles ... are not necessarily regarded as changes of musical style so long as these diversities are in conformity with the cultural practices which established the musical genre' (Vidal, quoted in Waterman 1990: 16). How, then, is novelty recognised and named? Which novelties can demand and attain new niches?

Hints in the literature and the fieldwork suggest a whole area of enquiry here for which there is little evidence so far. One mid-range farmer tried growing seed-yams for potential sale, which was a particular interest of technical agriculturalists at the time. His harvest was burned in the barn, an extremely uncharacteristic act. Is it not morally possible for a local farmer to develop a commercial niche in the development of planting material for the staple crops? Or perhaps there were other motives involved. Berry's descriptions of motor mechanics suggest very particular modes of niche definition: 'Most mechanics specialise in one aspect of motor vehicle maintenance and repair – engines, electrical systems, body work, tires – so that a customer may have to go to several different shops' (1985: 148). Rather than develop multiple skills, a mechanic develops a partnership with another who is an explicitly independent operator, even if he works on the same premises.

For the moment these questions about the initial carving out of a niche through nominalisation and monetary valuation remain to be further explored as social process. As Matory writes, in the different context of ritual life: 'money is the sine qua non of 'naming' strategies' (1994: 210). In whatever way this works at its generative moments, the process from then on builds towards, although not necessarily achieving, the establishment of an association and the institutions of apprenticeship whereby entry into the occupation and conditions of operation are controlled. Full membership is celebrated at the 'freedom ceremonies' for graduates. This entire complex of organisation, training and celebration went into a second growth spurt during the oil boom, when specialties proliferated, and freedom ceremonies became more numerous and more expensive than most other kinds of celebration in social life, excepting only funerals.

This level of social recognition has been achieved in agriculture only in the contract farming of tobacco, but the process of self-definition as a farmer (or a whole village) particularly skilled in this or that crop, or in operating a particular size of farm, is clearly in evidence. If people are now giving up the old occupational specialities they are nevertheless importing idiosyncracy into farming itself. And in this particular case, the variety may not break down neatly along familiar lines such as gender and age. Young men and women straddle the difference that can be discerned by an observer between full-time and side-line farming. Meaningful categories are being generated: by type of farm: (*aladanla* (owner of a large farm), *alabéṣékéré* (a marginal seller), and by type of crop: *olọbè/elewebè* (owner of a vegetable farm), *onikòkó* (owner of a treecrop farm), *àgbè onisu* (owner of yams), *àgbè onítomato* (tomato farmer), although not – apparently, or not yet – owner of egusi, maize or cassava.[1] Naming is, however, a restless and shifting process for the moment, with cross-cutting criteria, and with whole categories whose ongoing styles could still go in different directions; a shift of speciality is usually easier within agriculture than across craft specialisations. Farming, however, does belong to the niche dynamic, rather than lying outside it, as shown by the pervasive tendency towards narrow spectrum cultivation by individual farmers even in the context of the maintenance of a fully varied repertoire of diversity by the community.

The economy based on producer niches, named and framed in local conceptions and institutions, is a commercial economy. Its framework of technical and cultural predictability assumes pervasive exchange of the goods and services created through human effort via the medium of money. Every occupation and activity is founded on the notion that its services will be offered for cash in return for a livelihood. The more predictable and institutionalised is one occupational niche, the more possible it is for another to develop in relationship to it. The most important example in the farming economy is crop purchase at the farm by specialist traders who deal in bulk, that allows farmers some confidence in developing particular lines of production, instead of producing smaller quantities of varied crops that would be sorted by *pàràkòyí* in the wholesale markets. With technical and crop innovation the process towards niche establishment is quite relentless. For example, it is almost impossible for the owner of a tractor to protect it from others, not due to a 'traditional' adherence to a morality of communal obligation but rather to the pervasive assumption that its use should be open to commercial access through the *ẹgbẹ́*-type of organisation and price-setting. The morality of the niche economy is intolerant of enclaves that name their conditions of existence unilaterally of others in the community in which they are situated and make highly restrictive access a barrier condition to exchange. Everything should be accessible through commercial channels.

As long as the land frontier still exists, it may be the niche morality that accounts for any truculence and animosity towards the large-scale farmers rather than class conflict in a classic sense. Some have tried to operate as enclaves, naming terms rather than negotiating them, and dealing directly with sources and buyers outside the local arena. Farmers in the local economy can try to out-compete the large farmers, not just by the classic western process of self-exploitation that drives down returns to labour and makes their products cheaper, but by cornering the local labour pool through manipulation of the components of the wage. Even the corporate farming that comparative scholarship would see as rural class differentiation is seen and treated locally more like a set of new components in the economy, to be vigorously competed with, outwitted, kept within bounds, tapped into and ultimately got rid of if necessary, to some degree like any other.

The Yoruba literature is largely consonant with these principles. As Lloyd showed in his study of urban Yoruba approaches to inequality, there is no necessary resentment of wealth as long as others can tap into it. It is not wealth and power *per se* that are morally problematic, or the wages their holders may pay others, but rather 'their withdrawal ... from daily contact with the masses and the restriction of their generosity to their closer kin [that] are seen as being contrary to traditional values' (Lloyd 1974: 193). Peel reiterates the conclusion: 'What is demanded of the rich ... is that they should associate themselves with the town, build houses and spend money there ...' (1983: 260). This point is elaborated by Karin Barber, based on the study of oral texts. The premise of difference and the imperative for money to circulate are mutually implicated: '(W)hatever the differences of fortune and status, there are no separate spheres of exchange for the affluent and the indigent. All of them have to participate in the circulation of the same medium: money ... To be part of Yoruba humanity, it is necessary to take part in this cycle, which is mediated by money' (Barber 1995: 208). Everyone expects to negotiate these terms of engagement, as is epitomised by the Eleruwa's account of his confrontation with the teenage girl, a citizen of his own town, who kept her team of workers off the job of spreading fertiliser on one of his plots until she felt that the conditions were right. Everyone must submit themselves to the risks of loss by maintaining and furthering their differentiated place as performers of social and technical skills, not as passive holders of assets. Personal careers demand and encourage a variety that Fadipe noted, early in Yoruba studies, to go far beyond strict funcionality: 'In spite of the ... opportunities ... offered for a practically self-sufficient household economy, there are many occupations ...' (1970: 150–1).

The philosophical underpinnings of human multiplicity in Yoruba language and thought have been suggested by Akiwowo (1986) in an article on *iwà*. He glosses *iwà* as being or character. Bascom defines it as 'fate' (1951: 492) because in the indigenous religion each person chooses it before birth. A community is *asuwada*, a 'purposive clumping of diverse *iwà*' (Akiwowo 1986: 347). Difference and 'clumping' are logically mutually constitutive; there is no priority to either the element or the unit. This form of grouping is conceptually and linguistically distinguished from a boundless heap of fragments, such as seeds. Lawuyi and Taiwo (1990) have debated whether *iwà* refers to an initial state of being or the path forward to self-realisation. Either way, the point here is that the notion of a ramifying 'difference with access' that pervades economic practice, and that departs from an 'organic solidarity' image of a working whole divided into complementary functions, does find consonance with ideas in the philosophical corpus. Difference is wedded to career rather than to function.

NICHES AND CAREERS

While useful, the current analytical concepts are all somewhat lacking to depict the combination of multiplicity, finely graded hierarchy, relentless competition and ordered social process that are operative in combination here. The concept 'diversity' implies equality, whereas the concept of 'differentiation' implies structured hierarchy. Swindell's concept of 'mosaic' captures the sense of multiple points of connection amongst niches within local areas. The concept of '*filières*', or sequences of relationship, that is used in the French literature on particular products in urban provisioning systems,[2] or 'channels', captures a sense of the ramifying networks at the regional level. At one level this differs little from Jones' (1972) earlier concept of 'market chains', which he used to assess the efficiency of trade. Taken sociologically and historically however, *filières* can also address gradations of power by illuminating key links in the chain of connections. Cassava *filières* in Brazzaville are marked by very weak differentiation (LePlaideur and Moustier 1991: 153), whereas Yoruba local economies do not create equality. Rather there are many very small gradations on the basis of the income that is realisable through the operation of the negotiated prices within and between specialised lines of operation. A woman earns more as an egusi harvester than as a tobacco plucker. An Agatu labourer earns more than a Ṣaabẹ weeder. In general, those who precede stake out their terms; those who follow in the same general domain have to accept a notch lower, at least initially.

The social dynamic of niches creates and re-creates an open-ended roster of products, occupations and *filières* out of the novel opportunities that changing historical circumstances bring. The aspect of economic dynamics that the 'niche' adds to the other concepts is a focus on the order in the processes of creation and growth: synchronically (cyclically) with respect to foundation and development of a speciality, and above all diachronically under the fluctuating conditions of the larger political economy.

I have already discussed niche creation as a part of the economic competitive process. There is a concomitant process of career-building, that also has both repetitive and historically changing modes of realisation. Individuals can only advance within their niche by enlarging operations and by improving productivity through technical or organisational means, if and when conditions allow. Association fosters growth along these kinds of lines. But for a variety of reasons, including the exigencies of cultivating a stable pool of customers (see Berry 1985), the prohibitive expense of investment under unstable macro-economic conditions, and niche stabilisation itself, these means to ambition may be superceded by people simply switching specialities, moving up and down the graded income hierarchy by moving on. The local niche itself remains, with changed personnel.

Studies of crafts and trade offer several examples of career mobility of this type. The leader of the yam traders in the market becomes a beer trader (Trager 1985). Musicians move up within the band by switching instruments, until the point at which a successful band captain may want 'to move out of the music business altogether and into a more secure, higher status occupation, such a construction or trading' (Waterman 1990: 157,156). As Barber (1981) indicates for Yoruba religion, when their spirit is no longer powerful, the acolytes shift to another. The identity of person, craft and source of spiritual power is less complete than in the feudal model of guilds. Personal fulfilment can take precedence over loyalty to a specialty. Under unstable conditions the switches surely become more frequent.

Niche stabilisation places thresholds at both the upper and the lower levels of acceptable functioning. An example of the buffering against downward mobility is offered by Lawuyi and Falola (1992), which comes from ceremonial life which corresponds very closely to the qualitative bargaining modes described earlier for economic life. The authors tabulate the personal economies that the current economic crisis has brought to funeral celebration, showing how the cost of specific elements are manipulated so that the overall social effect on the person can be stabilised. '(E)ssential qualities of human beings and the means and mode of exchange are intricately interwoven such that goods and labour are representations of character, and character is a means of appreciating the worth of goods and labor' (Lawuyi and Falola 1992: 226). Their description bears repeating, so similar is the reasoning to the competitive processes in niche maintenance in the market economy. There are sixteen conceptually separate elements to the funeral ceremony, all costing money. In order to economise, some are dropped altogether, others are made less expensive by a qualitative narrowing of the social participation or selective curtailment of stages; others are retained at the same nominal level while the actual practice reduces the cost. The institution is thereby rendered far less expensive while retaining a form that preserves the personal standing of the celebrant, in a fashion that exactly parallels the intricacy of bargaining, adjustment, negotiation and stabilisation within niches, and the struggle to maintain them against pressures from without. In both, social standing is a central motivation.

The dynamics of difference and the value of persons lie at the heart of an understanding of the relationship amongst ecology, occupation and economic change in this society. Themes of nominalisation (of elements and persons), qualitative and graded valuation, competitive processes amongst niches and career trajectories that may cross them, run through the entire literature. Further horizons far beyond a farming study are opened up by the inferences I have drawn. What do skills consist of? What qualifies as a skill? How are 'character' and 'monetisation' linked for the relatively poor? How does wealth function in a late twentieth-century economy that is a market economy without being capitalist?. In Hart's (1982b) terms, it produces commodities for others, in a specialised division of labour, through market exchange mediated by money. Producers also invest their cash income in production, with a view to increasing their incomes. Interest rates and other returns to institutionalised capital do not however determine the level of production.

The disciplines of economic life inhere, rather, in the competitive conditions for career enhancement, for self-realisation (see Barber 1995) or 'character' (Lawuyi and Falola 1992), within what Bascom (1951) referred to as 'a pecuniary society'. As Belasco wrote, uncertainty 'is not focused on profit but on existential reversals' (1980: 32). Tellingly, he argues that it is Ifa divination that is thought to govern the key moments of economic life. Ifa is the mythical 'begetter of the traditional socioeconomic sectors of Yoruba life: he begat "Farm", "Market", "War", "Road", and "House"' (Belasco 1977: 67). Divination 'directed secular activity ... it could dictate an individual's occupational choice' (1977: 66). In a more general way, 'Ifa consultation transcends the mystification of the market' and renders its vagaries transparent (1977: 62–3).

We do not know how divination permeates economic decision making in the present, but, as I found in the analysis of labour profiles, farmers show in the limits they maintain as in the innovations that they make, that the intersection of life and work that makes the social career is an orienting ideal. There are clear boundaries to how much, and what, farmers will modify in order to maximise money returns because all the conditions of life have to be workable together and synergistically.

GROWTH, CHANGE AND COMPARISONS

I have argued that farming is a part of this larger dynamic, in a fashion that builds technical innovation around new crops and varieties, combined in new configurations that are anchored in the savanna agro-ecology of conservative land use. New configurations are mobilised at different historical moments, in different ways, by social categories within the producer population who are struggling to establish viable footholds in the commercial economy, their members shifting and sorting themselves across the spectrum of possibilities for specialisation: part-timing as the subsistence option, sidelining as the commercial option in complementarity to other income sources, narrow spectrum 'cassava-plus' farming on an individuated or localised collective model, and broad-spectrum commercial engagement. This economy has contained, and still contains, substantial potential for growth and change along market lines. The one thing it has not become is capitalist in its working principles. In fact, Mabogunje (1995) sees as a necessity *in the future* for strategic policy interventions in monetary management to initiate the changes that would turn savings into capital, in the Western sense. By implication, capitalism does not emerge by itself. His own strategy emulates the relatively peaceful process of 'institutional radicalisation' that he finds in certain phases and domains of the Western history of capitalism, as distinct from transformation by dispossession.

Places like Ibarapa are currently on the cusp of three possibilities: managing its own rubrics (defensively or expansively, depending on policy, the availability of crop and varietal innovation, and the state of urban demand); transforming slowly under key initiatives such as the community banks envisaged by Mabogunje (1995); or being essentially dispossessed or marginalised by interests embedded in formal capital of one sort or another, state or private. Other rural areas of Nigeria are linked to capital more profoundly than the West: the East through a strong private presence, and the North more predominantly through the state. A niche economy may not depend on large scale capital but it does depend on demand. Buoyant demand depends on incomes, which in turn implies a level of growth that can generate considerably more than the 15–20 per cent maximum real income growth per man – that is, not even per capita – over twenty years that these farmers have achieved. Dislocation from the centres of wealth in the economy and absolute impoverishment reduce all the possibilities: of occupational diversification, technical advance within stabilised niches, maintenance of the producer/consumer *filières*, and rising levels of diver- sified demand. The more that the state retreats from society into a mineral- financed enclave, the less relevant are any of the scenarios that create formal/ informal sector linkages – or any of the mosaic of multiple linkages to which practitioners in the niche economy avidly aspire – to the regional economic future.

Already by 1988, and in spite of vigorously expanding agricultural supply, declining urban incomes were being noted in the countryside as '*kò s'ówó*': 'there's no money' (see Williams 1991). The level of consumer demand, rather than bottlenecks in production *per se*, will certainly shape that future, as Thirsk (1985) argued that it shaped the expansion of English agriculture before the capitalist revolution. The central importance of demand conditions was noted by an earlier generation of scholars of African economies. As late as 1972 Jones was still addressing the argument that self- sufficiency in staple foods resulted in 'the inadequacy of demand' (1972: 12), which critically limited the potential for growth. Twenty years later rural Nigeria may be entering a period that was just on the horizon in 1988, where inadequacy of demand accounts for severe limits, not because of self- provisioning but because of the inaccessibility by the ordinary market dynamics of a differentiated society, of the enclave created by the rich.

Any tighter and more generative model of the dynamics of the niche economy and its engagement with regional and national forces demands further study on both sides of the 'formal/informal' interface. The funda- mental philosophical principles by which difference is defined in Yoruba, and other West African, economic cultures need more elaboration. The changing terms of operation of other market economies – capitalist, non- capitalist and newly-capitalist – need to be compared. The rapidly moving conceptual work on the sociology of markets needs to be assimilated, such as, for example, Burt and Talmud's (1993) work on 'market niche' in indus- trial economies. Ultimately, for those of us working in Africa and other 'marginal' economies of the world, the relationship *among* the structurally different economies that will define the conditions of life in the global future demands more study, in longer time frames. From a historical perspective, the complex that I have evoked here is not 'truly' endogenous but probably a historical creation of the powerful interfaces of the past: the Atlantic trade and vast cowry imports into local circuits. The fact that this is a historical creation raises the possibility that increasingly pervasive monetisation may mediate similar organisational and cultural elaboration in other societies. And the fact of a persistent, even if moving, interface between metropolitan and West African economies over several centuries encourages renewed attention to its dynamics.

The idea of a niche economy is a construct in our own contentions about how best to 'place' African economic change theoretically in an era when the idea of development has become so deeply suspect (see Watts 1993, for a summary). Even if these rural economies are not transforming along familiar lines, neither are they necessarily – at least for the moment – becoming increasingly anarchic, dysfunctional and environmentally destructive, as the 'crisis' literature implies. If there is order to routine daily phenomena such as urban provisioning, and if the non-hegemonic state (to use Berry's term) and world market frame, without determining, their dynamics, then analysis may not be well-served by reactive guiding concepts such as 'counter-modernity' or 'postcolonialism' or a generic 'informal sector'. African directions of social re-creation around commercial relations may be rendered almost as opaque if marginality, contingency and indeterminacy frame the enquiry as they are using the benchmarks of standard development. I suggest here, instead, that they may be working through logics, and at interfaces, that have yet to be adequately defined and theorised, and whose understanding rests on the renewed empirical endeavour of recent years, to which this study is a contribution.

NOTES

1. I am indebted to William Brieger for eliciting these terms after my fieldwork was over.
2. For example the Centre de Cooperation Internationale en Recherche Agronomique pour le Developpement (CIRAD) held a seminar in 1989 entitled The Filière Economy in Tropical Regions. Filiere is both a method of study that can be applied to any product and also a sociological finding, namely that the relationships that shape the market are 'peu capitalistiques' (LePlaideur and Moustier 1991: 155). Without comparative work such as Skinner explores for Chinese and other urban provisioning systems, we are not yet sure for Africa how varied the historical and socio-cultural dynamics are.

APPENDIX A

REMOTE SENSING STUDY OF THE AGRARIAN LANDSCAPE IN IDERE

Eric Lambin

Geographic coordinates: The image processed is a square of 512 x 512 pixels, each pixel having a size of 20 x 20 metres. The size of the image is thus 12.4 x 12.4 kilometres, or 153.76 square kilometres. It is centred on the town of Idere. The exact geographical coordinates of the corners are:

- NW: 7 degrees 35 minutes North; 3 degrees 10 minutes East;
- NE: 7 degrees 34 minutes North; 3 degrees 19 minutes East;
- SW: 7 degrees 25 minutes North; 3 degrees 9 minutes East;
- SE: 7 degrees 24 minutes North; 3 degrees 18 minutes East.

The data from the SPOT satellite were recorded at the end of the rainy season. In the multispectral mode (green, red, and near-infrared), these data have a spatial resolution of 20 x 20 metres. A subscene of 512 x 512 pixels (12.4 x 12.4 kilometres) has been defined to include Idere and its agricultural land. The data were corrected geometrically and radiometrically. A strong within-band line striping had to be removed by matching brightnesses and standard deviations of striped lines with the statistical parameters of neighbouring lines. Corrections also had to be performed to compensate for an atmospheric haze which reduced the dynamic range of image intensity.

A supervised classification was conducted on this subscene to produce a land use map. The different steps of this procedure include:

- the identification of discernible land use classes; these are the information classes;
- the estimation of the parameters of the classifier algorithm from the training areas; these parameters form the signature of the classes and are the properties of the probability model to be used;
- the selection of representative or prototype 'training areas' for these classes by using field work data and a reference map of physiographic units;
- the classification of the data by a maximum likelihood method; the classification algorithm quantitatively evaluates the mean, variance, and covariance of the category spectral response patterns when classifying an unknown pixel;
- the production of a tabular summary and a thematic map which summarise the results of the classification.

A vegetation index computed from the radiances in the red and near-infra-red channels (normalised difference vegetation index) has been used to improve the discrimination between vegetation types. This index is sensitive to the total biomass and the photosynthetic activity of vegetative cover.

The output of this classification is a land use map of the region around Idere. Six classes were discriminated:

- cultivated land;
- cleared land;
- granite outcrops;
- bottoms of valleys;
- savanna;
- dense vegetation.

The class 'cleared land' includes a majority of fields, but also some recent fallows and bare soils around towns or in eroded zones. It had to be defined separately from the class 'cultivated land' because the spectral response patterns of these two classes were significantly different. This could correspond to different mineral compositions, organic matter contents, or vegetation cover. The class 'bottoms of valleys' is characterised by a high soil moisture. The class 'savanna' also includes fallow land with a natural vegetation cover. Finally, 'dense vegetation' includes forest, wooded savannah, and dense cocoa plantations.

This supervised classification was the basis for an estimation of the areas and the proportions of the different land use types. This information was extracted by a computerised inventory of all pixels belonging to a specific class. The main landscape units were identified and delineated. Areas predominantly occupied by agricultural fields were distinguished from areas that offer a potential for an expansion of agriculture. The land use map was smoothed spatially to decrease the local spatial variability of the classification and create a more homogeneous map. A majority filter with a 3 x 3 moving window was applied to the data. This operation allows for a more accurate assessment of the extent and spatial distribution of land use types and makes the image more easily visually interpreted.

In addition to these interpretations of land use types and landscape units, a discrimination between tractor-cleared fields and hand-cleared fields was attempted in the area around Idere. These two types of fields have been discriminated by the application of a pattern recognition algorithm to the satellite data. Three spatial criteria have been defined:

- *the shape of the fields*: tractor-cleared fields have a geometric shape, with linear borders while traditional fields have a more heterogeneous shape;
- *their size*: tractor-cleared fields tend to be much bigger than traditional fields. To operate a tractor, a minimum size of the field is

required and the mechanisation of a field becomes more efficient for big clearings. In traditional farming, the size of the fields is usually small;

— *the transition between the field and the savanna*: for traditional fields, the transition from the field to the surrounding natural vegetation is usually a continuum characterised by a decreasing density of the crops and an increasing presence of natural vegetation. As opposed to this pattern, tractor-cleared land is characterised by a sharp and well-defined limit between the field and its surrounding. The transition between the field and surrounding can be detected with SPOT data, thanks to the high spatial resolution of this sensor.

To these criteria based on the spatial structure of the cultivated land, it is possible to add one criterion related to the spectral response of the fields. Tractor-cleared fields appear brighter (they reflect more energy) because tractor farming requires the removal of all trees and natural vegetation in the cultivated area. Thus, no shadow or woody biomass decrease the spectral signature of pixels. However, the difference in spectral response of tractor-cleared cultivated land and traditional fields is the less reliable element of discrimination and intervenes as a secondary criterion.

Indeed, these criteria applied to satellite data cannot perform a 100 per cent accuracy in the discrimination of tractor-cleared land and hand-cleared fields, but they certainly provide a good estimation of the proportion of these two types of farming practices. While it should be possible to computerise this pattern recognition method, a visual interpretation of the data has been performed in this case. Computerisation would require a rather complex approach which would be justified only if a very large area would have to be processed.

The proportion of the two types of fields has been estimated through a sampling technique based on a grid of 823 points spatially distributed in a systematic fashion. The estimation has been performed three times, with three different spatial arrangements of the grid. The results of these three separate estimations have been averaged. Their divergence was in a range of + or –0.5 per cent. Thus, we can consider that the sampling error is negligible. The only source of error occurs in the interpretation of tractor-cleared or hand-cleared fields. The proportion of tractor-cleared lands has been estimated in terms of the area under cultivation which has been cleared by tractor compared to the total area under cultivation. This proportion could also have been estimated in terms of number of fields cleared by tractor compared to the total number of fields in the region. This last approach is not possible at the small geographical scale of the SPOT data and would require large-scale aerial photographs or field measurements. These two proportions are expected to be different because tractor-cleared fields tend to be much larger than hand-cleared fields.

APPENDIX B

TOWARDS A HISTORY OF PRICES AND A CONSUMER PRICE INDEX

There are four price series most relevant to rural producers: the urban consumer price for their products, the local price of purchase, the price of goods that they regularly purchase, and the cost of transport. Each is officially collected in a different way and in ways that do not always inspire confidence. Each is subject to its own shaping forces, especially the prices of petrol and beer. Petroleum products have administered prices, and a reconstruction turned out to be more difficult than I imagined it would be. The official figures are not self-explanatory, so I set these prices aside for future attention.

As official figures, I include only those series that can be completed, namely the urban prices for farm products and consumer items. I complete this appendix with an indication of local market price history, as told by traders, and pieces of the history of 'big ticket' items of expenditure that people could still reconstruct: school fees and medical care.

A NOTE ON UNITS

Price and Weight

The units of both price and weight/volume have changed over the time period covered. The pound sterling was replaced by the Nigerian naira and kobo in 1972, at the rate of N2 to the pound (that is, a kobo was 1.2 pennies); the pound weight was replaced by the kilo in 1976; the use of standard local market measures (the *olódó* and cigarette cup) was no longer reported after 1974. One *olódó* of gari was 7.751 lb (3.5 kg); one cigarette cup of egusi was 0.381 lb (0.17 kg). For simplicity, the units of weight/volume have been converted to a uniform measure.

In 1985 egusi started to be reported explicitly as 'shelled'. For earlier years this is not specified. In view of the difficulty of accurate conversion, I take the entire series as if it were for the shelled seeds.

Seasonality

Wherever possible the month of June is used as the index month for the year; where not possible, July or August is used. No other month is reported because of wide seasonal fluctuations. For example, for 1986, when prices for every month are available, gari prices varied 100 per cent over the year from 43k per kg in February to 86k per kg in June. Egusi prices varied 90 per cent, from 513k in March to 975k in July. How typical these peaks and troughs are from year to year is not necessarily clear since they depend on climate and other variables, over the entire food supply region. Manufactured items show no marked seasonality.

OFFICIAL PRICES, 1968–86

Table B.1: Ibadan prices for Gari (a Cassava Product) and Egusi-melon, 1968–86 (Price per kg: in pence (to 1972), in kobo (to 1986). Year's price represented by June, unless otherwise indicated).

	Gari	Egusi
1968 (Aug)	4.6 pence	40.1 pence
1969 (Aug)	6.5	50.3
1970	12.1	65.8
1971	20.3	74.1
1972	16.8	88.4
1973	10.8 kobo	68.5 kobo
1974	10.4	55.8
1975	n.d.	141.9
1976	25.1	120.1
1977	34.4	170.9
1978–9	n.d	n.d.
1980 (July)	44.5	277.5
1981	127	256
1982–83	n.d.	n.d.
1984	137	273
1985 (July)	110	430 (shelled)
1986	86	784 (shelled)
Ratio, 1968–86 (*pennies:kobo*)	1:19	1:27

Source: Federal Office of Statistics, *Retail Prices and Consumer Prices Indices for Selected Urban Centres*.
Note:
1. The general price rise at the end of the Civil War in 1970.
2. The general price rise in 1974, said to be the result of the Udoji Commission Report and consequent rises in civil service salaries and pensions.
3. The 1980–81 rise which is particularly remembered by local farmers.

Table B.2: Ibadan Retail Prices, Consumer Items (Shirting, Bicycle Tyres, Star Beer, Kerosene) 1968–84.

	Shirting (10yd/m)	Tyres (1)	Beer (1 bottle)	Kerosene (litre)
1968	24.00s	11.38s	3.5s	8d
1969	29.00s	12.08s	3.5s	8d
1970	31.38s	25.11s	3.5s	8d
1971	27.50s	13.80s	4.5s	8d
1972	24.13s	13.18s	4.5s	8d
1973	N2.53	N1.28	N0.47	7k
1974	N2.7	N1.06	N0.35	8.33k
1975	N5.25	N1.45	N0.70	15.00k
1976	N6.02	N2.00	N0.65	16.67k
1977	N6.29	N1.60	N0.70	16.67k
1978	N15.00	n.d.	N1.05	16.67k
1979	n.d.	N6.75N	N1.03	33.33k
1980	N13.50	N6.00	N1.15	33.33k
1981	N14.00	N6.00	N1.13	33.33k
1982–3	n.d.	n.d.	n.d.	n.d.
1984	N30.00	N14.50	N1.23	25.05k
1985	n.d.	n.d.	n.d.	n.d.
1986	n.d.	n.d.	N1.23	17k
Ratio 1968–86 (*pennies:kobo*)	1:10	1:11	1:3	1:2

As an administered price kerosene moved up and stabilised in steps, maintaining an overall low rate of inflation. The price of manufactured beer was kept low by the rapid expansion of industrial beer production, in part through parastatal involvement, in the late 1970s. The national textile industry also expanded.

The price of food in the cities clearly rose faster than the price of basic consumer items.

LOCAL PRICES

Produce

The potential for inaccuracy is so enormous, given different types of crop preparation, different prices conditions for different size measures, differing production conditions due to rain, and farmers' own choice of where to sell, that only indicators are given here that can identify major shifts over time. All prices were elicited from traders in the Igbo-Ora markets by Nasiru Iṣọla.

Egusi

1977: N50 per bag in the rainy season and N60 in the dry season.
1979: many farmers sold straight to Lagos at N75 per bag because local prices were lower.
1981: N75 per bag in local markets.
1982–85: stabilised around N75 per bag.

1985–86: N80.

1987: especially noted for price rise to N95.

1988: N140 per bag.

1989: at N6 per *olódó* and N240 per bag (*alatika* type).

Summary: local wholesale prices probably quadrupled, 1977–1989, with most of the price rise after 1986 (comparable to the urban price history). Farmers received approximately one-third of the urban consumer price for the shelled seed.

Cassava

Gari: sold in units of *pebi, kongo, olódó, garawa* (measures) and *olotere* and *alatika* (bags).

Olabisi, trader since 1980. Interviewed 23 March 1988

1980: Olodo: N1.50 (alatika bag at N40).

1982: bag at N70.

1986–7: prices rose.

1988–9: Alatika bag at N234 in the dry season and N198 in rainy season.

Lafun (flour):

1978: N40–50 per bag.

1980: N60–65.

1981–85: N65–70.

1986: N80.

Fresh, by the pick-up load (approximately one-tenth of an acre, said to yield about 4–5 bags of flour)

1978: N65.

1981: N85.

1981: more or less stable.

1987: N100.

1988: N180.

Summary: local cassava prices doubled between the late 1970s and about 1985, then doubled again 1987–88. In general, the bad weather of 1987, as well as inflation, is responsible for the rapid rises after that year.

Major Expenses
School fees

See Table B.3

Antenatal/Delivery Fees, and Supplies, Government Clinic

1965: total clinic cost: 26s; supplies: 24s (few women delivered in the clinic in those days).

1975: all services but birth registration were made free.

1984: total clinic cost: N17.

1990: supplies cost: N33.

Table B.3: School Fees, Okedere High School (naira)

Year	Basic (per term, 3 per yr)	Uniform	Textbooks (*per session*)	Meal cost	PTA and other
1976	25	3	5	20k	Crafts (kind)
1980	free	15	free	50k	Crafts (kind)
1985	40	10	n.d.	50k	10
1990	40	30	60–80	50k	10

Annual, per child: 1976: N93 plus food.
                   1990: N340 plus food.

Examples of Farmers' Reports on Major Consumer Expenses for 1987

Apprenticeships: N280, for electrical work.
     N100, for carpentry.

Medical costs: N700 for adult daughter's surgery (she died).
     N700 for surgery.
     N600 for surgery.
     N260 for child's hospitalisation.

Debts on ceremonial: N600 on a wedding two years previously.
     N1,000 on a funeral.

Current ceremonial: N320 courts costs for divorce of prospective wife.
     N300 for child's naming ceremony.
     N500 for child's freedom ceremony.
     N1,000 for wife's father's funeral.
     N1,200 for father's funeral.
     N430 towards cost of feast for own taking of a minor title.

Fixing house: N120.
     N400.

BIBLIOGRAPHY

Abimbola, Wande (1976) *Ifa: An Exposition of Ifa Literary Corpus*, Ibadan: Oxford University Press.

Abraham, R. C. (1958) *Dictionary of Modern Yoruba*, London: University of London Press.

Abu, Bala Dan et al. (1989), 'Hands of vengeance', *Newswatch*, 9(11): 14–19.

Adebayo, Akanmu G (1996), 'Contemporary dimensions of migration among historically migrant Nigerians: the Fulani Pastoralists in South-western Nigeria', Paper presented to the conference on Refugees and Displacement, York University, Canada.

Adesina, Akinwumi (1992), 'Village-level studies and sorghum technology development in West Africa: case study in Mali', in J. L. Moock and R. E. Rhoades (eds), *Diversity, Farmer Knowledge, and Sustainability*, Ithaca: Cornell University Press, pp. 147–168.

Akinbode, Adefofu, Bryan Stoten and Rex Ugorji (eds) (1986) *The Role of Traditional Rulers and Local Governments in Nigerian Agriculture*, Ilorin: Agricultural and Rural Management Training Institute, University of Ilorin Press.

Akintoye, S. A. (1971*) Revolution and Power Politics in Yorubaland 1840–1893*, London: Longman.

Akiwowo, Akinsola (1986), 'Contributions to the sociology of knowledge from an African oral poetry', *International Sociology*, 1(4): 343–58.

Akiwowo, Akinsola and Arun C. Basu (1969) *Tobacco Growers in Northern Oyo Division and Adoption of New Farming Ideas and Practices*, Ibadan: Nigerian Institute of Social and Economic Research.

Alexander, Paul (1992), 'What's in a price? Trading practices in peasant (and other) markets', in Roy Dilley (ed.), *Contesting Markets. Analyses of Ideology, Discourse and Practice*, Edinburgh: Edinburgh University Press, pp. 79–96.

Allan, William (1965) *The African Husbandman*, Westport, CT: Greenwood Press.

Amanor, Kojo (1994) *The New Frontier: Farmer Responses to Land Degradation, a West African Study*, London and Atlantic Highlands, NJ: Zed Books in association with UNRISD.

Andrae, Gunilla and Bjorn Beckman (1985) *The Wheat Trap: Bread and Underdevelopment in Nigeria*, London: Zed Books in association with the Scandinavian Institute of African Studies.

Andrae, Gunilla and Bjorn Beckman (1987) *Industry Goes Farming: The Nigerian Raw Materials Crisis and the Case of Textiles and Cotton*, Uppsala: Scandinavian Institute of African Studies, Research Report No. 80.

Apter, Andrew (1992) *Black Critics and Kings: The Hermeneutics of Power in Yoruba Society*, Chicago: University of Chicago Press.

Austin, Gareth (1993), 'Indigenous credit institutions in West Africa, c.1750–c.1960', in G. Austin and K. Sugihara (eds), *Local Suppliers of Credit in the Third World, 1750–1960*, New York: St Martin's Press, pp. 93–159.

Awe, Bolanle (1967), 'Ibadan, its early beginnings', in P. C. Lloyd, A. L. Mabogunje and B. Awe (eds), *The City of Ibadan: A Symposium on its Structure and Development*, Cambridge: Cambridge University Press in association with the Institute of African Studies, University of Ibadan, pp. 11–25.

Babalola, Ademola (1992), 'BAT and the penetration of capital into Oyo State', *Review of African Political Economy*, No. 53, (March), 96–101.

Barber, G. Renate (1966) *Igbo-Ora, a Town in Transition: A Sociological Report on the Ibarapa Project*, Ibadan: Oxford University Press.

Barber, Karin (1981), 'How Man makes God in West Africa: Yoruba attitudes towards the Orisa', *Africa*, 51: 7224–45.

Barber, Karin (1982), 'Popular reactions to the petro-naira', *The Journal of Modern African Studies*, 20: 431–50.

Barber, Karin (1991) *I Could Speak Until Tomorrow: Oriki, Women and the Past in a Yoruba Town*, Edinburgh: Edinburgh University Press for the International African Institute.

Barber, Karin (1995), 'Money, self-realization and the person in Yoruba texts', in J. I. Guyer (ed.), *Money Matters: Instability, Values and Social Payments in the Modern History of West African Communities*, Portsmouth, NH: Heinemann, pp. 205–24.

Barnes, Sandra T. (1987), 'The urban frontier in West Africa: Mushin, Nigeria', in I. Kopytoff (ed.), *The African Frontier. The Reproduction of Traditional African Societies*, Bloomington: Indiana University Press, pp. 255–81.

Bascom, William (1951), 'Social status, wealth and individual differences among the Yoruba', *American Anthropologist*, 53: 490–505.

Basset, Thomas F. (1988), 'Breaking up the bottlenecks in food-crop and cotton cultivation in Northern Côte d'Ivoire', *Africa*, 58(2): 147–173.

Bates, Robert H. (1981) *Markets and States in Tropical Africa: The Political Basis of Agricultural Policies*, Berkeley: University of California Press.

Bates, Robert H. (1989) *Beyond the Miracle of the Market: The Political Economy of Agrarian Development in Kenya*, Cambridge: Cambridge University Press.

Bates, Robert H., V. Y. Mudimbe and Jean O'Barr (eds) (1993) *Africa and the Disciplines. The Contributions of Research in Africa to the Social Sciences and the Humanities*, Chicago: University of Chicago Press.

Bauer, P. T. (1954) *West African Trade*, Cambridge: Cambridge University Press.

Baumann, H. (1928), 'The division of work according to sex in African hoe culture', *Africa*, 1: 289–319.

Beer, Christopher (1976) *The Politics of Peasant Groups in Western Nigeria*, Ibadan: University of Ibadan Press.

Belasco, Bernard (1977) *Ethnomarketing and Entrepreneurs: The Apotheosis of Trade in Nigeria*, Ann Arbor: University Microfilms.

Belasco, Bernard I. (1980) *The Entrepreneur As Culture Hero: Preadaptations in Nigerian Economic Development*, New York: J. F. Bergin Publishers.

Bernstein, Henry (1986), 'Capitalism and petty commodity production', *Social Analysis*, 20: 11–28.

Bernstein, Henry (1990), 'Agricultural "modernisation" in sub-Saharan Africa', *Journal of Peasant Studies*, 18(1): 3–35.

Berry, Sara S. (1975) *Cocoa, Custom, and Socio-economic Change in Rural Western Nigeria*, Oxford: Clarendon Press.

Berry, Sara S. (1984), 'The food crisis and agrarian change in Africa', *African Studies Review* 27(2): 59–112.

Berry, Sara S. (1985) *Fathers Work for Their Sons: Accumulation, Mobility and Class Formation in an Extended Yoruba Community*, Berkeley: University of California Press.

Berry, Sara S. (1989), 'Social institutions and access to resources', *Africa*, 59(1): 41–55.

Berry, Sara. S. (1993) *No Condition is Permanent*, Madison: The University of Wisconsin Press.

Bevan, David, Paul Collier and Jan Willem Gunning (1990) *Controlled Open Economies. A Neoclassical Approach to Structuralism*, Oxford: Clarendon Press.

Bierstecker, Thomas J. (1987) *Multinationals, the State and Control of the Nigerian Economy*, Princeton: Princeton University Press.

Bohannan, Paul (1954) *Tiv Farm and Settlement*, London: H. M. Stationery Office.

Bohannan, Paul and George Dalton (eds) (1962) *Markets in Africa*, Evanston IL: Northwestern University Press.

Boserup, Ester (1965) *The Conditions of Agricultural Growth; the Economics of Agrarian Change under Population Pressure*, London: G. Allen and Unwin.

Boserup, Ester (1970) *Woman's Role in Economic Development*, New York: St Martin's Press.

Brieger, William and Jane Guyer (1990), 'Farmers' loss due to Guinea-worm disease: a pilot study', *Journal of Tropical Medicine and Hygiene*, 93: 106–11.

Brieger, William and Ramakrishna (n.d.), 'Census of Idere and Villages, Igbo-Ora Rural Health Center', Ms.

Brush, Stephen B (1992), 'Reconsidering the Green Revolution: diversity and stability in cradle areas of crop domestication', *Human Ecology*, 20(2): 145–67.

Burnham, Philip C. (1980), 'Changing agricultural and pastoral ecologies in the West African Savanna region', in D. Harris (ed.), *Human Ecology in Savanna Environments*, London: Academic Press, pp. 147–70.

Burt, Ronald S. and Ilan Talmud (1993), 'Market niche', *Social Networks*, 15: 133–49.

Byrne, Daniel (1985), 'Economic rationality in a competitive marketplace: when to mix apples and oranges', in Stuart Plattner (ed.), *Markets and Marketing*, New York: University Press of America, pp. 153–69.

Callaway, Archibald (1967), 'From traditional crafts to modern industries', in Lloyd et al. (eds), *The City of Ibadan*, Cambridge: Cambridge University Press, pp. 153–71.

Cantor, Robert, Steve Rayner and Stuart Henry (1992), *Making Markets: An Interdisciplinary Perspective on Economic Exchange*, Westport, CT: Greenwood Press.

Carney, Judith A. (1988), 'Struggles over crop rights and labour within contract farming households in a Gambian irrigated rice project', *Journal of Peasant Studies*, 15(3): 334–49.

Carney, Judith and Michael Watts (1990), 'Manufacturing dissent: work, gender and the politics of meaning in a peasant society', *Africa*, 60(2): 207–41.

Certeau, Michel de. (1964) *The Practice of Everyday Life*, Berkeley: University of California Press.

Chauveau, Jean-Pierre (1994), 'Crises, ajustements et recompositions en Côte-d'Ivoire: la remise en cause d'un modèle', Ms.

Chauveau, Jean-Pierre (1995), 'Les agriculteurs africains: évaluer la performance ou privilégier les processus?', *Marché tropicaux mediterranéens*, Hors série, December, pp. 44–8.

Chayanov, A. V. (1966) *The Theory of Peasant Economy*, Holmwood, IL: Richard D. Irwin.

Childs, H (1934) *A Report on the Western District of the Ibadan Division of Oyo Province*, Ibadan: National Archives.

Clapperton, Hugh (1829) *Journal of a Second Expedition into the Interior of Africa, from the Bight of Benin to Soccatoo*, London: John Murray, Albemarle Street.

Clarke, Julian (1981), 'Households and the political economy of small-scale cash crop production in South-West Nigeria', *Africa* 51(4): 807–23.

Clarke, William H. (1972) in J. A. Atanda (ed.), *Travels and Explorations in Yorubaland, 1854–1858*, Ibadan: Ibadan University Press.

Cristaller, Walter (1966) *Central Places in Southern Germany*, Trans. Carlisle W. Baskin, Englewood Cliffs, NJ: Prentice-Hall.

Cohen, Percy S. (1980), 'Is Positivism Dead?', *The Sociological Review*, 28(1): 141–76.

Coquery-Vidrovitch, Catherine (1972), 'Research on an African mode of production', in M. A. Klein and G. W. Johnson (eds), *Perspectives on the African Past*, New York: Little, Brown & Co.

Coursey, D. G. (1967) *Yams; An Account of the Nature, Origins, Cultivation and Utilization of the Useful Members of the Dioscoreaceae*, London: Longmans.

Daly, M. T., M. O. Filani and P. Richards (1981) *The Ibarapa Planning Atlas: Process and Problems of Rural Development in Ibarapa Division, Oyo State of Nigeria*, Ibadan: Department of Geography, University of Ibadan.

Dennis, Carolyne (1983), 'Capitalist development and women's work: a Nigerian case study', *Review of African Political Economy*, 27/28: 109–19.

Diagne, Suleymane Bachir (1993), 'The future of tradition', in Momar Coumba Diop (ed.), *Senegal. Essays in Statecraft*, Dakar: CODESRIA, pp. 269–90.

Dodd, George (1856) *The Food of London. A sketch of the chief varieties, sources of supply, probable quantities, modes of arrival, processes of manufacture, suspected adulteration and machinery of distribution of the food for a community of two millions and a half*, London: Longman, Brown, Green & Longman.

Dommen, Arthur (1988) *Innovation in African Agriculture*, Boulder, CO: Westview Press.

Dovring, Folke (1967), 'Unemployment in traditional agriculture', *Economic Development and Cultural Change*,15: 163–73.

Drewal, Henry John and Margaret Thompson Drewal (1983) *Gẹlẹdẹ: Art and Female Power among the Yoruba*, Bloomington: Indiana University Press.

Dupré, Georges (1985) *Les Naissances d'une Société. Espace et Historicité chez les Beembe du Congo*, Paris: ORSTOM.

Dupré, Georges and Pierre Philippe Rey (1968), 'Reflections on the relevance of a theory of the history of exchange', in D. Seddon (ed.), *Relations of Production. Marxist Approaches to Economic Anthropology*, London: Frank Cass, pp. 171–208.

Eades, J. S. (1980) *The Yoruba Today*, Cambridge: Cambridge University Press.

Ensminger, Jean (1992) *Making a Market: The Institutional Transformation of an African Society*, Cambridge: Cambridge University Press.

Fadipe, N. A. (1970) *The Sociology of the Yoruba*, Ibadan: Ibadan University Press.

Falola, Toyin (1989), 'Nigerian cassava starch production during World War II', *African Economic History*, 18: 73–98.

Falola, Toyin (1995), 'Money and informal credit institutions in colonial western Nigeria', in Jane I. Guyer (ed.), *Money Matters: Instability, Values and Social Payments in the Modern History of West African Communities*, Portsmouth, NH: Heinemann, pp. 162–187.

Fligstein, Neil (1990), *The Transformation of Corporate Control*, Cambridge, MA: Harvard University Press.

Flinn, F. C. and Paul S. Zuckerman (1981), 'Production, income and expenditure patterns of Yoruba smallholders', *Africa*, 51(4): 825–35.

Forde, Daryll (1934) *Habitat, Economy and Society*, London: Methuen.

Forrest, Tom (1981), 'Agricultural policies in Nigeria', in Judith Heyer, Pepe Roberts and Gavin Williams (eds), *Rural Development in Tropical Africa*, New York: St Martin's Press, pp. 222–57.

Forrest, Tom (1994) *The Advance of African Capital: The Growth of Nigerian Private Enterprise*, Edinburgh: Edinburgh University Press for the International African Institute.

Forrest, Tom (1995) *Politics and Economic Development in Nigeria*, Boulder, CO: Westview Press.

Fortes, Meyer (1958), 'Introduction', in J. Goody (ed.), *The Developmental Cycle in Domestic Groups*, Cambridge: Cambridge University Press, pp. 1–14.

Foster-Carter, Aidan (1978), 'Can we articulate "articulation"?,' in J. Clammer (ed.), *The New Economic Anthropology*, New York: St Martin's Press, pp. 210–49.

Francis, Paul (1984) '"For the use and benefit of all Nigerians": consequences of the 1978 land nationalization', *Africa*, 54(3): 5–28.

Frobenius, Leo (1913) (1966 edition), *The Voice of Africa*, New York: Benjamin Blom.

Galletti, R., K. S. Baldwin, and I. O. Dina (1956) *Nigerian Cocoa Farmers: An Economic Survey of Yoruba Cocoa Farming Families*, London: Oxford University Press.

Gladwin, Christina H. (ed.) (1991) *Structural Adjustment and African Women Farmers*, Gainesville: University of Florida Press.

Gladwin, Christina and Kathleen Truman (eds) (1989) *Food and Farm, Current Debates and Policies*, New York: University Press of America.

Gleave, M. B. (1996), 'The length of the fallow period in tropical fallow farming systems: a discussion with evidence from Sierra Leone', *The Geographical Journal*, 162(1): 14–24.

Goldman, Abe (1993), 'Population growth and agricultural change in Imo State, southeastern Nigeria', in B. L. Turner, Goran Hyden and Robert Kates (eds), *Population Growth and Agricultural Change in Africa*, Gainesville, FL: University Press of Florida, pp. 250–301.

Goldman, Abe and Joyotee Smith (1995), 'Agricultural transformations in India and Northern Nigeria: exploring the nature of green revolutions', *World Development*, 23(2): 243–63.

Goody, Jack (ed.) (1958) *The Developmental Cycle in Domestic Groups*, Cambridge: Cambridge University Press.

Granovetter, Mark (1993), 'The nature of economic relationships', in Richard Swedberg (ed.), *Explorations in Economic Sociology*, New York: Russell Sage Foundation, pp. 3–41.

Güsten, Rolf (1968) *Studies in the Staple Food Economy of Western Nigeria*, Munchen: Weltforum Verlag.

Guyer, Jane I. (1972), 'The organizational plan of traditional farming: Idere, Western Nigeria', PhD dissertation, University of Rochester.

Guyer, Jane I. (1981), 'Household and community in African studies', *African Studies Review*, 24(3/4): 87–137.

Guyer, Jane I. (1984) *Family and Farm in Southern Cameroon*, Boston University African Research Studies No. 15, Boston: African Studies Center, Boston University.

Guyer, Jane I. (ed.) (1987) *Feeding African Cities: Studies in Regional Social History*, Manchester: Manchester University Press for the International African Institute.

Guyer, Jane I. (1991), 'Female farming in anthropology and African history', in Micaela di Leonardo (ed.), *Gender at the Crossroads of Knowledge: Feminist Anthropology in a Postmodern Era*, Berkeley: University of California Press, pp. 257–77.

Guyer, Jane I. (1992), '"Small change": individual farm work and collective life in a Western Nigerian savanna town, 1969–88', *Africa*, 62(4): 465–89.

Guyer, Jane I. (1993) '"Toiling ingenuity". Food regulation in Britain and Nigeria', *American Ethnologist*, 20(4): 797–817.

Guyer, Jane I. (1995a), 'Introduction: the currency interface and its dynamics', in J. I. Guyer (ed.), *Money Matters: Instability, Values and Social Payments in the Modern History of West African Communities*, Portsmouth, NH: Heinemann, pp. 1–37.

Guyer, Jane I. (1995b), 'Women's farming and present ethnography: perspectives on a Nigerian restudy', in Deborah Fahy Bryceson (ed.), *Women Wielding the Hoe: Lessons from Rural Africa for Feminist Theory and Development Practice*, Oxford and Washington: Berg Publishers, pp. 25–46.

Guyer, Jane I. (1996), 'Diversity at different levels: farm and community in Western Nigeria', *Africa*, 66(1): 71–89.

Guyer, Jane I. (1997), 'Diversity and intensity in the scholarship on African agricultural change', *Reviews in Anthropology*, pp. 1–20.

Guyer, Jane I. and Olukemi Idowu (1991), 'Women's agricultural work in a multimodal rural economy: Ibarapa District, Oyo State, Nigeria', in C. H. Gladwin (ed.), *Structural Adjustment and African Women Farmers*, Gainesville: University of Florida Press, pp. 257–80.

Guyer, Jane I. and Eric F. Lambin (1993), 'Land use in an urban hinterland. Ethnography and remote sensing in the study of African intensification', *American Anthropologist*, 95(4): 839–59.

Hallen, B. and J. O. Sodipo (1986) *Knowledge, Belief, and Witchcraft: Analytic Experiments in African Philosophy*, London: Ethnographica.

Hansen, Karen Tranberg (1992), 'Introduction: domesticity in Africa', in K. T. Hansen (ed.), *African Encounters with Domesticity*, New Brunswick, NJ: Rutgers University Press, pp. 1–33.

Harlan, Jack (1980), 'The tropical African cereals', in Davis R. Harris (ed.), *Human Ecology in Savanna Environments*, New York: Academic Press, pp. 335–43.

Hart, Keith (1982a) *The Political Economy of West African Agriculture*, Cambridge: Cambridge University Press.

Hart, Keith (1982b), 'On commoditization', in Esther Goody (ed.), *From Craft to Industry. The Ethnography cf Proto-industrial Cloth Production*, Cambridge: Cambridge University Press, pp. 38–49.

Hart, Keith (1992), 'Market and state after the Cold War: the informal economy reconsidered', in Roy Dilley (ed.), *Contesting Markets. Analyses of Ideology, Discourse and Practice*, Edinburgh: Edinburgh University Press, pp. 214–27.

Haugerud, Angelique (1989), 'Food production and rural differentiation in the Kenya highlands', in C. Gladwin and K. Truman (eds), *Food and Farm. Current Debates and Policies*, New York: University Press of America, pp. 59–83.

Hibou, Beatrice (1996) *L'Afrique Est-Elle Protectioniste? Les chemins buissoniers de la libéralisation extérieure*, Paris: Karthala.

Hill, Polly (1963) *The Migrant Cocoa-Farmers of Southern Ghana; A Study in Rural Capitalism*, Cambridge: Cambridge University Press [reprinted LIT and James Currey].

Hill, Polly (1970) *Studies In Rural Capitalism In West Africa*, Cambridge: Cambridge University Press.

Hirschman, Albert O. (1986) *Rival Views of Market Society and Other Recent Essays*, New York: Viking.

Hodder, B. W. (1965), 'Distribution of markets in Yorubaland', *Scottish Geographical Magazine*, 81(1).

Hodder, B. W. and U. I. Ukwu (1969) *Markets in West Africa*, Ibadan: Ibadan University Press.

Hogendorn, Jan and Marion Johnson (1986) *The Shell Money of the Slave Trade*, Cambridge: Cambridge University Press.

Hopkins, A. G. (1973) *An Economic History of West Africa*, New York: Columbia University Press.

Idachaba, F. S. (1980) *Agricultural Research Policy in Nigeria*, Washington, DC: International Food Policy Research Institute.

Idachaba, F. S. (1984) *State-Federal Relations in Nigerian Agriculture*, MADIA (Managing Agricultural Development in Africa).

Idowu, Olukemi and Jane I. Guyer (1991), 'Commercialization and the harvest work of women. Ibarapa, Oyo State, Nigeria', Women's Research and Documentation Centre, University of Ibadan, WORDOC Working Paper No. 1, Ibadan.

Johnson, Allen W. (1972), 'Individuality and experimentation in traditional agriculture', *Human Ecology*, 1(2): 149–59.

Johnson, Samuel (1921) *The History of the Yorubas*, London: Lowe and Brydone Limited.

Jones, William O. (1959) *Manioc in Africa*, Stanford: Stanford University Press.

Jones, William O. (1972) *Marketing Staple Food Crops in Tropical Africa*, Ithaca: Cornell University Press.

Kautsky, Karl (1988) *The Agrarian Question*, London: Zwan.

Kopytoff, Igor (ed.) (1987) *The African Frontier: The Reproduction of Traditional African Societies*, Bloomington: Indiana University Press.

Kowal, Jan M. and A. K. Hassan (1978) *Agricultural Ecology of Savanna: A Study of West Africa*, Oxford: Clarendon Press.

Kranendonk (1968) *A Preliminary Report on the Rural Changes in the Savannah Area of the Western State of Nigeria, with Special Reference to Tobacco Production*, Ibadan: Nigerian Institute of Social and Economic Research.

Lambin, Eric F. and Jane I. Guyer, 'The complementarity of remote sensing and anthropology in the study of complex human ecology', Boston: Boston University African Studies Center, Working Papers No. 175.

Lawal, Babatunde (1985), 'Ori: the significance of the head in Yoruba sculpture', *The Journal of Anthropological Research*, 41(1): 91–103.

Lawrence, Ben (1988), 'Texaco's Gari dream shattered', *The President*, 3 July: 20–1.

Lawuyi, Tunde and Toyin Falola (1992), 'The instability of the naira and social payment among the Yoruba', *Journal of Asian and African Studies*, XXVII: 3–4.

Lawuyi, O. B. and Olufemi Taiwo (1990), 'Towards an African sociological tradition: a rejoinder to Akiwowo and Makinde', *International Sociology*, 5(1): 57–73.

Lele, Uma and Steven W. Stone (1989) 'Population pressure, the environment and agricultural intensification', MADIA Discussion Paper No. 4, The World Bank.

LePlaideur, Alain and Paule Moustier (1991), 'Dynamique du Vivrier à Brazzaville. Les mythes de l'anarchie et de l'inefficace', *Cahiers des Sciences Humaines*, 27(1–2): 147–57.

Linares, Olga (1992) *Power, Prayer, and Production: the Jola of Casamance, Senegal*, Cambridge: Cambridge University Press.

Little, Peter D. and Michael J. Watts (eds) (1994) *Living Under Contract: Contract Farming and Agrarian Transformation in Sub-Saharan Africa*, Madison: The University of Wisconsin Press.

Lloyd, P. C. (1953), 'Craft organization in Yoruba towns', *Africa*, 23: 30–44.

Lloyd, P.C. (1974) *Power and Independence: Urban Africans' Perception of Social Inequality*, Boston: Routledge and Kegan Paul Ltd.

Lloyd, P. C., A. L. Mabogunje and B. Awe (eds.) (1967) *The City of Ibadan: A Symposium on its Structure and Development*, Cambridge: Cambridge University Press in association with the Institute of African Studies, University of Ibadan.

Mabogunje, A. L. (1968) *Urbanism in Nigeria*, London: University of London Press.
Mabogunje, A. L. (1977), 'Issues in Nigerian urbanization', *Nigerian Economic Society. Urbanization and Nigerian Economic Development. Proceedings of the 1977 Annual Conference of the Nigerian Economic Journal*, pp. 39–56.
Mabogunje, Akin L. (1995), 'The capitalization of money and credit in the development process: the case of community banking in Nigeria', in Jane I. Guyer (ed.), *Money Matters: Instability, Values and Social Payments in the Modern History of West African Communities*, Portsmouth, NH: Heinemann, pp. 277–95.
Mabogunje, Akin L. and Michael B. Gleave (1964), 'Changing agricultural landscape in southern Nigeria', *Nigerian Geographical Journal*, 7(1): 1–15.
MacArthur, J. D. (1980), 'Some characteristics of farming in a tropical environment', in Hans Ruthenberg (ed.), *Farming Systems in the Tropics*, Oxford: Clarendon Press, pp. 19–29.
Mamdani, Mahmood (1996) *Citizen and Subject: Contemporary Africa and the Legacy of Late Colonialism*, Princeton: Princeton University Press.
Mandala, Elias C. (1990) *Work and Control in a Peasant Economy: A History of the Lower Tchiri Valley in Malawi, 1859–1960*, Madison: University of Wisconsin Press.
Matory, J. Lorand. (1994) *Sex and the Empire that is No More: Gender and the Politics of Metaphor in Oyo Yoruba Religion*, Minneapolis, MN: University of Minnesota Press.
Mbembe, Achille (1996) *La Naissance du Macquis dans le Sud-Cameroun (1920–1960)*, Paris: Karthala.
Meillassoux, Claude (1978) (1960), '"The Economy" in agricultural self-sustaining societies: a preliminary analysis', in D. Seddon (ed.), *Relations of Production. Marxist Approaches to Economic Anthropology*, London: Frank Cass, pp. 127–57.
Meillassoux, Claude (1991) *The Anthropology of Slavery*, Chicago: University of Chicago Press.
Miracle, Marvin P. (1966) *Maize in Tropical Africa*, Madison: The University of Wisconsin Press.
Mkandawire, Thandika and Naceur Bourenane (eds) (1987) *The State and Agriculture in Africa*, London: CODRESIA Book Series.
Moock, Joyce Lewinger and Robert E. Rhoades (eds) (1992) *Diversity, Farmer Knowledge, and Sustainability*, Ithaca: Cornell University Press.
Moore, Henrietta L. and Megan Vaughan (1994) *Cutting Down Trees: Gender, Nutrition, and Agricultural Change in the Northern Province of Zambia, 1890–1990*, Portsmouth, NH: Heinemann.
Morgan, W. B. and R. P. Moss (1965), 'Savanna and forest in Western Nigeria, *Africa*, 35(3): 286–94.
Morrison, T. U. (1984), 'Cereal imports in developing countries: trends and determinants', *Food Policy*, 9(1): 13–26.
Mortimore, Michael (1993) 'The intensification of the peri-urban agriculture: the Kano, close-settled zone, 1964–1986', in B. L. Turner, Goran Hyden and Robert Kates (eds), *Population Growth and Agricultural Change in Africa*, Gainesville, FL: University Press of Florida, pp. 358–400.
Ndiulor, Tony (1995), 'CBN can't account for N87.4b in circulation', *The Guardian*, 31 October: 36.
Netting, Robert McC. (1968) *Hill Farmers of Nigeria: Cultural Ecology of the Kofyar of the Jos Plateau*, Seattle: University of Washington Press.
Netting, Robert McC. (1993) *Smallholders, Householders: Farm Families and the Ecology of Intensive, Sustainable Agriculture*, Stanford, CA: Stanford University Press.
Netting, Robert, M. Priscilla Stone, and Glenn D. Stone (1989), 'Kofyar cash-

cropping: choice and change in indigenous agricultural development', *Human Ecology*, 17(3): 299–319.

Nigerian Tobacco Company (1976) (1978) (1980) *Annual Reports*.

Ogunlesi, T. O. and C. R. Barber (1965), 'Igbo-Ora: demographic report', Ibarapa Project Report No. 3, University of Ibadan.

Olatunbosun, 'Dupe (1975) *Africa's Neglected Rural Majority*, Ibadan: Oxford University Press for the Nigerian Institute of Social and Economic Research.

Olowu, Dele (1990), *Lagos State: Governance, Society and Economy*, Lagos: Melthouse Press.

Omeje, Kenneth (1992), 'Structural adjustment and the politics of human rights violations in rural Nigeria: implications for the peace process', Research Paper, Social Science Research Council, Committee on International Peace and Security.

Omotola, J. A. (ed.) (1982) *The Land Use Act. Report of a National Workshop*, Lagos: Lagos Unversity Press.

Onitiri, H. M. A. and Keziah Awosika (eds) (1982) *Inflation in Nigeria: Proceedings of a National Conference*, Ibadan: Nigerian Institute of Social and Economic.

Oyo State, Agricultural Surveys for 1976, 1979.

Peel, J. D. Y. (1978) 'Two cheers for empiricism', *Sociology*, 12 (2): 345–59.

Peel, J. D. Y. (1983) *Ijeshas and Nigerians: The Incorporation of a Yoruba Kingdom, 1890s–1970s*, Cambridge: Cambridge University Press.

Peil, Margaret, Stephen K. Ekpenyong, and Olotunji Y. Oyeneye (1988), 'Going home: migration careers of southern Nigerians', *International Migration Review*, 22(4): 563–85.

Phillips, T. A. (1964) *An Agricultural Notebook (with special reference to Nigeria)*, 2nd edition, Ijeka: Longmans of Nigeria.

Pingali, Prabhu, Yves Bigot and Hans P. Binswanger (1987) *Agricultural Mechanization and the Evolution of Farming Systems in Sub-Saharan Africa*, Baltimore and London: The Johns Hopkins University Press for the World Bank.

Plattner, Stuart (1982), 'Economic decision making in a public marketplace', *American Ethnologist* 9(2): 399–420.

Rey, Pierre-Phillippe (1975), 'The lineage mode of production', *Critique of Anthropology*, 3: 27–79.

Richards, Audrey (1939) *Land, Labour, and Diet in Northern Rhodesia: An Economic Study of the Bemba Tribe*, London: Oxford University Press for the International African Institute [reprinted LIT and James Currey].

Richards, Paul (1983) 'Ecological change and the politics of African land use', *African Studies Review* 26(2): 1–72.

Richards, Paul (1985) *Indigenous Agricultural Revolution*, London: Hutchinson.

Richards, Paul (1986) *Coping With Hunger: Hazard and Experiment in an African Rice-Farming System*, London: Allen and Unwin Ltd.

Richards, Paul (1990), 'Local strategies for coping with hunger: Central Sierra Leone and Northern Nigeria compared', *African Affairs*, 89(355): 265–75.

Richards, Paul (1992), 'Landscapes of dissent: Ikale and Ikaje country, 1870–1950', in J. F. Ade Ajaye and J. D. Y. Peel (eds), *People and Empires in African History: Essays in Memory of Michael Crowder*, London: Longman, pp. 161–183.

Richards, Paul (1993), 'Cultivation: knowledge or performance?', in Mark Hobart (ed.), *Anthropological Critique of Development: The Growth of Ignorance*, London: Routledge, pp. 79–99.

Richards, Paul (1996), 'Agrarian creolization: the ethnobiology, history, culture and politics of West African rice', in R. Ellen (ed.), *Redefining Nature*, New York: Berg, pp. 291–318.

Rimmer, Douglas (ed.) (1988) *Rural Transformation in Tropical Africa*, Athens, OH: Ohio University Press.

Robertson, A. F. (1987) *The Dynamics of Productive Relationships: African Share Contracts in Comparative Perspective*, Cambridge: Cambridge University Press.

Roseberry, William (1989), 'Peasants and the world', in Stuart Plattner (ed.), *Economic Anthropology*, Stanford: Stanford University Press, pp. 108–26.

Ruthenberg, Hans (1980) *Farming Systems in the Tropics*, Oxford: Clarendon Press.

Schlippe, Pierre de (1956) *Shifting Cultivation in Africa. The Zande System of Agriculture*, London: Routledge and Kegan Paul.

Schultz, Marc (1982), 'Habitus and peasantisation in Nigeria: a Yoruba case study', *Man* (N.S.), 17: 728–46.

Scott, James C. (1976) *The Moral Economy of the Peasant: Rebellion and Subsistence in Southeast Asia*, New Haven, CT: Yale University Press.

Scott, James C. (1985) *Weapons of the Weak: Everyday Forms of Peasant Resistance*, New Haven, CT: Yale University Press.

Shipton, Parker. (1994), 'Land and culture in tropical Africa: soils, symbols, and the metaphysics of the mundane', *Annual Review of Anthropology*, 23: 347–77.

Siddle, David and Kenneth Swindell (1990) *Rural Change in Tropical Africa. From Colonies to Nation-States*, Oxford: Basil Blackwell.

Skinner, G. William (1964–65), 'Marketing and Social Structure in rural China, Parts I, II, III', *Journal of Asian Studies* 24(1):3–43; 24(2):195–228; 24(3):363–99.

Slicher Van Bath, B. H. (1963) *The Agrarian History of Western Europe, A.D. 500–1850*, Translated by Olive Ordish, London: Edward Arnold.

Snrech, Serge (1995), 'West Africa long term perspective study, Summary Report', Provisional Document, CILSS, CINERGIE, OECD/OCDE.

Stone, Glen (1993), 'Agricultural abandonment: a comparative study in historical ecology', in C. Cameron and S. Tomka (eds), *The Abandonment of Settlements and Regions: Ethnoarchaeological and Archaeological Approaches*, Cambridge: Cambridge University Press, pp. 74–81.

Stone, Glenn Davis, Robert McC. Netting, and M. Priscilla Stone (1990), 'Seasonality, labor scheduling, and agricultural intensification in the Nigerian Savanna', *American Anthropologist*, 92(1): 7–24.

Stone, M. Priscilla, Glenn David Stone and Robert McC. Netting (1995), 'The sexual division of labor in Kofyar agriculture', *American Ethnologist*, 22(1): 165–86.

Swindell, Ken (1985) *Farm Labour*, Cambridge: Cambridge University Press.

Swindell, Ken (1988), 'Agrarian change and peri-urban fringes in tropical Africa', in Douglas Rimmer (ed.), *Rural Transformations in Tropical Africa*, Athens, OH: Ohio University Press, pp. 98–115.

Thirsk, Joan (1978) *Economic Policy and Projects. The Development of a Consumer Society In Early Modern England*, Oxford: Clarendon Press.

Thirsk, Joan (1985), 'Agricultural innovations and their diffusion', in J. Thirsk (ed.), *The Agrarian History of England and Wales*, Vol. II, Cambridge: Cambridge University Press, pp. 533–89.

von Thünen, Johann Heinrich (1966) *Von Thünen's Isolated State*, Oxford: Pergamon Press.

Tiffen, Mary (1976) *The Enterprising Peasant: Economic Development in Gombe Emirate, North Eastern State, Nigeria, 1900–1968*, London: H. M. Stationery Office.

Tiffen, Mary, Michael Mortimore and Francis Gichuki (1994) *More People, Less Erosion: Environmental Recovery in Kenya*, West Sussex: John Wiley and Sons.

Tosh, John (1980), 'The cash crop revolution in tropical Africa: an agricultural reappraisal', *African Affairs*, 79: 79–94.

Trager, Lillian (1981), 'Customers and creditors: variations in economic personalism in a Nigerian marketing system', *Ethnology*, 20: 133–46.

Trager, Lillian (1985), 'From yams to beer in a Nigerian city: expansion and change in an informal sector activity', in Stuart Plattner (ed.), *Markets and Marketing. Monographs in Economic Anthropology, No. 4*, New York: University Press of America, pp. 259–78.

Turner, B. L., Robert O. Hanham and Anthony V. Portaharo (1977), 'Population pressure and agricultural intensity', *Annals of the Association of American Geographers*, 67(3): 384–96.

Turner, B. L. II, Goran Hyden and Robert Kates (eds) (1993) *Population Growth and Agricultural Change in Africa*, Gainesville, FL: University Press of Florida.

Udry, Christopher (1990), 'Agricultural credit in Northern Nigeria: credit as insurance in a rural economy', *World Bank Economic Review*, 4(3): 251–69.

Udry, Christopher (1994), 'Risk and insurance in a rural credit market: an empirical investigation in Northern Nigeria', *Review of Economic Studies*, 61: 495–526.

Vansina, Jan (1990) *Paths in the Rainforests*, Madison: The University of Wisconsin Press.

Voss, Joachim (1992), 'Conserving and increasing on-farm genetic diversity: farmer management of varietal bean mixtures in Central Africa', in J. L. Moock and R. E. Rhoades (eds), *Diversity, Farmer Knowledge, and Sustainability*, Ithaca: Cornell University Press, pp. 34–51.

Waterman, Christopher (1990) *Juju. A social history and ethnography of an African popular Music*, Chicago: University of Chicago Press.

Watts, Michael (1983) *Silent Violence: Food, Famine and Peasantry in Northern Nigeria*, Berkeley: University of California Press.

Watts, Michael (ed.) (1987) *State, Oil, and Agriculture in Nigeria*, Berkeley: Institute of International Studies, University of California.

Watts, Michael J. (1989), 'The agrarian crisis in Africa: debating the crisis', *Progress in Human Geography* 13(1): 1–41.

Watts, Michael J. (1993), 'Development I: power, knowledge, discursive practise', *Progress in Human Geography*, 17(2): 257–72.

Watts, Michael and R. Schroeder (1991), 'Struggling over strategies, fighting over food: adjusting to food commercialization among Mandinka peasants', *Research in Rural Development*, 5: 45–72.

Wiggins, Steve (1995), 'Change in African farming systems between the mid-1970s and the mid-1980s', *Journal of International Development*, 7(6): 807–48.

Williams, Gavin (1988), 'Why is there no agrarian capitalism in Nigeria?', *Journal of Historical Sociology*, 1(4): 345–98.

Williams, Gavin (1991), 'What disequilibria? People, land and food in Nigeria', in F. Gendreau, C. Meillassoux, B. Schlemmer and M. Verlet (eds), *Les Spectres de Malthus. Deséquilibres Alimentaires, Deséquilibres Démographiques*, Paris: EDI, pp. 375–96.

Woldemariam, Tekalign (1994), 'A city and its hinterlands: the political economy of agriculture, land tenure, and food supply for Addis Ababa, Ethiopia, 1887–1974', PhD thesis, Boston University.

Wrigley, E. Anthony (1985), 'Urban growth and agricultural change: England and the continent in the Early Modern Period', *Journal of Interdisciplinary History*, 24(4): 683–728.

Wrigley, E. A. (1987) 'Early modern agriculture: a new harvest gathered in', *The Agricultural History Review*, 35(I): 65–71.

Zeleza, Paul Tiyambe (1993) *A Modern Economic History of Africa, Volume 1: The Nineteenth Century*, Dakar: CODESRIA.

INDEX